16.47

SUPER SEARCHERS GO TO THE SOURCE

The Interviewing and Hands-On Information Strategies of Top Primary Researchers—Online, on the Phone, and in Person

Risa Sacks

Edited by Reva Basch

CyberAge Books

Information Today, Inc.
Medford, New Jersey

Super Searchers Go to the Source:
The Interviewing and Hands-On Information Strategies of Top
Primary Researchers—Online, on the Phone, and in Person

Copyright © 2001 by Risa Sacks

Super Searchers, Volume VII
A series edited by Reva Basch

Liability
The opinions of the searchers being interviewed are their own and not necessarily those of their employers, the author, editor, or publisher. Information Today, Inc. does not guarantee the accuracy, adequacy, or completeness of any information and is not responsible for any errors or omissions or the results obtained from the use of such information.

Trademarks
Trademarks and service names have been used throughout this book. The names are used with capitalization in the style used by the name claimant. The exception is the use of the trademarked name "LISTSERV." Many of the searchers being interviewed used this term generically and their usage has been retained in this book. Rather than insert a trademark notation at each occurrence of the name, the publisher states that all such trademarks are used in an editorial manner without any intent to infringe upon the trademark.

Library of Congress Cataloging-in-Publication Data

Sacks, Risa, 1946-
   Super searchers go to the source : the interviewing and hands-on information strategies of top primary researchers-online, on the phone, and in person / Risa Sacks ; edited by Reva Basch.
      p. cm. – (Super searchers ; v. 7)
   Includes bibliographical references and index.
   ISBN 0-910965-53-6
   1. Interviewing. 2. Research--Methodology. I. Basch, Reva. II. Title. III. Series.

   BF637.I5 S22 2001
   001.4'2—dc21

                                        2001042190

Printed and bound in the United States of America

Publisher: Thomas H. Hogan, Sr.
Editor-in-Chief: John B. Bryans
Managing Editor: Deborah Poulson
Copy Editor: Dorothy Pike
Production Manager: M. Heide Dengler
Cover Designer: Jacqueline Walter
Book Designer: Kara Mia Jalkowski
Indexer: Enid Zafran

Dedication

To so many who brought wonderful gifts to my life, especially:

To Jessie Cohen for spirit and courage,
Sylvia for curiosity and love of learning,
Bert for striving for ideals,
Barbara for hope and faith,
Jane for unflagging enthusiasm and encouragement.

To Sue and Mary for friendship across time and space,
and beyond measure.

To my husband Larry Smith—an uncommon man with a
common name—for laughter, caring, and seeing me through.

About The Super Searchers Web Page

At the Information Today Web site, you will find *The Super Searchers Web Page*, featuring links to sites mentioned in this book. We will periodically update the page, removing dead links and adding additional sites that may be useful to readers.

The Super Searchers Web Page is being made available as a bonus to readers of *Super Searchers Go to the Source* and other books in the Super Searchers series. To access the page, an Internet connection and Web browser are required. Go to:

www.infotoday.com/supersearchers

Table of Contents

Foreword

A few years ago, while flying to a business meeting, I sat next to an engineer from a company that makes computer chips. I told him I worked for a competitive intelligence consulting firm, and he told me that he was in charge of a project to commercialize a gallium arsenide computer chip that his company made for the U.S. Air Force. Gallium arsenide chips are potentially faster than silicon chips, but it's hard to grow pure gallium arsenide crystals. As a result, the chips are very expensive. My seatmate said that the Air Force used these fast but expensive chips in on-board electronic warfare and anti-missile systems for jet fighters. I have some general knowledge of chip making, so I asked him a couple of questions to pass the time, and he told me just about everything I could ever have wanted to know about his project. As we neared our destination, he wrapped up by taking the twenty-inch square photomask out of his briefcase to explain the features of the chip's design. (A photomask is like a big color negative of the chip's innards.) As the plane began its descent, we were holding the photomask up to the airplane window to get some good backlighting, and I wondered whether it was marked *Top Secret* or just *Secret*.

You won't learn here how fast the gallium arsenide chip ran, or the diameter of the crystals the company could grow, or the target price for the commercial version of the chip. No harm was done to my chatty seatmate's company or to our country's security—it was just another airplane conversation, and the details he revealed went no further than my own head. And indeed, most of us have been on airplanes, engaged a seatmate in a conversation to while away the time, and learned more than we ever imagined we could about that person's business or personal life. That sort of conversation can be enjoyable if your seatmate has an interesting story to tell, and it can be irritating if you'd rather sleep or read a book. If you're reading this book you're probably interested in one form or another of information-gathering, so, more often than not, you probably enjoy conversations of that sort.

A casual airplane conversation is a very unstructured form of primary research. Whether we use it casually or deliberately, primary research is the way to get at the vast reservoir of non-confidential information that is not available in secondary form, which means that it will never be published—not in newspapers or trade journals or professional journals, or even on the Internet with its billions of pages.

Many information professionals rely almost totally on what is published. Published information is readily accessible, inexpensive, and easy to obtain anonymously. Of course, the problem with calling the author and the people cited in the article, asking them for referrals to other knowledgeable sources, looking up the terms of a grant that funds the research, finding the environmental documents filed by the company that developed the technology, is that it takes time and it can be scary. And really, the scary part is what keeps most researchers from getting past the limitations of secondary research.

This book is the perfect antidote to the uncertainty that grips people when they try to make the jump to primary research. It is full of practical advice from experts, and the advice is delivered in dosages your brain can absorb and retain. I suppose someone could publish a four-page, single-spaced bulleted list that would encompass all of the lessons taught in this book. You'd read them and absorb nothing; the lessons would be forgotten the next day. The value of this book is in the way it teaches. Risa Sacks is an outstanding primary researcher, and the chapters in this book, in and of themselves, are excellent examples of the interviewer's art.

Moreover, the easy, conversational style of the interviews makes absorbing the lessons an enjoyable mental exercise. Reading this book is like eavesdropping on a series of delightful and informative discussions between two experts sitting at the next table in a restaurant. The concepts will stick with you. It is possible to learn an enormous amount about any topic through primary research. Like anything else, this type of work requires the right skill set. You have a great resource for acquiring those skills right here in your hands. If you want proof, keep reading.

Michael A. Sandman, Senior Vice President
Fuld & Company, Inc.
Cambridge, MA
msandman@fuld.com
www.fuld.com

Acknowledgments

My first and most grateful acknowledgment goes to my "distinguished dozen"—the twelve Super Searchers interviewed in this book. They gave generously of their time and expertise, spending countless hours talking with me on the phone. They talked while their houses were literally being moved out from under them, while their own deadlines approached, while spouses and offspring awaited their arrivals and dinners. They talked through their own lunch breaks and gave up their infrequent and treasured free moments. And through it all, with warmth, humor, and patience, they provided an incredible wealth of information. It was—in the best sense of the phrase—an awe-inspiring experience.

To Patty Shannon of The Work Station, who transcribed the hundreds and hundreds of pages of interviews, heartfelt thanks. If you want good feedback on interviews, ask a great transcriptionist!

Mike Sandman, of Fuld & Company, graciously agreed to write the foreword. On trans-Atlantic flights he read those hundreds of pages of rough manuscript, then provided great feedback and encouragement, as well as a foreword that I found both touching and delightful.

To Reva Basch (editor extraordinaire) and John Bryans (publisher pluperfect), I'm grateful for your effort, skill, and for always believing in the project, even when I couldn't.

Finally, to family, friends, and colleagues, deep appreciation for your encouragement, support, and forbearance through these months.

Introduction

Since the basic goal of research is to solve each problem in the optimum way possible—most efficient, most complete, fastest, cheapest, etc.—Super Searchers know how critical it is to use the right research tool for each situation. The most comprehensive searchers have an arsenal of research methods at their disposal, and have honed their skills in each of them. Sometimes the answers are online, but sometimes you need to go to the source—talk to an expert, see for yourself, or dig through archives or case files for documents. In fact, Super Searchers in every previous book in this series have mentioned that there are times when primary research is the best way to go, and times when it's the only way to go.

How else can you get the data that didn't make it into the published article, or have the statistics re-run to meet your needs? With primary research, you can talk to the experts who will answer your exact questions, give you the reasons behind the opinions, or help resolve discrepancies you've found. You can go and see that the plant is only running at half capacity or that the "big business" is a little shack or a mail drop. You can discover that the handwriting on the documents shows that Mr. A and Mr. Z are really the same person. You can tap a large body of information and perspectives that you can't find online—and that may provide critical pieces of a research solution.

In some ways a Super Searcher book that isn't focused exclusively on online techniques may seem like an aberration. In other ways it's a perfect fit, an important adjunct to an online series. As other books in the series show, Internet and commercial database searching provide information, sources, and benefits that complement each other. In a similar way, primary research provides the "third leg" of the research triangle. It's important to provide the link between the online world and the rest of the information universe.

I fervently believe in the importance of primary research; of considering a variety of methods to reach an answer, then using the best combination of methods to get the most complete solution; of using online and offline resources interactively and synergistically so that each complements and enhances the other. At the drop of a hat (or a URL), I'll hop up on my soapbox to preach the importance of expanding research beyond online answers, of not limiting your research horizons.

Still ... now that the time had come to put my money where my mouth was, suddenly the task was daunting. "You have really done it this time!" I told myself yet again. How in the world could I integrate coverage of online skills, in-person and telephone interviewing, hands-on public records searching, and direct observation in a single book? Even though I wasn't planning to tackle basic library research or marketing research using focus groups and surveys—either of which would have been an entire book in itself—the territory I contemplated was huge.

There was only one thing to do—exactly what I always do when faced with an impossible task: I went to the experts. Just as Reva Basch, Mary Ellen Bates, T.R. Halvorson, Amelia Kassel, and the authors of every other book in the Super Searcher series did, for my answers, I "went to the source."

In a way it's serendipity, I suppose, that the Super Searcher series itself is a great example of primary research—specifically interviews—in action. How else could you get the combined wisdom of so many experts exactly targeted to the specific topics you want to address? In fact, the whole series is based on using primary research to get the best answers.

The keys are knowing what is needed and how to get it, either yourself or from others. This book shares the secrets of integrating online skills with primary research to create a total research approach. It covers how Super Searchers determine when primary research is appropriate. It looks at how to use commercial databases and the Internet to prepare for primary research and, conversely, how to use primary research to supplement or validate database and Web research. Since it encompasses such a broad scope, it can't go into great depth on each topic, but it gives you a taste of a variety of different areas.

"Broad scope" also applies to our experts—and what a set of experts they are! Because primary research cuts across all subjects and settings, I sought out a "distinguished dozen." From the boardrooms of America's top corporations, to the halls of academia, to the pressroom of *The New York Times*, researchers in a wide array of situations share their knowledge.

Whether you're a novice researcher, an experienced online searcher who would like to improve your primary research skills and increase your research options, an experienced primary researcher, or someone who hires information professionals, this book provides invaluable tips, sources, and methods.

Why Now?

In a strange way, the growth of the Internet has contributed to the reemergence of primary research. In the beginning, there was the expert and there were your eyes. Long before computers or the Internet, even before paper and the printed word, when you needed an answer, you asked someone who knew, or you went and looked for yourself.

With the development of books, journals, and libraries, the world of paper was off and running. With computers came the growth of commercial online services and databases on CD-ROM, and their enormous power to find and organize published information. Online searching, justifiably, became the new kid, and the superstar, on the block. It was a formalized, hierarchical world, where organization and data ruled. Then came the Web, which was people-driven—and which blew the world of information wide open. Suddenly, technology was bringing people back together in new and revolutionary ways, including virtual communities, chat rooms, and instant messaging.

Robin Yarmovsky, the Market Research and Business Services Manager at SunLibrary, Sun Microsystem's corporate library, puts it this way:

> I think technology now helps that human connection. There was a phase of online where it was third-party resources and fee-based services, which wasn't interactive in the same way; you were interacting with data. This way you're interacting with data and people. The Internet gives you that human connection where you not only get to look at data, but then you can usually email someone or connect with someone or talk to somebody. It was like moving from getting no information online, to getting all of it online, to this place, now, where the two genres are melding together.

During the early years of online, primary research was often seen as not glitzy or sexy. It was ignored or sent off, like Cinderella, to sit by the fire and pick through the ashes. Now, increasingly, there is the recognition that primary research has something important to offer—Cinderella gets to dress up and come to the research ball.

Realizing and exploring the power and scope of what online has to offer has also highlighted the limitations and holes that exist. You may need something that is too old, not yet, or never to be loaded on a system—or something that's too new. If a story just broke in the last fifteen minutes, now's the time to go to the source. People require "soft" information; they want to know how someone thinks or feels, the "whys" of a situation, the "where are they going next?"

In one Super Searcher book after another, the problem of the validity of online information comes up. Primary research often provides ways to cross-check and confirm or disprove online information. Alex Kramer, a researcher and licensed private investigator in Washington D.C., who specializes in public records searching and competitive intelligence, provides one view:

> The way I look at it is, there are three steps to every investigation. There's the online, the database search, which develops the leads. There's the public records step, which fills in from the leads and follows up, and then there's the interview process, which is confirming, denying, getting the flavor, or getting the meat of everything else that you've been building up to.

Does primary research replace online? Never. Does it exist in a vacuum apart from online? Not on your life. Does it take you places online just can't go? It can. Do online and primary research complement and reinforce each other? That's what we're here to explore.

Going back to the primary-research-as-Cinderella metaphor for a minute, she may not always wear the glass slipper and reign as belle of the ball, but neither can she be sent back to oblivion with impunity. To switch metaphors—enough of Cinderella, already—primary research deserves a seat at the table, a voice in the research decision making. And today's world both facilitates that interaction and requires it for complete research solutions.

Trends and Themes

In talking to a dozen experts across a number of fields and settings, I found many areas of agreement and disagreement. One researcher might love ProfNet [108, see Appendix], one might hate it. Some researchers use online sources to lead them to people, others use people to lead them to online sources. Still, a number of common themes emerged. They include the following.

The Importance of Primary Research

While the role of primary research in their jobs and its place in their research approach differ from researcher to researcher, the one thing the researchers all agree on, not surprisingly, is the importance of primary research. Not a single one feels that the job could be done properly or completely without it. That doesn't mean that primary research is necessarily part of every single research project, or that it should be. If the complete answer is available online, go for it. But it does indicate a universal awareness of what primary research can contribute, a willingness to think outside the box and to consider all the options when approaching any research issue.

Along with this goes a willingness to integrate all their research methods and, as much as possible, select the best tool, or combination of tools, for the job. To quote Robin again:

> The way I've always looked at questions is not "Where is the information?" in terms of online or primary. It's "What is the answer to my question?" There may be a variety of different ways of getting that answer. The whole reason for research is to find the answer to a question, and so I use different strategies and techniques to get to my end goal. You learn to hone all of your research skills so that you can meet the end goal. If the answer is in a file drawer, on a shelf, online, in someone's brain, it really doesn't make a difference as long as you achieve the goal.

Researchers use online and offline synergistically, interactively, iteratively. They might start with online to find the names of experts, then, in talking to the experts, be led to surprising Web sites. An online public records search might lead to going to a courthouse to retrieve a case file. Information in the file might lead to an online search of a new corporation or an interview with an old employee. And serendipity plays a role in both online and offline research. Being open to where your research might lead you is a theme that came up over and over.

There's No One Right Way; It's Okay to Fail; We've All Been There ...

Fortunately (or not), there's no magic key for when to use primary research, or one right way to do it. Experiment and find which approaches, methods, and procedures work best for you. Understand that research is always a "work in progress" and be willing to re-evaluate as you go along. Joe Flower, a healthcare futurist, columnist, and author, puts it this way:

> My advice to people who are doing research is, don't swim upstream. Recognize what you're really good at. A lot of it really is about the personal style of the researcher, what works best for you. Of course, in order to know that, you have to try out a lot of different styles. For example, I have found over time that I can work with primary documents, but I absorb things better if I talk to someone.

And don't be afraid to fail. We've all been there. Are there times when you hate to pick up the phone, or when the thought of talking with someone terrifies you? Welcome aboard. In this amazing collection of talented and accomplished experts who, taken together, have conducted probably well over ten thousand interviews, are there still calls that are hard to make? Absolutely.

Had a bad experience or blown it big time? You're in good company; join the club. Called and called only to find out weeks later that the person you were trying to reach left that company two years ago? So have the experts. Ever spent too much time on the phone when the answer was online, or too much time online when the answer was a one-minute phone call away? We have, too.

Because every interaction is different and involves so many factors, you never know for sure how something will go. And that's part of what makes the research adventure both intimidating and exhilarating.

Do your homework!

Some of my least favorite words are "It's just one quick call." While you can't control all the factors in primary research, and you do not have to know everything about a topic, for example, in order to interview someone, you still need to do your part. Before you pick up the phone to ask someone questions, ask yourself some questions. Have you read what they've written? Have you done the background research that will allow you to bring something of value to the interchange? Can you offer a quid pro quo with some valuable information to share? Again, sometimes you're limited in how much you can, or should, do. But preparation frequently has a huge influence on the outcome of primary research.

Tenacity, Curiosity, and Caring

Tenacity, curiosity, and caring were recurring themes. Primary research requires incredible tenacity—the image of a bulldog or a terrier comes to mind: Grabbing hold of something and not letting go until you get the answer. Going over, around, and through gatekeepers and obstacles to the information. Finding alternate routes, sources, and approaches, and always being willing to think outside the box. Persevering in a way that online research doesn't require. For example, as Té Revesz of FIND/SVP once did, "trying to get somebody in Sweden, I called them every morning for a month between 5 and 6 A.M."

The driving force behind this tenacity (aside from Dan Tynan's "Usually you have an editor with a whip" or Wendy Grossman's "I'm driven by fear, because if I don't make the deadline, they won't hire me again") is an enormous sense of curiosity about the world and people. A fascination with the amazing things you can find, and a real enjoyment of the hunt, the chase, the adventure.

If the Super Searchers gave one piece of advice consistently, it was something on the order of "be nice, be appreciative, be interested—really care about what you do and the people you interact with." Whether it's the CEO, the clerk at the court, or the temp on the switchboard, treat them with respect, and strive for that personal connection that will stand you in very good stead. Sometimes you'll find that taking a hard line is the way to go, even being aggressive or abrupt, but those times are the exception, not the rule.

Referrals

Referrals are one of your strongest tools—and a good reason to treat people well, by the way. No matter whom you speak with, always ask "Who else could help me with this?" "Who else would you suggest I talk with?" "Who do you think is the expert in this area?" Referrals introduce you to sources you would never have found otherwise; they grease the wheels of information-gathering, and they can even increase your credibility. A number of experts have made calls to other people first, just to get referrals to the person they really want to talk to. The importance of referrals can't be overestimated. Seeing everyone as a source of referrals can even help you handle rejection. Marjorie Desgrosseilliers states it like this:

> Marjorie rule number 568 in telephone research: Never, never leave somebody without asking for a referral. Even if it's just the temp person who's answering the phone. And when you call the next person, say that you were recommended by the previous person. People respond so well to recommended calls.

Primary Research Can Be Costly, Complex, Time-Consuming ... and Worth It.

Sometimes primary research is both quick and inexpensive, the fastest, cheapest answer on the block. Many of us have had those wonderful experiences where a surprisingly quick phone call delivered the absolute gold. Frequently, however, primary research takes time, effort, and resources. You're dealing with people, not just databases, and while computers can get viruses, people get viruses, flu, vacations, meetings, and just plain cantankerous streaks. So it's important to weigh the costs against the possible results. But the returns can be tremendous. Primary research can pinpoint trends, debunk myths, correct errors, and provide information you can't get any other way.

Evaluating Sources and Information

With primary research, just as with online research, it's critical to evaluate both the sources and the information itself. Who said it? Where are they coming from? What are their biases or filters? How about their credentials? How does their information compare with everything else you're learning? How about the internal consistency of what you're hearing or seeing? The Super Searchers in this book offer a number of tips for evaluating information, from keeping your bullshit meter on, to "right-braining it" or following your gut instinct, to cross-checking information with someone who's not in the same loop. All of them stressed the importance of constant ongoing evaluation.

North Carolina

You may notice a number of references to North Carolina, so I'll let you in on it. My husband and I, after living for many years in the San Francisco area, moved to a tiny town in the Blue Ridge mountains of North Carolina—nearest store, nine miles. So you'll encounter remarks about "Podunk N.C." and so on. One of the wonderful things about our modern world is that, sitting on my hilltop, I can reach out to this incredible group of people across the U.S. and England ... that is, if the power stays on and "the creek don't rise."

Organization and How to Use This Book

There are unique advantages in using primary research techniques to explore primary research. Using interviews to talk about interviewing works on a number of levels. You not only get to read about interviewing techniques, you get to see them working, both in my interviews with the Super Searchers and in their many examples and anecdotes. You get to see the exact words and phrases they use when doing primary research, to experience how they deal with various situations, and to share in their trials and triumphs.

Because both the process and the information presented are important, I wanted you to see not only the wonderful tips and suggestions that each interview elicited, but also how we got there, how the interview itself progressed and flowed. As in every Super Searcher book, the interviews are edited from substantially longer transcripts, but in this one we let you in on more of the "behind the scenes" view. I decided (after a certain amount of soul-searching) that it was important for you to see when I had to admit to Wendy, "I don't know who that person is," or to ask Robin to define a term for me. There I was saying to Lynn Peterson, "So you can get most of that online?"—and discovering in the next sentence that, no, actually you can get very little of "that" online. Part of the interview process with John Schwartz was for me to have to return to an issue I'd started earlier. Not exactly neat, but that's how it really goes.

Other instances you might look for include my asking Alex and John Nolan two or three times or more, "Is there anything else?" In one instance, Andrew Pollard chooses to limit information and I agree, saying, "I'll ask the various questions and, if there's any of this is you don't want to talk about, we'll move on." At times I'll "share back" information—another technique that facilitates the interview process—or chime in with experiences of my own.

I didn't preserve every occurrence of interview-technique-by-example, but I did leave illustrations. I asked everyone for permission to tape, but you don't need to see it twelve times. I left the words in Alex's interview, so you would see that I really did it, and how. Similarly, Té provides an example of asking if I can call her back with further questions. I tell John Schwartz he's been wonderful, and in fact "just a peach." Of course, every Super Searcher I interviewed was wonderful and I thanked them all. No, I didn't call every one of them a peach ... that just popped out and, again, I left it for you to see.

You'll frequently see me rephrasing, rechecking, making sure I got it right. And sometimes I didn't. One of the great things about interviewing is the chance to recheck and correct. You'll see "hanging questions" and incomplete sentences—again, all part of the real world. Jeanne Barone warns about the dangers of multiple questions, where you ask more than one at a time. I'm guilty as charged, as you'll see.

It may be that interviewing, like sausage making, is a process that's not so gorgeous to observe. But limiting your view to the finished, cleaned-up product doesn't give you an accurate understanding of what the process is all about.

For a number of reasons, I include considerable information about each Super Searcher's background and history. As Jeanne says, "There is a quote by G.K. Chesterton, 'The only two things that can satisfy a soul are a person and a story, and even the story has to be about a person,' because we learn best by connecting information to the individual lives and experiences of others."

I want you to start "hearing" the voices of these people in your mind's ear. To see how each expert's experiences, "filters," views of the world, affect what they have to say. This gives you a chance to begin the evaluation process that is such an integral part of primary research: How does it fit for you? How does it relate to what the other experts say?

Finally, so many of their stories were so much fun that I couldn't bear to cut them. We have a poet turned futurist, a theologian turned researcher, a lawyer turned reporter, a folk singer turned journalist. These people undertook wonderful journeys to get where they are, and you can see how they bring pieces of their past experiences to bear on the work they do today.

Of course you can read this book in any order, but there are some underlying reasons for the order I selected. In general, the first three chapters introduce primary research within different types of research settings—a small independent research company, the large research firm Find/SVP, and the library of Sun Microsystems, a major corporation. The focus in these chapters is on interviewing, but other topics are covered as well. These chapters provide an introduction to primary research, and some opportunity to observe the interviewing process that comprises the book.

With that experience under your belt, you can look at the next two chapters, which focus on some techniques and theory, again within the interviewing arena. Here, two educators present methods that you will not only use yourself, but that you will see illustrated throughout the book in the specific examples given by interviewees as well as in the interview process itself as it unfolds in each chapter.

The following three chapters focus on the hands-on aspects of public records research and direct observation. This section is geared particularly toward the competitive intelligence—or CI—world, with a little PI folded in, because it was such a kick. Private investigation brings a different perspective to direct observation, including some techniques and situations that are useful to consider in the broader research world.

The last four chapters look at how journalists, reporters, and writers use primary research. We have a *New York Times* reporter, a former features editor for *PC World* magazine, an American freelancer based in London, and a futurist who is an author, columnist, and freelance writer. They often combine all the elements of primary research—documents, direct observation and interviews—and they have some wonderful stories to tell, including some award-winning investigative journalism. They also provide tips on how to approach journalists as sources.

Various sections of the book also provide an international view. Té brings in Europe and Asia in the first section; Andrew offers an outlook on the U.K., the U.S., and the European continent in the third section; and Wendy, in the last section, gives us the perspective of an American operating in England.

For the sake of readability, I did not include in the text the Internet addresses or other identifying information for the references mentioned in the interviews. Instead I have compiled all the resources in the Appendix. The first mention of each resource in a chapter is noted with a number corresponding to its listing in the Appendix.

This is your book. Use it however it works best for you. Read it in chapter order or pick and choose; read it for hard information; read it for procedures; read it for stories. Read it to practice your evaluation skills; evaluate the sources and evaluate the interviews themselves. Ask yourself questions: How might you have handled something differently? What would you have liked to ask? If you were there, what would you have spent more time following up on? What would you have skipped or glossed over? What works for you? What can you take away?

Every researcher is at some level a primary researcher. Every time you do a reference interview or talk with your client or boss, you're involved in a form of primary research. To quote Robin one more time, "As this profession has known for a long time, you're not only interviewing experts to get information, but you're also interviewing the person that you're doing research for."

You may never, in your research career, leap for the phone or go look at a building. If this book gives you nothing more than an increased general awareness of what primary research can do, that's fine. If you hire someone else to pick up some of those pieces, that's fine. If you increase your use of primary research or improve your primary research skills, that's wonderful.

However you use this book, come along as we go to the source and see what the experts have to share.

Photo by "The Coeur d'Alene Press"

Marjorie Desgrosseilliers

Small Firm, Primary Focus

Described as "one of the industry's foremost telephone researchers," Marjorie Desgrosseilliers, president and founder of AccuSearch Information Services, Inc., is an experienced investigative writer/researcher specializing in difficult-to-find information. She writes and speaks on the topic of telephone research and other non-online ("nonline") information-gathering techniques. AccuSearch is a virtual company based in Coeur d'Alene, Idaho, with offices in Philadelphia, Pennsylvania, and a network of researchers and subject experts across the country and around the world.

marjorie@iea.com
www.accusearchinfo.com

Marjorie, why don't you begin by telling me a little bit about your background and how you came to end up with AccuSearch.

I was a kid who started out asking a lot of questions. My mother said my first word was "why." I was born asking questions. And the very first present I ever got was a book. So, ever since then, I've been interested in reading and information and wanting to know why. I always thought I knew everything anyway. When I was in high school, I volunteered at the library, and I liked it so much that I ended up working at the library in college. I had no background or research experience at all; I didn't have a clue how to do research.

They were looking for volunteers for a reference librarian, so I ended up getting trained. I became the reference librarian while

I was a student at Ambassador College in Pasadena, California. Part of my job was clipping articles on different topics. I came across articles by Marydee Ojala, Mary Ellen Bates, and Reva Basch. I started seeing that there was actually a viable business behind this research thing; I could get paid to do things I liked.

When I left college, I went to work for the *Plain Truth* magazine. I was the sole librarian there for six years. Part of the reason why I started my business was a combination of wanting to do something that really appealed to my independent, entrepreneurial side, and wanting to move from Southern California. I took a leave of absence from my job for a month, and started my business as AccuSearch Information Services, Inc.

At this point I only take projects that I really like to take, and I farm out the rest. I have taken my company from a sole proprietorship, where I was the only person doing all the research, all the marketing, all the you-know-what, to where I have a stable of about eight researchers who work for me regularly.

Were your degrees in library science, or some other research area?

No, I have no degree in research whatsoever. I have a bachelor of arts in theology. I actually started to do an MLIS (master's in library and information science). I took the five core classes, and I did very well in them, but I decided that just wasn't where I wanted to be. I found it too restrictive for some reason, and I thought, well, I know I can do this, because I had a lot of practical experience.

Tell me a bit about what your clients and your projects are like at AccuSearch, though that may be a moving target.

It is a moving target. When I first started doing research, I really didn't know what I would be, what I would fit into. People always told me, "you gotta find a niche, you gotta find a niche." I kind of rebelled against that, because I didn't want to get stuck.

They would say, "find yourself a niche, right now, and get into it." But you know, until you have a little experience in this kind of business, you don't know where you're going to fit. I think it's important to do a lot of different things until you find something you like.

I kind of fell into doing telephone research, which is really funny, because I hate talking on the phone. I started out initially as a subcontractor for a larger information brokerage firm. The phone research part was looked upon as garbage collection. People hated to do it. But it's like "what would we do without sanitation engineers?" I was always the kind of person who thought, "nobody wants to do it, so I'll do it." I found that I had a knack for it, and I did very well. I wish I could say it was something I planned, but I just fell into it.

When I first started, seventy to a hundred percent of my business was subcontracting for other researchers. Now subcontracting's about thirty percent. Our projects range all over the map. Our other clients include consultants, public relations firms, and Fortune 500 and 1000 companies. We do market research, competitive and business research, and intelligence. Projects can go anywhere from the $400-600 range to ones lasting several months and costing thousands of dollars. On the short end, we have a "Get Smart" package that gives a client an overview of a particular company or industry. An example of a long complex project was one dealing with data disaster preparedness, looking at programs that various states and countries had in a number of major areas such as transportation and medical information.

What kinds of offline research do you do aside from telephone research? Do you do any face-to-face interviewing or digging in public records, or is it mostly telephone?

It's mostly telephone. I've not had a research project where I've had to go face-to-face with somebody. I'd much rather do it on the phone. If I'm trying to get information out of people, it depends on how sensitive the project is, but if it's CI (competitive intelligence), I don't want to talk to anybody face-to-face.

That's interesting. What differences do you find between interviewing somebody face-to-face and interviewing someone on the phone?

In person there's so much body language going on. If I were having a difficult time trying to get someone to talk to me, and it was face-to-face, I probably would be more inclined to turn tail and run than I would be on the phone. It's like, I can't see them, I don't know who they are, they don't know who I am. It's totally anonymous on the phone; it's a whole different ball of wax. However, after saying that, I do feel that if I had to go face-to-face with someone, I could do it and probably do it well.

So the anonymity of the telephone provides the freedom to do what works for you. Are your projects all phone research, or do you use a combination of research methods?

When I first started, it was all pretty much phone research. Then I started getting a lot of quick-and-dirty online research: "I have 300 bucks; get me what you can within this time and budget." I got very good at online research, developed strong online skills. I just don't market online as much as I do phone research, because I truly believe that primary research is where the real information is.

Sometimes projects are mainly or completely online. But now I'm finding that almost all of our phone projects involve an online element at some point, if only to give us some direction as to where to go.

In terms of your feeling that primary really is the gold, what do you think primary gives you

that you just can't get online using the Net or commercial databases?

What primary gives me is depth. What we read in books or newspapers or journal articles or whatever is two-dimensional. With telephone research, you get that three-dimensional picture; you get feelings. Let's say you're trying to find out about a person's philosophies as far as business is concerned. When you're talking to someone, you can tell if they do not like person XYZ. Then you go digging around to find out whether it's that they don't like them personally, or that they don't like their business sense. There are so many nuances, if you know what you're looking for. You can feel the body language coming through the phone. Phone research is so important because it is the soft information that is not available in print.

How do you usually get your requests for projects? Do clients come to you because they know they want primary research, or do they just say, "we need this question answered" and you decide which part might be primary, which part might be secondary?

We have a couple of advertisements, like in The Librarian's Yellow Pages [81, see Appendix]. But most of our requests come through email and word of mouth. People call us and say, "So-and-so said that you do this kind of thing." I also follow up contacts with people that someone else has suggested might be able to use my services. When I get a project by word-of-mouth, the client has pretty much figured out that it's going to take some primary research. But most of my requests are just people looking for information.

When a request comes in, do you do a reference interview with the requestor to pin

down what they need, as opposed to what they think they need or what they say they need?

Exactly. When somebody calls, the first thing I do is make sure they understand that it's a fee-for-service situation. Then the question I ask is not "What do you need?" but "What are you trying to accomplish?" and I make notes. Then I'll say, "As a company policy, especially for first-time clients, I'd like you to send me an email outlining in a couple of paragraphs what you've told me. This helps me make sure that I understand exactly what you want, and helps me put together an estimate." Our estimate is actually a contract that we have our clients sign. Our terms and conditions are on the back; they explain who we are, what we do, what we will not do. We say that we make a reasonable, good-faith effort to find them what they want.

If you're asked to estimate the cost of a project, how do you do that?

It just so happens that I wrote an article for Price Watcher [106] on that. I give an overall range based on an hourly rate, and that hourly rate depends on the type of work, the amount of analysis needed, and so on. I figure that, if a project involves calling ten companies, and you need to ask three or four questions at each one, and it looks like the same type of person should be able to answer all of them, that means talking to ten people, and I allow at the very least an hour per company. If it were three or four questions and ten companies, and it looked like I'd have to talk to three different people at each one, I would go to an hour and a half. I add up the hours and multiply by the hourly rate for that kind of project, and I add a percentage on top of that. I don't estimate phone costs; that's an additional expense.

One of the things about telephone projects is that they're more expensive, overall, than online projects, because of the time and effort involved. And I'm not afraid to say that to clients.

How long do your projects usually take, and what kind of turnaround time do you have?

It depends, sometimes, on the urgency. With telephone projects, especially if they want a good, thorough job, I ask for ten to fifteen business days; it typically takes anywhere between one and two weeks to get it done. In the summertime, it sometimes takes longer because so many people are on vacation. I usually ask for six to eight weeks and try to turn it around in four.

When you look at a project, are there flags that say, "hmm, primary research" or that indicate that you might use primary and secondary research synergistically, say online and telephone, to support each other?

There is no magical answer. Some of it's instinctual. There's no formula for when to do phone research as opposed to online research. I don't know why I think this is a phone research project, why I think that one is online. But what I do know is that I know.

Let's say somebody calls and says, "I would like information on a company; I'd like some of their financials, I'd like to know a bit about the industry." We have the "Get Smart" package that I mentioned, and I know right away I'm going to go online for that. Or they'll call and want to know what's been happening in the last year with this company. That's online, no question.

However, if they say, "I'd like to know what this company is thinking, what their market strategies or philosophies are," that is a two-fold research project. I would see what I could find online, and then I would augment that with telephone research.

As far as doing a total telephone research project is concerned, that might happen if I'm asked to update a report that I had done before, or that somebody else had done. Sometimes I have a gut feeling that we'll probably not find a whole lot online. That's true of anything that I know is an emerging field, especially new technical information, high-tech and telecommunications industries.

For most of that, the first place I go is the phone. Actually, that's not true. The very first place I go is company Web sites.

Are there decision points, a sort of research triage where you say, "for this part, I'll go to the Net first, and then maybe a bit on the commercial databases, and then I'll go to the phones?" Can you think through your decision process for me, when you've got a brand-new project? Or is it by now just a gut reaction?

It's a gut thing. And it's hard. More and more, it depends on the question that someone is asking.

Often a client is looking for a new twist on an age-old question. For instance, they might know a company's market share, but they also want to know how they got there. They might say, "I've heard that XYZ company has a bit of a different investment philosophy. They used to do this and now they're taking their company to go do that. I need you to find out if that's true or not and, if so, why they are doing it." I know that, more than likely, I'm not going to find that kind of information online; my experience has been that I'm going to get the critical stuff on the phone.

One of the main reasons I go to the phone is when it looks like more touchy-feely information—how are they thinking, what are they feeling, what are the trends in this area of the industry. You can pick up some of that online, but the problem with online is that you are tied, you're restricted. Online tools put you at the mercy of what someone else has written and the way they've chosen to answer the questions.

For the real soft stuff, the innuendos, the feelings that people have, I use the phone. Because the excitement doesn't come through in an article—are they excited about it, are they worried about it? I know I haven't answered your question yet; it's a struggle. I've done it for so long now that I just know.

Do other factors come into that decision, like budget or turnaround time?

Yes. Budget is a big thing. What I'll do with a client when they have essentially no money is give them an estimate. I'll say, "Well, we can see what we can find online. It'll probably cost you between"—and I give them a range—this is just pulling numbers out of my hat—"three and five hundred dollars to do the online part. If we come up with nothing, I can give you an estimate for doing more work on the telephone." If I have a strong sense that it will more than likely end up being phone research, I tell them that up front.

More and more, though, I am running into people who are willing to spend the money, and they're not interested in just what's out there in print. They want to know what makes a company tick. They want to get to the heart of the matter.

Do you find any difference in your interaction with clients that you're doing primary research for, versus the ones that you're doing secondary research for?

I have a lot more contact with people that I do phone research for, because different directions emerge. Or somebody says something in a conversation that makes me think, "this seems to change the whole tenor of your question."

Sometimes clients ask me to find information based on their criteria, and I find that their criteria are not what the information is based on, but something completely different. One client told us that chemical companies were developing new products to deal with allergens, and wanted us to find out what those new products were. We found out that the companies weren't concentrating on developing products to deal with allergens, but were focusing on making whatever products they developed fall within the regulations set out by particular governing bodies like the National Institutes of Health [90], OSHA [101], and EPA [48].

As soon as I get any indication that we're dealing with completely different issues, I get back to the client and say, "Okay, this is what we're finding." Once you get to the point where you're saying, "Look, you're not going to like this, but this is really how it is," you know you've got a real working relationship going.

As long as we're talking about clients, have you found any major client misconceptions concerning primary research?

That it's cheap, and that it's fast. You can get it cheap, fast, or good. You can have two of the three, but you can't have all three. You can have it good, and you can have it next Wednesday. But you can't have it good, next Wednesday, and cheap. You have to educate your clients. The key to all this is to manage your client's expectations.

Tell me what's involved in managing a client's expectations.

It is so vitally important to do that. My knowledge is a mile wide and about an inch deep on a lot of things. Sometimes, especially if it's a subject I've never heard of before, I just know that there are going to be some difficulties, and I make that clear to the client. I can give you an example of this with a new diet products study we got. I told the client, "I have a feeling we're not going to get any of this online." However, they were convinced that we would. I just said, "I don't know what we're going to get there. We may get this and this." And I give a percentage probability. Especially if they've given me a list of questions they want answered, I'll say, "Well, I believe we have about a twenty or twenty-five percent probability of getting this, and this, and this." I don't go much above fifty percent, unless I know I've seen it somewhere before and I'm sure I'm going to get it.

Are you giving it a twenty-five percent probability that you'll get it online, or that you'll get it at all, using whatever combination of methods works?

Get it at all. I'm very honest with them. I'll say, "We'll do what we can to get the information that you're looking for. We'll do the secondary, online phase, but I doubt we're going to find anything there. Then we'll do the primary telephone research. That is where we're going to find most of our information." Because I managed the client's expectations, what we ended up giving them so far exceeded what they were looking for that I became an overnight hero. That's what I like about this business. Being a telephone researcher is kind of like being Superwoman. You feel like a Marvel comic hero.

How do you prepare for the telephone phase of projects?

To be a good telephone researcher, you can't just get on the phone and start asking questions. You have to know a little bit about what you're looking for, the subject at hand, trends in the industry, who the players are. You might not know who all the top companies are, but you need to know enough to ask intelligent questions. If you're going to do business or competitive intelligence research, you can't just know how to do the research. You've got to understand how business works, how industries work, how businesspeople think. Because things come up in conversations, and you think, "Oh my goodness, I can't believe you just told me that."

I think of it as learning to walk the walk and talk the talk. Let's move on to some specifics of how you go about finding your sources and acquiring "enough knowledge to be

dangerous." Say you've got a new project on a topic that you know zilch about. Where do you start in terms of print resources, favorite Net sites, commercial databases?

The very first thing I reach for is National Trade and Professional Associations, the NTPA, by Columbia Books [92]. They list the top associations in any given subject area. I think it's an awesome source. I also love Headquarters USA [61], which used to be called the Business Phone Book USA, and before that, the National Directory of Addresses and Telephone Numbers. It has a section that's divided by industry, and that's very helpful.

I like the *Encyclopedia of Associations* [47], which I use if the NTPA doesn't work. I don't use the online version. I have tried it, thinking I should because it's online. But I much prefer, when I'm looking for phone numbers to call, to go through books if I can.

I find that when you're physically browsing, a phenomenon takes place where you're looking at one thing, but your fingers are walking through the pages and you find other, related things. It's like a treasure hunt.

Right. You know, computers are computers, and they only spit out what we ask them for. But when you're looking through the *Encyclopedia of Associations*, you flip through going, "Oh, you know, that section would be good, or this one might be good." I can't tell you how many times that's happened.

Sometimes, for instance if I want to find experts, I'll look at the *Standard Periodical Directory* [122], *Ulrich's International Periodicals Directory* [130], and the *Gale Directory of Publications and Broadcast Media* [55]. I'm looking for what publications cover a certain industry. Then I call those publications. It's like locating authors of journal articles, but on another level. I talk to the editors to see if they know anything. These guys are covering the industry; they should know what's going on. And they do.

Do you find that you can also call the editors and ask, "Okay, who on your staff is the expert in thin-film lithography?" or whatever, and there's that one person who really eats and drinks the subject?

Exactly right. That's actually one of the phrases I use: "Who lives, breathes, and sleeps this?" A lot of times you can go to a journal and find out who the authors are in those particular areas; they tend to be pretty knowledgeable people.

Another source that I use is investment analysts. People are kind of afraid of them, but they're great people. They're busy, and sometimes rather abrupt, but if you get someone who will talk to you, they're very well-informed. To locate analysts, I use *Nelson's Directory of Investment Managers* [93]; they call it the Red Book. I get into that, the *Gale Directory of Publications and Broadcast Media*, and the *Encyclopedia of Associations* when I'm really digging to the bottom of the barrel. On some research projects, you just cannot find anybody who will either (a) talk to you or (b) know anything.

And those are definitely two factors that you have to consider. One, will they talk to you, and two, if they are willing, is it going to be useful?

That's exactly right. So much for finding associations and business and industry sources. As far as government sources go, I really like Congressional Quarterly's *Washington Information Directory* [136]. That's the only source I buy every year, because those telephone numbers change so much. They do an amazing job. You discover when you're doing government research that the left hand often doesn't know what the right hand is doing. Quite often you'll find, let's say, an office in the Justice Department that does exactly the same research as somebody in the Bureau of Labor Statistics, and they don't even know it.

But in a way that's fine, isn't it, because if Justice won't talk to you, Labor might. From our point of view, it gives us more avenues in.

Absolutely. It works for me. The state *Yellow Books* [145] are also good. I pick those up at library sales. I have some that are so old, but even old editions are good because they're a starting place, at least. The numbers for state offices don't really change that much.

Do you use CDs at all?

I did. American Business Information, which is now called infoUSA [72], put out a CD called 16 Million Businesses Phone Book; it's old, but I like CDs like that; I never throw anything away because I want to make sure I can find the information again. Now, typically, I find what I need on the Internet rather than on a CD.

That brings us to our next question. What have you found the Net useful for, particularly when you're having to do primary research as well? And have you found that the Net has changed the way you do primary research?

I first started using the Internet in 1991 or '92. It wasted so much time up front; I just said, "Forget it." But now, the Internet helps me a lot. I use it all the time. I absolutely love company Web sites because they'll often list names. Those are stepping stones to me. I don't care if they're out-of-date names or not. At least it gets me an in with the company: "Oh, so-and-so's not there anymore? Okay, who's taken over his position? Well, I'd like to talk to them."

When people started putting their Web pages up on the Internet, the information you could find on companies was amazing. Sometimes it was rather proprietary information, too. That's changed; for the most part, it's very sanitized now. At the beginning people must have thought they were invisible. They put everything about their companies on their Web site; I don't think they realized the global ramifications of the Internet—that anybody, anywhere could look at your business and see who you were and what you did. Later people started scaling back the information that they put on their Web sites. Still, if you know what you're looking for, you can make some educated guesses about a company even if they don't include the proprietary stuff.

I prefer Northern Light [97] and AltaVista [8] search engines, which probably goes against everything my colleagues say. I've gravitated toward those two because I felt they were reliable, and they're different enough from each other that what one won't pick up, the other probably will. I find that if I use a meta-search engine, I get too much, and I don't have the time to spend on that.

Those are my two favorite search engines, too. On AltaVista, what search strategies do you use? Do you use the advanced search option? Do you start broadly or narrowly focused?

It depends. Sometimes I'll just put in a word—for instance, if it's something I don't have a clue about, like a pharmaceutical industry drug that I've never heard of before. I'll type in the name of the drug, just to see what's out there. A billion hits later, of course, I will narrow it down from there. But I usually start pretty broad. I also use quotes a lot, to search on an exact phrase.

I don't tend to look up phone numbers on the Internet, unless I'm looking for a company that I thought was in a particular state or location and it's not. Then I'll use an Internet phone list like 555-1212.com [1].

I like the reverse business phone books, where you search by telephone number instead of company name. You can do that with 555-1212.com, too. This is a little trick that I've picked up; it's so easy, but it took me a while to figure this one out. When I first started making lists of phone numbers, I would write down the name of the company and the phone number, and let it go at that. But sometimes those phone numbers were wrong, and then I'd have to waste time looking up the state. So now I always write down the name of the city and the state to the side when I make these lists. I know it sounds like a stupid little thing, but boy, I save myself a lot of headaches doing that.

I do the same kind of little trick that you'd think would be dumb, but that really helps. When I'm calling all over the country or all over the world, I write down time zones. You'd think we'd know, after all the time we spend on the phone, exactly where the time zone lines go. But that way I can tell who I can start calling at nine in the morning, who's going to come online at noon, who's going to have lunch at three, East Coast time. You sort of phone your way across the country, or around the world.

That's right. Also, I discovered, much to my surprise, that not all time zones change to daylight saving time.

I do use international phone lists on the Net, especially if I don't have a clue what country or city a company is located in. I don't use one source in particular. Typically, if I'm looking for international numbers, I'll plug a search into Northern Light that includes the name of the country and the word "telephone" or "directory." Recently a client said, "I need information on this company, and I know that it's in Israel; I have no idea where." So I did a quick search and found out that it was in Haifa.

Do you use online mailing lists or discussion groups or FAQs at all?

Unless I am specifically asked to monitor them, I typically don't. I've found that people can say a lot of things, and it ends up being worth absolutely nothing. You might get that nugget of information, but it takes more work than it's worth, as far as I'm concerned.

Let's go on to commercial databases. Do you have favorite online services, favorites files, favorite strategies when you're using online in conjunction with primary research? What sources do you like for industry background, location data, leads on people to follow up with phone research?

My favorite commercial service when I first started was Lexis-Nexis [80], because I feel that I can do a lot of searching fairly cheaply. Many people have a mindset about Nexis, that it's just too expensive. If you search it the way you search Dialog [39], then yes, it is. If you come at it a different way, then it's probably one of the cheapest services going. Using functions like Focus is really helpful, but what I found most useful of all is using the session record function in Nexis' proprietary software to download articles and avoid the cost-per-line imposed by Nexis if you use its download option. There is a bit of cleanup and reformatting involved but, all in all, I've found it to be a better option.

Sometimes I start with Dow Jones Interactive [41]. I can search to my heart's content, since searching is free, and I can sometimes get data such as company locations, phone numbers, and contacts, or get pointed in the right direction, essentially for free. I was looking for a company somewhere in Denmark. I went into Dow Jones, plugged in that company name, and one of the article titles was "XYZ company based in Viborg, Denmark." I didn't have to pay for it, since you can look at the list of titles for free. That was very helpful.

But my favorite is Dialog. I can get in and out quickly, and know exactly what I'm doing. I'll go into file 411 (DialIndex) [38] first, and do a brief search to find out if anything's been written on my subject. I can then transfer that search automatically into the eight or nine databases that will probably contain some information—most likely files 15 (ABI/INFORM) [2], 16 (PROMT) [109], 148 (Trade & Industry Database) [128], 9 (Business and Industry) [18], and 636 (Newsletters) [96]. Those are the major business files I use.

Okay, you've looked in your favorite reference books, and you've gone online to learn a little bit about the industry or the topic, and you've found some sources that you're going to call. How do you prepare for your calls and how do you decide who to call first?

Usually I have a paragraph in front of me that spells out what the client wants. I also have a list of questions, and some info tidbits or research results I can use to sound somewhat educated. I do not adhere to a script of any kind. I'm not a great proponent of scripts, because I feel that they inhibit the flow of a conversation.

If I'm interested in ten companies, I'll often stay away from the top five until I've talked to the tenth, ninth, or eighth. I want to figure out who I have to talk to to get the information I need. Are they regular employees or are they management types? How do I approach them? How are they responding to my questions? Am I asking the right questions? I want to get all the bugs worked out of my approach, make sure it's the right approach, before I start tackling the ones I think are going to be my best targets.

If Fred Jones' name keeps coming up, then I'll wait until I've done one or two interviews, to see where I'm going, before I tackle him. I never want to leave my best people until last, because telephone research is such a long process to begin with. Once I feel comfortable with my approach, I'll go right to the people I think will give me the best information.

And how would you identify these best targets? Let's go back to that for a minute. How would

you identify, say, the ten top companies or the leading expert in the new process you're researching?

Sometimes you just get a gut feeling about a person. Or the people I'm talking to recommend them; I keep hearing, "Have you talked to so-and-so? You really need to talk to him, he's the expert in this whole area." But usually people write about them or mention them in a phone conversation. They show up in the press; my online research tells me, over and over again, that XYZ company is a groundbreaker in this industry.

Do you tend to go to the journalists who write about your topics?

Yes, I do. We did a project involving an investment company that, from what our client had heard, had recently changed investment strategy, turning more toward high tech. To confirm this, we found some business journals that specialize in high-tech areas, and talked to a couple of the news reporters there. They were very helpful, pointing us to the right people on the inside, because those are the people that they talk to. They would give us a little background and hints like "This guy is not really talkative, but if you talk about golf, you'll be in."

So you're at the point of calling someone on the phone. Tell me a little about phone techniques, skills, observations that work for you.

I sometimes come across a little scatterbrained, but that's a great tool for a phone researcher, because I come across as pretty harmless, too. It really does depend on how you come across. Always remember that the people you're talking to are human beings. Be friendly. Just let your personality come out. That's me, anyhow, because I'm a very people-oriented person. But I know of a phone researcher who does a great job and she's not like me at all. She's more to the point, but she reaches one side of people and I reach the opposite side.

One of the little tricks I use is trying to find something in common with these people, some little thing. Also complimenting them, but doing it sincerely. For instance, after you've done some research and the same name keeps coming up, you say, "I have been doing some industry research and I keep getting your name; people have been telling me that you're it, you're the person to talk to. I'd like to know if you can point me in the right direction." You have to mean it, because people can sense flattery. They can tell if you're being hypocritical.

One big thing that helps me in telephone research is that when I'm talking to people I have a smile plastered on my face. Let me read you a couple of good statistics from George Walther, who wrote *Phone Power: How to Make the Telephone Your Most Profitable Business Tool* [166], back in 1987. He says, "Only seven percent of the feeling communicated in a spoken message is conveyed by the words we say. Thirty-eight percent comes from things like our tone of voice and how loud we talk. A whopping fifty-five percent comes nonverbally through body language." And believe me, body language projects through the telephone.

It's really important, when you're talking to people, to come across confident and not apologize for anything. Just remember that everybody puts their pants on the same way in the morning, whether you're talking to the janitor or the CEO. Depending on my state of mind I may say, "I know you're really busy, but ..." That's okay, but for the most part it's "make those phone calls and go after it like you know you're going to get it." Still, I have to do it in such a way that it's not obnoxious—although I will lean on them if I have to.

What are some of the ways you get through gatekeepers?

I've looked at four different ways of getting into a company: switchboard operators, customer service, related departments—

or what I call dialing for dollars, where you just start dialing random numbers in the same area—and secretaries. There are others, but those are my major ways to identify contacts within companies. It's really hard, because sometimes one or more routes into a company are blocked to you, or don't work for some reason. So it's helpful to think of alternate ways to get to the people you need.

The first category is switchboard operators. It's their job to help callers get to the right place within an organization. It's getting harder and harder to get anywhere within a company these days, because switchboard operators often don't know people's names. They basically know departments, and if you don't have somebody's name, they won't put you through. But I'll talk about that in a second.

Essentially, the key to successful calls with operators is to be patient and positive. It's their job to answer the phone, so you're going to get interrupted. They might have to put you on hold several times before they can really answer your question, and the answer might be no.

We've all run into cranky operators. Cranky people are often just in a bad mood, and sometimes you can turn those people around by being really positive. If an operator refuses to help you, you say, "Thank you very much," and ask if there's somewhere else that you can call … and they'll usually say no. So, call back at lunchtime, or after hours, or before hours. With larger companies, you can probably call back right away and get a different operator.

If I can't get through the operator, I'll see if I can find a customer service number. Customer service is kind of a back-door approach, but their job, too, is to provide service. You tell whatever rep you reach, "This is the only phone number I can find for your company." Another approach I use is "I've just been in a voicemail black hole. I really need to talk to a live body. Who is the best person I could talk to about XYZ?" I don't always ask directly for what I'm looking for, but I try to find something nonthreatening, like "I'm looking for the marketing department. Who would I call?" People instinctively want to help, so they do.

Throwing yourself on someone's mercy works really well. With operators, I frequently say, "I'm not sure who to talk with, but perhaps you could help direct my call." Then you're making a partner out of them.

Exactly. I'll also try related departments, anything I can think of. I've spoken to security, the sanitation engineer, or the janitor's room. Calling after hours, calling at midnight, who answers the phone? Some companies do have a person answering the phone twenty-four hours. Sometimes calls go to the security department automatically. You can just say something like, "I'm sorry. Maybe, if you could just help me, this would save me a phone call. Who is the person who's in, I know it's something like blah-blah-blah." And they'll say "Oh, no, no, that's not him. He's in blah-blah-blah. It's so-and-so you want to talk to."

In fact, these security guys are so bored sometimes that they'll really talk. Once at five o'clock in the morning I called a company in the fasteners, bolts, and nuts industry. This high-school guy answered the phone. We had a nice little chat, and I found out all sorts of things.

And there are times when, seriously, I'll sit there and just dial for dollars. I did a project not too long ago that involved finding out about a new company that was supposed to be setting up to provide a certain kind of artificial intelligence software. Using the Internet, I had found a phone number but I didn't have a location; I didn't even have a company name. I ended up in a university think-tank that was a sort of business "incubator." The company hadn't actually gotten off the ground yet, but people in the industry had heard about it already. It turned out that the people involved with this company were all over the place, nobody knew who they were, nobody knew where they were. I just started dialing extensions that were close to the one that I had found. After the sixth extension, I found a person who had what I was looking for. He was an assistant to the guy I wanted to talk to, but he told me everything I needed to know. The clients were just beside themselves.

How about secretaries?

They're always fun. They can either be my dream come true or a full-blown nightmare. I had to learn to live with the fact that it's the secretary's job to screen the boss's phone calls. Don't be afraid of that. It's their job to help their boss, but they can also be a big help to me. They're a good source of names of other people to speak with if their boss isn't available. They can point you to other departments or organizations. This is where a compliment can be really useful, and that comes naturally to me. For example, I notice a person's accent, particularly if they're from England because I grew up in an English household. So right away there's a common thread. I'll say, "How long have you been in the United States? Wow, you have a great accent. I love hearing you talk." And then talk a little bit about that while feeding in questions, as you can, about who the best person might be to talk to.

George Walther, the author of *Phone Power*, clued me in to the fact that secretaries are, as a whole, underappreciated. So it's important to give them sincere compliments, when we can, on their role. I had a really intense project on automotive parts. I was getting to the point where I wanted to pull my hair out, because I couldn't get through to the person I needed to talk to. I was having a really hard time getting past the secretary. I tried everything I could think of. She was very polite, but very firm: "No, you can't talk to him." I finally gave up—and I didn't plan this, but I started laughing. "You know what? Your boss is so lucky to have you," I said. "You are amazing, you do such an excellent job of screening calls." She was shocked. She didn't say anything for ten, fifteen seconds. Then she said, "Thank you so much." And she went on, "You know what? I'll bet there's some-body else in the company who can help you." So, even though she wouldn't let me talk to her boss, she found me a person who helped me. Through that person, I got an inroad to his boss, who was the guy I was trying to reach in the first place.

That's a great example of how useful it is to be able to say, "I was just talking to the president's office, and they gave me your name and number to call." It's the power of referrals.

Exactly. Even if you're just saying, "I called somebody in the Sanitation Engineering Department and they said you were the expert in this area." I use that a lot. It's one of my favorite tools. Networking within a company is an awesome way to get to the person you need.

I ask everyone I talk to if they can refer me to someone else. That is Marjorie rule number 568 in telephone research. Never, never leave somebody without asking for a referral. Even if it's just the temp person who's answering the phone. When you call the next person, say that you were referred by the previous person. People respond so well to calls when someone has referred you.

Here is an example. I was working on a project for an executive search firm, for which I had to contact the human relations directors of several large companies across various industries. It was difficult to get through to the directors, so I started asking for their assistants or someone in their office. It turned out that, in all the companies I called, it wasn't the human resources director I needed after all, but someone else in the company. The great thing was that I could approach those people using the referral. I didn't have to say, "Mr. Human Resources Director recommended I call you," but "Mr. Human Resources Director's office recommended I call you."

Once you've gotten through to your source, what about the interview itself? How do you introduce yourself, how do you manage the flow of the interview?

I just say, "My name is Marjorie and I'm an independent researcher." My favorite approach, once I've introduced myself, is "I'm doing industry research on XYZ." Sometimes it's across multiple industries, sometimes it's a single topic. "Researcher" is okay, but I try to avoid the term "study" or anything like that. It really turns people off. It pushes a little button inside their head and they say, "I'm sorry, I don't have time for a survey." Then you have to backtrack and say, "It's not actually a survey. I'm trying to identify some trends in the industry. I've talked to several people already, and from what they're saying, you're the expert."

Sometimes they'll ask, "Who are you doing this research for?" It's usually safe to say, "I'm working for a consulting firm," and if my target is a company that is way off in Seattle and the consulting firm is in New York, I say, "based in New York, and we're doing this research for our client." A lot of times I ask my clients not to tell me certain things, so I can honestly say, "I don't know."

Or I might say, "My boss has asked me to call. We've already talked to XYZ company," And I'll continue with, "You know, they told us that your share of the market is ten percent, is that true?" or "The trend in the widget industry is toward bright purple. Are you noticing the same thing?" Typically, people will want to correct you if you have wrong information. Sometimes, the answer is no answer at all, but you can tell a lot from their body language as to whether you've hit it right or not.

Do you control the interview, or do you find it takes on a life of its own?

Often it takes on a life of its own. I do direct the conversation, but in subtle ways. Sometimes I'm looking for benchmarking information, which is not necessarily competitive; then it's straightforward. You pretty much hammer through one question at a time, and that's what people are expecting.

I'm always after qualitative information more than quantitative, though that's important too. So I just let people talk. I say things like, "That's really interesting. You know, one expert told me this; what do you think about that?"

This brings up the whole area of using comfort and discomfort. I've heard you mention letting interviewees know that you can stay within their comfort zone. How do you do that and how does that work for you?

If it seems like they're getting a little antsy, I'll say, "Look, I just want you to know that you do not have to answer any questions that you don't feel comfortable with. You do not have to tell me anything that you don't want to. I want you to know that up front. You don't have to tell me anything proprietary." I am very sincere when I tell them that.

I'll talk about trends in the industry, industry projections, and industry information. They'll use their company as a focal point, because that's where they're talking from. It helps them relax a bit. But information does come out in the conversation that I'm going to be able to use.

When people say, "I can't talk about that," I say, "I totally understand; thanks very much." And then I figure out how I can ask this question a different way, and come back to it later. When you're doing telephone interviewing, the best way I can describe it is like a ballet, or a tennis match going on inside your head. You're focused on what's being said, but at the same time you're always thinking ahead: "Okay, he didn't answer that, how am I going to ask that the next time?"

Right. I think of it as a chess game. You're making your current move, then everything they say is going to shape your next response. But what if someone won't talk to you at all?

Sometimes I will lean on them. Then I try to give them something to respond to. I'll say something like, "Let's just cut to the chase. In talking with other companies in the industry, I've heard that your profit so far this year is 1.5 billion. Is that right?" Silence on the other end of the phone. Then, "Why won't you answer that question?" And sometimes they will. But that's kind of a last resort; I'm not into burning bridges.

Talk to me for a minute about the use and importance of silence.

Ask the question, and then shut up. That's something I've learned, and the reason it works is that people don't like silence. They start talking to fill it. Once, that technique backfired on me. I asked the question, and I sat there. And the other guy sat there. Just sat there. And there was silence for a full minute. And I said, "Well, we both know that technique, don't we?" He started laughing. So, I find another one of the weapons in my research arsenal, or whatever you want to call it, is humor. You know, when I'm caught, I'm caught. So I figure, what have I got to lose?

Absolutely—busted, big time. I love it. Once you do get a response, how do you evaluate the value or credibility or reliability, the trustworthiness of a source?

In all projects, it's really important to understand the viability of sources, to know that they are who they say they are, and that they know what they say they know. I have three ways of determining that. You can pretty much tell when you're talking to them whether they know about the industry or not. A second way is to find out what their actual credentials are. In competitive intelligence projects, we actually seed questions into our interviews; we ask things like "Oh, and where did you go to university?" or "Oh, okay, I see. How long have you been with the company? How long have you been in this industry?" With all our CI interview transcripts, we include information like the name of the person, company, title, university attended or degree held, how long they've been with the company, how long they've been in the industry. A third way to measure credibility is how many times they've been recommended by other people. And are other people corroborating their information? Does the same information come up all the time?

How do you decide when a particular interview is over, when you've got to call it quits?

That's tough. There's a side of me that, being a researcher and a librarian who wants to go to the ends of the earth to find the answer, doesn't fit with budgets and the real world. One way I know it's over is when the same things are being said over and over. Another way, of course, is if the interviewee himself says, "You know, I just don't have any more time," or "I'm really busy." You can tell by their body language, and their voice over the phone. When it gets to the point where I feel like I'm losing their interest, I'll hit them with the last questions, if I haven't gotten to that point yet.

And how about for a project as a whole? How do you decide when you've done all the research you can for a particular project?

Again, when the same information keeps coming up over and over again from different people, from online sources. When everything points to the same thing, then we've probably found the answer. That's when we stop. But often, the biggest factor is budget.

Is there anything else you want to talk about regarding the interview process?

I'd like to make just a couple more points. I know this one is going to sound incredible coming from me, but I have a rule: "Be concise." By that I mean that I don't go into a lot of detail about who I am and what I want until I reach the person I really want to speak to.

Another rule deals with getting around "no" or "I don't know." When a person says, "I don't know," I always ask them to make an educated guess: "What would you say? You've been in this industry long enough. What would your educated guess be?" Some people balk at that, but you can usually get them to do it—and their educated guesses are often in the ballpark.

Also, when people say "no" it doesn't always mean "no"; sometimes it means, "I don't know," or it means they didn't understand the question correctly. So I do a lot of rephrasing, or asking questions a different way later on. If I've gotten permission from the client, sometimes I'll offer to share back a sanitized version of our research when it's completed, in order to get people to talk to me. Sometimes, though, "no" is "no." In any case, I never leave them without asking, "Who else can I talk to?"

And also thanking them for whatever they did give you, so you've set up your relationship for the next time you need them.

Saying "thank you" is amazing. I try to always send thank-you cards to people. I get a call back from them thanking me for the thank-you card. So many people are unappreciated; any time you can say thank you, or do something nice for someone, I think it's important.

On the opposite side, how do you handle rejection or frustration, especially since you have to be "up" and positive on the phone? You can snarl at your computer but you really can't snarl at the person on the phone.

I know that some days I just should not be on the phone. I've learned to build that into my estimate. Some days are just soap operas and ice cream. I don't actually watch soap operas, but I've learned that I don't always do my best work. I can plow through days like that, power my way through, and sometimes I have to. But if I have a choice about it, I don't.

Once I was working on a horrible, horrible competitive intelligence project, hammering away at this one HMO company, calling every office, every division, CEOs, vice presidents, talking to salespeople in the field. I got an amazing amount of information, but the guy I was working for wanted more and more. Finally, I felt that I could not get any more information without lying. So I found somebody else who I knew was really good at phone research, and I paid them to take over the project. That was the only way I could handle it.

Another time, I had all my stuff together, but I wasn't prepared. I called this guy but I wasn't expecting to get him. I had papers and pens everywhere, everything was everywhere. I said, "Oh, can you just wait a second ..." and I'm shuffling papers. It was embarrassing; I mean, it was like thirty seconds of silence. And he said, "You know what, if you can't be prepared to do your interviewing, I just don't have the time to talk to you." Click. Oh my goodness. Then I've had people actually yell at me on the phone, just basically "Who the hell do you think you are, trying to find information about my company blah, blah, blah?"

The one thing I never do is react. Never. It took me a while to learn "do not take it personally." I think that's why I prefer phone interviews to face-to-face interviews. Any kind of rejection, or any time somebody says "no," I get up, walk around, shake it off, go have a cup of tea or whatever, and then come back and start again. Get back on the horse.

How do you present your results? Are they usually transcribed interviews, or summaries, or reports, or what?

All of that. We have a report template that we use. Typically it includes a table of contents and a research overview showing where the information came from. Then we do an executive summary, in which I outline the client's questions and answer them. If it's one of those projects where the questions haven't been answered exactly, I include a bigger section about what we found, touching on the different areas, then bringing out the point that really turned out to be more the issue. Next I include a transcript of all the interviews and information on why the people I spoke with are qualified to answer the questions. I don't tape interviews. I have my own method of shorthand. Then I include any articles that we've found. At the very end I include a contact list and a list of sources searched.

Are you finding that you usually email your results now? Is email taking over from paper?

I never send anything in hard copy anymore. Even where marketing is concerned, it's usually word of mouth, phone, and email. I do have an in-person appointment with a client tomorrow—one of the first, actually, in several years.

I know people I've had relationships with for years, whom I've never seen face to face. It's amazing. How about an example of a success story where you used both offline and online research, but where the primary research really came up gold?

One was the project I mentioned with the "incubator" company. That was a real success story in that I was able to find this company before it even existed. Somebody had heard a rumor about the software and asked "Could you find out who this company is, and can you find out whether they're going to look for outsourcers?" I ended up doing the dialing-for-dollars thing, finding the right person, having them tell me exactly what I needed to know—and much more, including when they were going to start, what they were going to do, what their focus was going to be, whether they were looking for people, whether they were going to do outsourcing, exactly what these outsourcers had to present, what they had to send, what they were looking for. There's no way we would have found all of that online. The client was ecstatic.

Can you think of an example of a call that was really difficult for you to make, or that you really dreaded making? One where you thought, "I don't know how I'm going to do this one?"

I can think of several. There was one call during that HMO project I mentioned. I had to talk to a vice president, and I had to get the answers I needed, and I didn't know how to do it. I was in a kind of mind frame too, where I was thinking, "I don't know if I can take being blown out of the water again."

So I just sat down and dialed and said, "Really, honestly, I just need your help. I have a couple questions, and I don't want to be so rude as to assume that you have the time now to talk to me. But if you could see your way clear for about five minutes, or if I can call you back at a certain time, I would really appreciate that." He gave me ten minutes right then, and I was able to call him back, and he did tell me some of the things I needed to know.

Sometimes I find that "You're my last resort" helps.

Another call that I really dreaded making was when we were trying to find out whether a certain company was going to build a chemical facility and manufacturing plant in Texas. I did everything I could and couldn't find the answer. Something inside me figured "damn the torpedoes." So I called the PR person, and said, "Look, I'm coming to the horse's mouth. This is the rumor that I've heard. Is it true?" The woman was so flabbergasted that she said, "Well, yes, it is. This is when we're starting construction on it, this is what we're going to do." I said,

"Well, thank you very much, I appreciate that, goodbye." And I sat there, my heart rate was going like mad, and I thought, oh my goodness, look at that. There are times when asking straight out for what you want is very effective.

What do you like best about phone research?

It's different every single time. And even though I hate being on the phone, I personally love talking to people. I love that it's like a mystery I'm solving. I'm on the hunt. When I finally bag what I'm looking for, sometimes I just get up and I dance around my chair.

Yes! It's funny; it's a different feeling when you find the answer online as opposed to actually getting it from the source's mouth.

Yes, it is! You've got to think the way your quarry thinks. You never know how they're going to react; you never know what's going to happen. It's always a crap shoot.

What do you like least, or hate most, about phone research?

I hate the competitive intelligence aspect of telephoning. Actually, it's a love/hate relationship. I hate it when I have somebody on the other end of the phone and they are just spewing for all they're worth. I'm sitting there thinking, "Why are you telling me this? You should not be telling me this." Sometimes I have a tough time with that. I used to do a lot of CI work, but I farm that out now. I try never to lie to anyone, but I'm struggling with the issue of misleading by omission. It's not just my struggle; I think we're all struggling with the ethics of this. John Levis wrote an article on the subject in *Connections* [33].

Do you see any technology changes that might affect phone research?

I remember once saying, "If they ever come out with video-phones, I'm dead." Because we make this thirty-second commute to our offices in our pink fuzzy slippers. If we ever have to do the videophone thing, that's going to change the face, literally, of phone research.

The one thing I really hate right now is Caller ID. For the most part, you're damned if you do and damned if you don't. If you put a block on your number coming in, people who actually notice will think, "I don't know who you are, I'm not going to talk to you, I'm not going to pick up the phone." If you don't put a block on your number, people may recognize it and decide that they don't want to talk with you. Or they may decide they don't want to talk to you because they don't recognize the number. I'm not quite sure what to do about that. I like the element of surprise. I don't like to leave voicemail. I never leave voicemail messages.

That's interesting. You absolutely never leave voicemail messages, or very rarely?

Very rarely, and in competitive intelligence situations, I never do. In even slightly competitive situations, I never, never leave voicemail. Because it gives people an opportunity to start wondering, "Who is this person, and what does she want?" Maybe they don't do that on a conscious level, but subconsciously, it raises questions. I like to avoid creating questions in people's minds that I could have prevented by not leaving voicemail.

What would you say are the characteristics of a good phone researcher, and how do they compare to the characteristics of a good online researcher? Do you have any suggestions or recommendations for someone going into phone research or primary research?

A lot of people are afraid to go there. They don't want to do it; they don't want to talk to other people. I don't think everybody can do it. It does take certain personality traits. There's an innate need in us to know why. I know that's the same with online researchers, but there's some determination in us to find the essence of the information. It takes a pit bull approach where you stick with something until you bleed it dry. When somebody says "no," it doesn't mean that there's no answer to the question; it just means you've got to find somebody else who's going to give you the answer.

You have to take a personal interest, invest yourself as though it were your company. One thing that makes me good at what I do, that distinguishes me from other telephone researchers—and I don't mean this in a vain way; I've seen it over and over and over again—is that I am willing to chase after information. It's like I have a sixth sense about things that people say that tells me, "Okay, let them talk about that for a little while." Sometimes a person I'm interviewing will go off in a different direction that seems totally unrelated to the topic that we're talking about—but, you know, it turns out not to be.

Often I'll get a research study back from a subcontractor, and they've given me exactly what the client has asked for, which is fine. But much better is not just sticking with what you think the client wants, but figuring out what the client needs. That's the big question. So many clients call me back saying, "Where did you find XYZ? This is so good." They're just falling all over themselves, because they didn't ask for it, but we've provided information that was critical to some business decision they needed to make.

You have to be resourceful and inventive. We need to think on our feet in doing online research too, because you don't want to rack up the costs. But the phone is much more "real time," and the question of ethics comes in—the issue of "I don't want to lie to this person." You have to consider both your personal ethics and the law.

You need to have some human relations skills. You almost have to become a chameleon on the other end of the phone. You become whatever you need to be, to be able to talk to different types of people. I have pictures of people in my head when I hear their voices. If I'm talking to someone who is a strait-laced stuffed shirt, I don't act flippant, though sometimes I'll infuse a little bit of humor.

You have to have a certain amount of compassion. I might say, "You sound like you're having a bad day. I'm really sorry about that. Is there something I can do? What's going on?" Sometimes the gates open; no one's ever asked them that before.

It takes perseverance to do telephone research; sometimes it's boring and you can't just let it go. And sometimes it's a very creative process. Online searching is, too, but with phone work you sometimes come to the same point that you do with painting or writing—you have a complete block, and you can't get past it. And you know that, if you keep hammering away at it long enough, the dam will break with that "aha!"

If you could look in your crystal ball, how would you see the role of telephone or primary research changing over the next five years?

I think there's going to be more and more need for it. When I first started doing research, probably three-quarters of my work was online and the other quarter was telephone research. It has completely flip-flopped over the last seven years, because people are after soft information. They want to know the ethereal stuff, the intangible stuff. They want to get inside people's minds, companies' minds. They're trying to predict where they're going to move, and you can't do that by number-crunching. Some aspects you can, but people want intelligence, they want analysis, they don't just want a few articles. People need to know the inner workings of what's going on; they need to know why people make the decisions they make.

I really feel that primary research is the research of the future. The other day I was talking to a colleague and I quoted my hourly rates. They had different rates—for online research maybe $90 an hour, for telephone research $60 an hour. I said to them, "That's really backwards, don't you think?" Online is going to be around forever. But there is a desperate need for good phone researchers.

Five or six years ago, researchers were up in arms about not having clients anymore because, with the Internet, that would be it. What the Internet has done for us, really, is blow the doors open. People have seen the amount of information out there and realized that's why they need us—to go through all that information, to boldly go where no one has gone before and sort it all out. To know what is real, to know what is true, to know what is viable information.

On the flip side, because of the perception that people can go on the Internet and get whatever they want, there's a consciousness emerging that "I need to know what the other guy's thinking." Well, he's not writing his thoughts out anywhere. So it's "I need somebody who can dig them out for me." And that's where we come in.

Super Searcher Tips

➤   What primary research gives me is depth, because books or newspapers or journal articles are two-dimensional. With telephone research, you get that three-dimensional picture; you get feelings.

➤   In a reference interview, the question I ask is not "What do you need?" but "What are you trying to accomplish?"

➤ To be a good telephone researcher, you can't just get on the phone and start asking questions. You have to know a little bit about what you're looking for, about the subject at hand, trends in the industry, who the players are—just enough that you can ask intelligent questions.

➤ The very first thing I reach for is *National Trade and Professional Associations*, which lists the top associations in any subject area. For industry analysts, I like *Nelson's Directory of Investment Managers*, and for government sources, Congressional Quarterly's *Washington Information Directory*.

➤ In interviewing, I stay away from the top five until I talk to maybe the tenth, ninth, or eighth. I want to make sure the people and the approach are correct before tackling my best targets.

➤ Secretaries can be my dream come true or a full-blown nightmare. It's their job to screen their boss's calls, but at the same time, they can be a big help. They're a good source of names of other people to speak with.

➤ Never, never leave somebody without asking for a referral. And when you call the next person, say that you were referred by the previous person.

➤ Company Web sites frequently list names. Those are stepping stones even if they're out-of-date. At least they get me an in with the company: "He's not there anymore? Who's taken over his position?"

➤ I might say, "I've just been in a voicemail black hole. I really need to talk to a live body. Who is the best person I could talk to about XYZ?" People instinctively want to help, so they do.

➤ When a person says, "I don't know," I always ask them to make an educated guess. Some people balk at that, but you can usually get them to do it—and their educated guesses are usually in the ballpark.

Té Revesz

Large International Research Company

Therese R. (Té) Revesz is a Senior Project Manager and International Practice Coordinator with FIND/SVP's Strategic Consulting & Research Group. Her favorite projects are best practices/benchmarking studies. In addition to research and consulting, she teaches a seminar on interviewing techniques, has been a lecturer at Baruch College of the City University of New York, and a speaker at various conferences. Before joining FIND/SVP, she was an international business journalist.

trevesz@findsvp.com
bantercom@yahoo.com
www.findsvp.com

Let's start with something about your background.

I've always liked primary research. When I was doing my thesis, I didn't want to rehash things that other people had done. I wanted it to be purely original. I like going places no one has gone before, and I also like people. People are interesting. So I really started my interviewing career back in college.

What were your degrees in?

International Affairs and Economics. And the thesis I did was on cross-cultural communications. There was one book on the topic at the time, and I had never even taken a course on cultural anthropology. So before I started, I read a whole bookshelf on the subject. Then I did interviews with U.S. diplomats and AID (Agency for International Development) officers who had been posted to Southeast Asia, and with Southeast Asian diplomats who were posted to the U.N. and the U.S. That was my first effort at in-depth interviewing, and I've done it ever since.

When you went into the working world, where were you before FIND?

The AFL-CIO. I did a book for them called *The Union Counselor's Handbook*. It was a book of resources. One of the things I included was a whole step-by-step guide on how to telephone a government agency and get information.

So you were already training primary interviewers back then.

Next I worked for Citibank in their international banking group, and then in their Washington office. I did a lot of primary research there, talking both within the government and with other businesses. At that time there was a lot of controversy about international trade investment legislation. Then I worked briefly for Pru-Bache. I honed my interviewing skills when I worked for Business International, which became the Economist Intelligence Unit [45, see Appendix]. I spent almost ten years as a business journalist. Sixty to seventy percent of what I wrote was based on interviews. We did a couple of large studies as well. The largest was on transborder data flow. I did most of the hundred corporate and hundred expert interviews around the world. That one took me to Japan and Europe. I did some private consulting for a couple of years, and then I came to FIND.

What are some of the differences between interviewing in the U.S. and interviewing in Europe or Asia?

In Japan, interviews tend to be more formal. Also, you usually have more than one person present, the person you're interviewing plus two or three subordinates who may or may not speak—at least not directly to you, although your principal respondent may consult with them, in Japanese, before answering you.

For most of the interviews, I was working with an interpreter. You have to be very careful of the phrasing, particularly in Asia. You cannot ask questions that can be answered "yes" or "no" because people will tend to answer "yes." They are very polite. It's not a question of lying, but there are different concepts of politeness. There's a whole concept of "face."

In Japan—and this was a while ago—although my interpreter was a woman, there was not one corporate woman. At the time I went, the women were all serving tea.

Another big issue with phrasing is, you have to be careful and make sure that you're understood. You have to be very careful about your slang, because Americans tend to use a lot of sports slang, football and baseball slang in particular—like an "end run" around something—which is not always understood. The more specific your question is, the more likely you are to get an answer.

The Japanese have very strong school affiliations, so if you can find a way to tie into that, that's helpful. Usually—and this really works in other countries too—there's a quid pro quo in sharing information. People want to get information, if they're going to give it. The Japanese like to get competitive intelligence, although they don't like to give out a lot of intelligence. This is true, much more so, in other countries like Korea, where competitive intelligence may be considered tantamount to spying.

Japanese place a very high value on information. A professor at Tokyo University told me how the Japanese spend hours and hours and thousands and thousands of yen with a tea master, not just to learn the ritual, but to learn it to the nth degree. And finally they'll get that one little thing and they'll feel it has great value because they put so much time and energy into acquiring it. So information is very, very precious.

How about some of the European countries?

It varies. Europeans were not as different, in my experience, as the Japanese. But there were differences among business

interviews, political interviews, labor interviews, and interviews with bureaucrats. The labor interviews tended to be
much more hostile; they had certain expectations since I'd
come from a business-oriented publication. Each had its own
culture, in a sense, within their country culture.

The German corporate culture is more formal, a little bit like
going to Japan. Cologne was a lot more formal than Hamburg,
where everything was very open and people tried to anticipate
what I was going to need before I ever asked for it. The French like
to do the interview in French. I did them partially in English and
partially in French; I took notes in a mixture of French and English.
I found that they were more forthcoming in French. I don't speak
German, but I didn't find a similar situation in Germany.

Now tell me what you do at FIND.

I am a Senior Project Manager and I work for our Strategic
Consulting and Research Group. I do everything from a real
quickie "try and call someone to do a quick interview," to business intelligence, market research, and, my absolute favorite,
best practices studies. Benchmarking, best practices—those are
always the most interesting to me. And that's where I do most of
the real in-depth interviewing. Obviously I do secondary
research as well.

You also do some training of other people at FIND?

I do a seminar for people at FIND on interviewing techniques.
I put it together for two reasons. I think it's good to contribute to
the skill set of the people I work with. And people used to come
to me and say, "But it's just one phone call. Can you make just
one phone call?"

In the seminars I spend a lot of time on preparing for the
interview: How do you find the right person to interview? How
do you manage your client's expectation about what you can get?

If you're doing a large project, how do you schedule the interviews? Then I get into specific interviewing techniques.

What do you tell people about taping?

The absolute first thing you do is test your tape recorder. For an important interview you use new batteries. Even if you're going to plug it in, you want to make sure that there are working batteries in there because you can always kick out a plug. I usually test it with my voicemail. On a really important interview, I will call someone and record both sides of the conversation, just to make sure it's working in both input and output. That's the physical side of it.

Just as important, you never tape without letting the other person know. You may be able do that legally, but I think it's very bad ethically. As you did with me, I always ask, "Do you mind if I tape?" Or I'll say, "I'd like to tape you." If I'm going to use the actual transcript or give the transcript to a client, I let them know that. If it's a very complex subject, sometimes I will tape for background purposes, and then I say, "I'm taping for background; we will destroy the tape when we're finished. And if there's something you want to say that you don't want taped, let me know."

Once I've asked permission, the other thing I do is never rely on the tape. I always take detailed backup notes as if I did not have the tape on, because if you don't, the tape will break and you won't notice it. Or you're going to get to the end of the side, or the tape will foul, and you didn't notice it. I've had static on the line so bad that I could not hear the other person on the tape, even though the respondent sounded just fine on the phone and the tape looked like it was going perfectly. Check your tape every few seconds during the interviewing process to make sure it's going, but never trust your tape. I will say, for the times that I leaned back and trusted the tape, I paid. I had one interview where we got into a discussion and I stopped writing notes and my batteries went. When I played it back, his voice got softer and softer and softer. I lost part of the interview.

I've experienced everything I've described—tapes breaking in the middle of interviews, fouling within the recorder, all of them—so I always take notes as if I didn't have it. And I tell people that, even though I've asked their permission to tape, I'm also taking notes while we're doing this. I give them the reasons: "Because if I don't, I know the tape's going to break or something." And it gets them to laugh and relax a little bit.

I also tell them that I'm typing the notes because I can't read my own handwriting, which is true. I can't read my writing so, whenever I can, I type all my notes on the computer. In Microsoft Word, under the Tools menu, I use Autocorrect, and I put a lot of shortcut words in there. When I'm interviewing on a specific subject, I'll temporarily put specific words in there.

That makes your note-taking go more quickly?

Yes. It gives me much more legible notes at the end.

That's great. Now let's talk about finding the right person to interview.

First of all, I find out if the client's got anybody specific in mind; that's always helpful. With companies, I ask whether they know anybody in the company. Very often they'll have some names to start with.

I do some secondary research as part of my preparation. I look for names of people who have been quoted in articles or who have written articles, because it's great to call someone and say, "I saw you quoted in Pulp and Paper Journal and you were saying this, and I'd like to just ask you some more about that." Or "I saw you quoted in this publication and it looks like you're super-knowledgeable in this area."

On a company's Web site you may find names. You can find names in an annual report, but it's tricky because you only get the really senior person, and that's probably not the person you're going to interview. But you can find names and, if you can get to the right division, go to the office of whoever runs it to get the name of the right person to speak to. Also, if you've got something that a company has said in an annual report, it's easier to follow up: "Well, you said it in the annual report!"

The other way to find names is to ask at the switchboard, and try to be very specific. That works in some companies, but in others it's extremely hard to find people without knowing their names. In fact, there are a couple of companies that I won't even tackle, usually. Unless you know somebody at Procter & Gamble, you can't find anybody because they will not give out names by title and they won't put you through to a department. The only department they'll put you through to is public relations.

You can also use directories. Retailing has a series of *Chain Store Guides* [26]. They work beautifully. There's a *Chain Store Guide* for the automotive aftermarket, the supermarket industry, apparel stores, and so on. They list all the buyers and lots and lots of other names. Those are great sources if you happen to be working in the retailing area.

What are your favorite print sources for finding experts?

Industry publications. If you're doing a secondary search you can find them on Dialog [39] or Dow Jones Interactive [41]. Sometimes people are quoted in the local press, so any source that picks up local press is good. Very often you can find names in little items in the local press, somebody from the company who doesn't make it to the national press or the industry press, but you find them quoted in the local newspaper or the local business press.

The *Carroll's Directories* [23] are very good sources for government personnel. They have five reference books. The federal government one is really good. I can usually find the right person within three phone calls. The state directory is not as complete, but at least you can get some good office numbers and you can usually find the right office. Then you have city and county directories, but the information is even more sketchy in those.

Do you use associations as sources?

Industry associations are great sources to interview, and to find members, people who have spoken at conferences. There is an association for practically every industry. Sometimes I just go into HotBot [66] and put in the subject I'm interested in and see what comes up. The best way to find an association is the *Encyclopedia of Associations* [47]. Or I ask a colleague in our Quick Consulting & Research group; they very often have contacts within associations in the area they specialize in. We have teams in various areas—food teams, high-tech teams, and so on. We're members of certain associations ourselves, which is also helpful. The caveat is that you have to be judicious about calling associations, or you wear out your welcome.

So it helps to have a referral and a name. How about favorite Web sources and commercial online vendors?

I mentioned HotBot. It's one of the few search engines where you can request an exact phrase, they actually come back with a page containing that exact phrase. It has an advanced search feature, which lets you narrow things down by adding words that must or must not be included. Ninety percent of the time I can find what I need on HotBot.

For company information, the other Web source I like is Yahoo! [141], particularly when I want to get company profiles. In Yahoo!'s stock section you can find the company's profile and usually a good clickthrough to their Web site. Hoover's [65] is another good site for company information, and so is Edgar [46]. I keep bookmarking sites that come in handy eventually. I must have over a thousand bookmarks.

As far as commercial online services are concerned, I tend to use Dow Jones Interactive and Hoovers. Recently I've started using Reuters' Web version [112], which is really strong on the international side.

With secondary research, do you tend to start broad or narrow?

It depends on the time I have available and the subject. If I know zilch about the subject, I start a little bit broader. But I'll get into whatever I have to so I'm knowledgeable enough to do the interviews intelligently.

What kind of clients do you have? And how do their projects come in to you?

Our clients are primarily corporate, some government, some associations. Some clients call me directly, or the switchboard will send them to me. Others send in requests via the Web site. Consultants in our Quick Consulting & Research group refer clients to us. I get a lot of the international requests. Normally we send the client a proposal outlining the project specifications, the methodology, cost, and timing. In a large project, with multiple interviews, very often we work with the client to design a discussion guide for structuring the interviews.

Can you tell me a bit more about the types of relationships clients have with FIND?

Some clients come to us for single projects or engagements, but most of FIND/SVP clients have a retainer relationship with us, giving them access primarily to our Quick Consulting & Research Service. About 2,500 distinct companies or organizations have retainers, and about twenty thousand executives within those companies have FIND/SVP cards.

Our Quick Consulting & Research Service deals with inquiries that can be handled in three hours or less. My group, the Strategic Consulting and Research group, handles inquiries—custom research, best practices/benchmarking studies, customer satisfaction measurement—that are more involved and can range from five hours and $600, to engagements that take months and cost well over $100,000 to $200,000. We will work with retainer clients or non-retainer clients.

When a project comes to you, do you get to talk to the client directly to do a reference interview?

Of course. You always need to know the objective. What is your client trying to accomplish? Diagnosing the client's needs is one of the most important parts of the process. If you can't get the client to be really clear about her objective, she might ask you to find things that won't accomplish what she's trying to do. Also, we make it clear that we will not misrepresent FIND in any way; this is company policy. We subscribe to the SCIP code of ethics [115]. That's very important.

I will very often ask a client to think about her questions and outline them in an email or fax. That makes the client organize her thoughts. I also try to get them to prioritize the information that they want. And I review the questions with the client to make sure that I am clear about the meaning.

Before I write a proposal on anything, especially if we are dealing with an area I don't know anything about, I'll do some preliminary research very quickly. I'll talk to one of the industry specialists in Quick Consulting & Research; I'll see what in-house resources we have. I want to get a feeling, first of all, for whether the topic is well covered in secondary sources or not. In other words, I want to get a feeling for what it's going to take to do the project. We're not always right, but that first step is helpful.

Do you find that clients usually know what they want, or do they think they want one thing and they really need something else?

It depends on the client. Some are very, very precise and some are all over the place. They may change their minds twelve times, including after you've started the research. Sometimes it's because they've developed new needs. They see preliminary information and want follow-up. Sometimes it's because they haven't thought it through. That's why I like to get the client to put something down in writing if I can. If not, I take very literal notes. When I outline for the client what we're going to do, I'm almost spieling back their own words.

How do you estimate project costs?

I try to get a feel for the time it's going to take, the resources I'm going to need, how much of our research will be secondary. What does the client want? This can be all over the place, with anything from one or two interviews to a hundred. Then, what kind of depth are we looking for? How much secondary research will we do? How much primary? What is the deliverable? Is the deliverable a one-page memo? A written report? A presentation? Based on all that, we have time guidelines.

With in-depth executive interviews, you have to factor the time it takes to set up the discussion guide. Depending on its length, that can be five or six hours. If you're going back and forth with your client, it can take even longer. When I write the discussion guide, I say the questions out loud to make sure that these are "sayable" questions. And structuring the questions is really important. If I have the freedom to do it, I structure the discussion guide so that the least threatening questions come first.

I tend to figure that a one-hour interview is going to require five hours of my time. At least two are going to be in finding the person and in trying to connect and actually get the interview. So it's at least a two-to-one factor; it could be a three-to-one factor. I had one project where I was trying to get somebody in Sweden and I called them every morning for a month between 5 and 6 A.M. Then, of course, when you finally connect with your target she might not be the right person.

There's the time for the interview itself, and then, if you're writing up some notes, whether you're taping or not, you have to figure it's a two- or three-to-one factor. For every minute of your interview, it's going to take you two to three minutes to write up the interview.

So you factor that all in and then multiply it by some cost.

Right. If my deliverable is the interview, that's one thing. If my deliverable is an analysis and a report, then the time for preparing the report should be almost equal to the time you spend getting the interviews. People always underestimate the time that's going to take. Ordinarily, it should be about fifty percent of your project.

Do you find that you're doing a lot of value-added work for your clients—analysis, creating tables, providing your own take on the information that you're getting?

Even when the clients just want the interviews, they usually ask for a summary of what I got from it, and what the key points were. Even if they don't want a formal report, they do want to know what your key findings are. The value-added can come in the interviews themselves, depending on what you can get a respondent to say and the kind of analysis that you can provoke your respondent into making. But we also do a lot of value-added analysis.

I also try to manage the client's expectation about deadlines, reminding them that this is not like going online. You're trying to find someone who is at his or her desk, and is free to speak with you. Depending on how much time you need from someone, that can be difficult. We also remind them, if they want proprietary information, that the respondent's perfectly free to say "no." They may not reveal proprietary information, particularly if it's a small, privately held company. Very often we will say to the client, "Would your company give out this information?"

What are major client misconceptions?

"It just takes one phone call." I have to remind them that these are live people, and they're probably as busy as he, the client, is.

People travel a lot. They go to a lot of meetings. It takes time to get somebody to carve out time for you.

I try to get clients, in a big study at least, to give me something to make it worthwhile for the respondent to spend his valuable time speaking with me. For example, can we give respondents a summary of the findings? Usually that's what they want. Sometimes we might offer a gift certificate, or a small honorarium, or a small donation to a respondent's favorite charity. You try to have something to offer.

I also remind them that many companies have adopted a policy of refusing to take part in surveys. They do that to protect confidential information, and to conserve employee time.

Do you have favorite ways of finding phone numbers?

Through the directories, sometimes through *Duns Business Locator* [43], or the *Thomas Register* [127]. Often I'll just go to a company's Internet site, although sometimes they bury their phone numbers.

Phone sites I've used include Switchboard [125], Anywho [10], The Ultimate People Finder [131], The Real White Pages [111], and Yahoo! People Search [144]. Some are good, some are not. They seem to work well at different times. The ones that allow you to search nationwide are usually better than the ones where you have to know the state in advance.

How about preparing for the interview?

I think preparation is critical to doing a successful interview. The more you know, the more you can bring to an interview, the more you get from it. I get as smart as I can about a company, about a subject. I look into the secondary literature. I interview our clients to find out what they already know. It depends on the size of the project, of course, and how much time I have to do it.

You just don't plunge into these things. Acquiring a knowledge base is sort of my security blanket, but it also means that I can bring something to the interview if I know what's being written about a subject, what the current articles are saying. I like to go in with some kind of trading beads, something I know that will interest the person I'm talking to. I'll try to find some numbers I can quote, so I have something to go in with. That way they'll still feel they've gotten a benefit from talking to me, even if I'm not doing a formal report that they can share in.

Also, if I'm doing a major interview project, I tend to read my questions aloud before I start so I feel comfortable with them. It's like making a speech. Then the interview feels more like a conversation; it makes the respondent, and me, more comfortable.

I think of what some of my backup probes, or follow-up questions, are going to be. I usually write them down so I don't forget them. That's all part of getting ready.

When you use a discussion guide, do you stick to those questions word-for-word?

It depends on the project. People don't like questionnaires, and I usually say, "I have a few questions." When we do write a discussion guide we also put probes in. Depending on the project and the subject I try to get through the whole discussion guide, but I very rarely say everything exactly as it's written unless there's a specific point to doing it, or the client has instructed us to do so.

Do you find that interviews take on a life of their own, even if you have a discussion guide?

Absolutely, and an interviewee might answer question seven when you're at two. So you take notes on that and try to keep it in mind. That's another reason to go through your questions several times in advance—so you know them well enough to realize that the respondent is answering question seven.

When I feel that the questions are repetitive, I may actually say, "I think you may have answered this before, but ..." or "I think we may have covered this when I asked you about such-and-such, but …" And then they say something totally different anyway, so you're still getting new information.

Let's look at how to get through the gatekeepers.

Sometimes you never do get through the gatekeeper. I try very hard to get someone's direct dial number, if I can. Sometimes you can get it, sometimes you can't. I will often just say, "I saw her quoted in an article and I'm following up on this." One of my other little tricks when I'm looking for someone is to go to the office of the Executive Vice President or the President. You don't get the EVP, but you get their secretary and you ask, "Who's knowledgeable about this? Who should I be talking to?" You get a name, so then you can call and say, "So-and-so's office told me you're the person I should be speaking to." Or "So-and-so's office suggested I call you."

Also, if the company has multiple branches, try calling one that's outside New York City; people in New York are always too busy.

Do you find there are best times or days to call, or worst times or days to call?

Worst time, Friday afternoon. Other than that, it is better to try early in the morning—7:30 or 8 in the morning. Try calling at lunch hour, calling when the gatekeeper is going to be away. Of course, if you're making calls around the world, early in the morning can be very early, your time.

When you do get a gatekeeper, do you have approaches that you use to try to get through?

Be really nice, but not subservient. Act like you have a right to speak with them. I don't say I want to interview them; I just say, "I would like to speak with so-and-so." If you really need an "about," say, "I'd like to speak with them about x."

A lot of times I'm very spontaneous, responding to the situation. "I really need to speak with her." "I'm told she's the absolute only person …" "Can you help me?" Sometimes you can enlist their help, get them on your side.

The other approach that works beautifully once in a while is the corporate public relations department. I just did a Nike interview. We were so sure we would have trouble with Nike, but the woman in PR got me the perfect interview subject and really smoothed the way. In fact, I called her back afterwards to thank her. Treat the gatekeepers like people and professionals. If somebody is going to refer you, and goes out of their way to look up a phone number or anything, say, "Thank you so much. I really, really appreciate your taking the time to do this for me."

I use that so much myself, and I mean it! I really do appreciate their taking the time. Once you've gotten to the right person, what approaches have worked particularly well?

Generally I state what I'm looking for and say, "I've been told that you are the best person on this," or that "this is something you're really good at." Usually I'm telling the truth; this is the person. I also ask, "Is this a good time?" Depending on whether I've got just one or two questions, or I really want to talk with them in depth, I ask, "Can I set up a time at your convenience?" I always make sure that the person knows we can do it at their convenience. I tell them, "If you want to do this at 5 A.M., we'll do it at 5 A.M. If you want to do this on Sunday morning, we'll do it on Sunday morning." And I've done that. Then, when I call, even if I've set up the interview in advance, I still recheck to make sure that it's a good time.

It depends on how formal the situation is, but when we write up a discussion guide, we usually include a little formal qualifier to make sure we're talking to the right person. We describe what the project is about and what we're looking for, and then we ask, "Would you be the person in charge of this?" Then we often begin with general questions to get a comfort level going.

I treat a phone interview as if I were there in person. You smile at the interviewee. They can hear a smile over the telephone. They can tell your energy level. You should be pouring your energy into the interview. It's like going on stage. You have a sense of looking the person in the eyes. You try to get a feel for whether they're going to speak very quickly or not. As people are talking, I encourage them to keep talking: "That's so interesting." And I mean it! It's not something you fake. Sometimes I'll pick up on something they say and then push further. You give the person you're talking to positive feedback all the time.

During the course of a discussion, I always try to establish some kind of personal relationship with the person on the other side of the phone. I always think of them as people. And I almost always think of them as potential clients, and I treat them the same way I would treat a client. I never cut people off. I learned this from a transcription typist I work with. She told me that one of the differences between me and other interviewers is that I don't cut people off. I let them talk, with these sort of encouraging murmurs, and they keep talking.

People will talk to fill up a silence. So you should not be afraid of a little silence. When I'm being silent, it's usually because I haven't caught up with what they're saying and I'm madly taking my notes, but they'll often keep talking and provide more interesting information without my asking for it.

Another useful tactic is to bring something of interest to the respondent. I've talked with so many companies and dealt with so many subjects that I can very often tell someone, "Oh, what you're saying is like x, or like what another company has done, or like what they're doing in another industry."

Also, you appeal to the person's expertise. You ask their opinion. If they are quoted in an article you can quote from it. That really works. I'll say, "I saw that Pharmaceutical News Weekly said that your such-and-such division had seventy-four million dollars in sales last year. I know the press often gets things wrong, so I want to verify that."

Great. So you come in with a figure and you ask them to verify it.

Yes. People like to teach. I very often interview on subjects I know nothing about. I will say, "I'm not an expert in the field; can you define that concept? I want to make sure I understand what you're saying." I ask about acronyms. "I deal with so many industries and they've all got acronyms and sometimes they overlap. What's that one?"—because it could mean any one of twelve different things.

Very often I'll ask, "Am I correct in understanding that you have said ...?" And I'll repeat what I think I heard in my own terms, so I know I'm getting it right. That reassures people that you've been listening to them.

And if you got it wrong, you find out right away. How do you deal with issues that might be sensitive?

If I think it is really sensitive, I may actually preface my question by saying, "This may be proprietary but I'd like to ask ..." They'll either answer it or they won't. I don't always do that; it depends on my sense of the interview. Also, once I've gotten somebody involved in the subject, they do tend to talk more. One of the things that works for me, aside from being polite, is that I get really interested in what people are saying. Everybody is interesting, even switchboard operators, but especially the people that you are interviewing.

How do you handle objections? What if someone says, "I don't want to talk about this?"

"You have an absolute right not to." I may ask the question three different ways, and sometimes they'll say, "Well ..." Then I admit, "Now, I figured you probably wouldn't answer, but I had to ask it."

The other thing I tell people is that different people at different companies have different thresholds of what's considered proprietary. What one company puts in its marketing literature is, to another company, totally proprietary. That's true, and you never know till you ask.

And that seems to make them feel more comfortable?

Yes. I may also tell them, "I think it may be proprietary but I don't know ..." I always use this example: One year Merck did a major corporate reorganization, forming world units—like world R&D, world manufacturing—and they detailed the entire reorganization, including all the top people, in the annual report. That same year, I was trying to find the head of one of the five major divisions listed in the annual report for either Lilly or Johnson and Johnson, and it was proprietary; they wouldn't tell me who it was!

When you have a number of people to call, how do you decide whom to call first?

The least important one, if you can. Sometimes it's the first one you were actually able to get, and who's willing to talk. But I always want to get some practice by starting with the least sensitive or least significant contact, because that way I'm building up some knowledge. I have more to bring to the next interview. Each successive interview may not be getting easier, but at least you know more. Your questions get better. The probes get better. And sometimes you can say, "I can't tell you who said this, but one of my other interviewees said ..." Again, you're bringing more to the interview.

When you're doing an interview, what tells you that you're done?

When I've answered all my questions, or I think I have. Then usually I'll have a last question where I ask, "Is there anything that I should have asked you that I haven't?" or some variation on that. Sometimes you get nothing and sometimes you get lots. Then I'll also ask: "If I think of something else, or don't understand my notes, can I call you back? Is there anyone else I should speak with?"

So there's "anything I didn't think to ask," callbacks, and referrals. When you're teaching people to do interviews, what do you stress most to begin with?

Be interested. Be knowledgeable. Novices may not have a lot of knowledge to bring to an interview, especially if they're new to the field. So the emphasis is on the prep time; the more they prep the more comfortable they'll be.

We need to warn them: Don't lie. It will come back to bite you. You can't misrepresent yourself or FIND. For example, you absolutely do not represent yourself as a student. You can get a client into trouble by doing it. We have a client who hired another consultancy where a young woman misrepresented herself as a student to a competitor, and the competitor found out and sued the company.

Do you have a favorite success story, or a favorite horror story, in your primary research experience?

The worst is when you've called forty different companies and you can't get anybody to do the interview. We've had this happen. Or clients want something that nobody's tracking, and think they can get an answer without spending many thousands of dollars themselves. The best—my favorite—interviews are ones where I really learned something new and in-depth. I meet somebody who gives me a sense that I've had this wonderful intellectual experience, and it's totally exciting. I did one with a top person at Texas Instruments DSP Division. When we started out talking, I think he was in Sweden; then he was in London. I finally finished it up when he got home on a Sunday. I got a complete, detailed picture of how they had created the market and the infrastructure for the digital signal processor. It was fascinating stuff. Or the interview with the Japanese professor who described himself as a simple electrical engineer, but who gave me such profound insights into Japanese culture that, when I left, I couldn't help bowing and saying, rather reverently, "Sensei."

The wildest experience was when I walked into a trade union in Great Britain and the guy just snarled at me like he was going to eat my head off because I was from the business community. I started that one off by saying, "I really want to talk to you about your increased worker participation; I think that's such an exciting development and so important that it happened." He just looked at me like, "Where is she coming from? This isn't what I expected."

You always try to be sympathetic to the person you are interviewing. You're trying to get information from their point of view. You have to assess what that point of view is, and where they're coming from.

Another crazy interview happened some years back. I had been trying to interview the head of the EU's foreign affairs directorate. He wouldn't talk to me on the phone from Brussels, but we wound up at the same weekend conference at the Wye Plantation in Maryland. I latched onto him and finally got him to promise me the interview. But he kept saying "later." Then in the afternoon we were in the swimming pool, and he suddenly turned around and said, "Okay; what are your questions?" Fortunately I had already interviewed his two top aides in Brussels, so all I had to do was remember his really pungent, quotable comments. He thought I was brilliant and I never had trouble getting through to him after that.

Are there any types of calls or interviews that you particularly don't like, that are really hard to make yourself do? How do you get over that?

I usually get stage fright before any major interview, anyway. I look at my notes, I start reviewing things aloud again, and I pick up the phone.

I don't like competitive intelligence. I find it very, very hard to do. I keep the SCIP code of ethics up by my desk, and I let clients know ahead of time that I'm going to abide by that. It's difficult when you're talking to a company and you feel that somebody's telling you too much and they shouldn't. Sometimes I'll either stop them or I simply will not take notes. I'm not in business to hurt a company. You can do damage, and that is not where I want to be.

Absolutely. We were talking before about phone interviews and in-person interviews. What major differences do you find between the two?

In person, you're even more on a stage. Your body language is so important. Your body language has to sort of mirror your respondent's. Also, I don't take my computer to in-person interviews; I take notes by hand, and I have to figure out a way to do it so that I can read my handwriting afterwards. You have to relate to people differently in person. Usually there are more preliminaries. You set up the relationship ahead of time, because you've met in person. You've shaken hands, you've made a little small talk. When I tape, I stick the tape recorder in between us and I just say, "Anytime you don't want to be taped you turn it off." But it also makes it harder to watch your tape and make sure that you haven't run out on one side.

With the telephone, where you don't have those body language clues as much, do you compensate in some way, or do things differently?

You still have the body language. You sit forward, you smile at the person. You kind of pretend you're there. It's just that when you are there, they can see everything you do.

Sometimes it's easier to get people really talking on the phone. Very often—and I do this in person, too—I tend, briefly, to get off into something personal. One whole stint I wound up talking about opera with a lot of people, and that worked well. Sometimes that happens in the middle of the interview; you go off and come back.

When you look at a research request, are there keys or cues that say to you "for this we might be able to get secondary information, but for this we're going to need to go primary?"

You don't always know ahead of time. There's no magic solution for that one. Given my own personal orientation, I tend to think everything should be done primary. My instinct is just to call up the association, call up this, call up that. It's my phone trigger finger. I have to make myself remember to try secondary sources first.

The modus operandi is, you do the secondary and then you do the primary. It makes more sense to see what's there, as part of the prep. I do what you'd call triage. Either I consult with a colleague or I quickly go onto Dow Jones Interactive, throw in the key words, and see if I get one article or a lot. My group's in a unique situation because we deal with so many different industries that, unless you've done a similar assignment, you just don't know what you might be getting into. So I very often go to colleagues in our Quick Consulting & Research group. I can just send an email or go over to one of our industry experts and say, "I have to propose on this; is this well-covered or not? Might we get a lot of secondary?"

We have people who specialize in certain areas, who know the HMO industry, who know pharmaceuticals, who can tell me, "Yes, this one is well-covered," or "No, I've had this question before and nobody is writing about it." Sometimes they'll say, "It's got a great industry association that does lots of research, but you have to be a member for them to do anything for you." Or "They've got a great researcher and we talk to them all the time, and it's covered in the press." And we have some internal databases where, if we get the right search phrase, we can see if questions on a particular subject have been handled in Quick Consulting & Research.

Of course, if the client says, "We want you to talk to people," that's a big cue that we'll probably go primary. How detailed and specific the individual questions are often provides a clue: Is somebody going to write about this? Well, maybe so; maybe there's a Harvard case study. That would be great.

With certain kinds of questions, I just sort of know. If somebody wants a best practices study, that will involve primary research. You know with competitive intelligence that they're not going to find that online. Sometimes I'll look at the questions and think, "Nobody in their right mind is going to answer those questions, but we'll try." So I have a sense that primary won't always do the trick, either.

And sometimes the subject might just be too new. If this is a brand-new service or this company is in the midst of reorganizing, that's your key that very little information is going to be available in secondary sources. You can hope that maybe there's a press release. By the way, that's another thing I'll look for—press releases, just to see if there's any way I can refer to their content in interviews, or pick up other sources they might mention.

And then some stuff just never gets covered because it's of interest to like, five people in the whole world.

Once you know you need it, are there situations in which it's particularly difficult to do primary research?

I can think of two problems when you're doing market research. One is when you've got only one or two large companies in the industry. Your chances of getting anything decline precipitously, because why should they talk to you? They're not likely to give out a lot of information, and they're even worse if they're privately held.

The other is when you've got lots of small, privately held companies. That's also a big problem. I had a major project like that last year, and I had to piece it together like a mosaic. Initially, nobody wanted to talk to me on the phone. So I wound up going to a trade show and I met some people there and actually did a number of interviews at the show. I also collected names of people that I could talk to afterwards and follow up with. If you visit a trade show, meet a person, introduce yourself, and collect business cards, then later you can call and say, "I met you at the trade show." That's a big help.

Speakers at trade shows are also a great resource. Going to trade shows is one way to learn about the industry too.

Do you have some favorite sources for identifying the best trade shows for a particular industry, or do you go to your industry experts?

It depends on the industry. There are directories of trade shows but, very often, my process is to just go to the association; they will tell me about the trade show. Or I look at the association's Web site.

How has the Net changed the way you do primary research?

I love it. It's a lot easier. It doesn't replace interviewing, but it's easier to find people and companies, and to find out about a company. It's easier to say, "Gee, I saw this on the Net, but could you go into it a little more?" Because you're talking about it on the Net; therefore you obviously want people to know about it.

What people don't understand about searching on the Net is that the same search can produce very different results. Of course, you get different hits from every search engine, but you can do the same search a week apart and get different answers. Clients don't understand that. It's not like doing a search in Dow Jones Interactive where, if you put in your search terms, it comes up with every article within your parameter. But if you use the same keywords on the Net, you get all kinds of things that may or may not fit.

Sometimes there's serendipity, something fortuitous; you find something you wouldn't even have imagined. Other times you're wading through piles of junk.

Some clients will say, "I searched the Net." Okay, but what search engines did they use? Sometimes we say, "We searched the Net and didn't find it," and then the client does find it. You can try some of the meta-search engines. I've tried Dogpile [40], which brings up a lot of stuff, but it's so imprecise. It's very time-consuming to go through.

I'll use the Net for other things. I use it to look at a company's employment section on their Web site. Job postings can tell you a lot about a company. I don't know whether you'd consider that primary or secondary research.

It's a very fuzzy line these days. It's not as cut-and-dried as it used to be. Even considering the blurring of the lines, what do you get from primary research that nothing else will give you?

Personal interaction. Aside from that, insights, the ability for me to make the analysis rather than relying on somebody's pre-digested opinions. The catnip for me is getting to do a project where nobody's really looked at the subject before. I can't get enough of those. When you talk to people, find out their insights, and bring together a lot of different experts' insights, you can really come up with interesting things.

Absolutely; it's so much fun. If you look down the road, how do you see primary research

changing over the next five years? Do you think that the need for it will increase or decrease?

It's a mix. It's getting harder to do certain kinds of research. I don't think the interview is going to be replaced by computer. The worry is that people are so pressed for time. A lot of my interviews on best practices can run an hour and a half. It's the demands on people to carve out the twenty minutes for you or, for the more in-depth interviews, the hour or hour and a half. It's very hard, unless you can really offer something, give people a reason to talk to you so they feel they're getting something out of it. You have to make sure they stay interested in the interview, and that's partly where your preparation comes in. Hopefully you have enough information about other, related subjects that you can drop little pearls along the way to keep them interested.

I think it will become harder and harder to do competitive intelligence. Companies are becoming more and more aware of it. Companies learn how to get more defensive. The use of phones that tell people where you're coming from worries me a little bit—anything that makes it easier for people to avoid talking to you. And I don't want a minicam on my computer because, while we do not misrepresent, I role play just ever so gently when I'm interviewing. Not fully—just a hint, for example, of playing the sweet young thing or the brisk professional. You can't do that when they can see you. I just don't like the idea of video; I may come to like it, but I don't think so.

How do you feel about leaving voicemail? How do you deal with that?

A couple of tips: It's fine to leave a message, but I rarely leave more than two or three, at least not in the same week. Although, when I'm trying to reach somebody, I may call six or eight times a day until I finally get them. When I get a gatekeeper instead of voicemail, I will leave a message but I'll also say, "What's the best time to call back, because I'm on the phone all the time and I hate to throw somebody into telephone tag." I call it "dancing tape to tape."

Also, when you leave a message for someone and the voice-mail says, "I'm away from my desk" or something like that, you should not assume that the person actually is somewhere in the office. People often don't change their voicemail message. So if you haven't heard back or been able to reach somebody in a week or so, try to find someone else in their office to ask what's going on. Are they traveling? Are they out sick? Once I was trying to get someone for weeks and they were never there, although the voice on the voicemail promised to get back to me soon. It turned out that the person hadn't worked for the company for two years—but his voicemail was still there. Another time, a marketing executive was out for six months on maternity leave, and wasn't working from home. But her voicemail didn't mention that fact and was still taking messages.

So it's very important to find out whether the person is actually in the office, because you could wait for weeks to get them—and then it turns out not to be the right person and you have to start all over again.

I've had that experience and I love that you brought it up.

Another thing is that, going in through the switchboard, you can get sent to someone who isn't the right person. That person then sends you to someone who sends you to someone who sends you to someone. You can lose an amazing amount of time. If I'm on that kind of treasure hunt and I can't reach the person I've been referred to within a day or two, I'll call their assistant to ask, "Is this the right person?" So often it turns out not to be. Companies get reorganized so much.

How about sending questions or discussion guides ahead of time?

It depends on what I'm doing. Sometimes I will send a discussion guide ahead, but only a cleaned-up version where I've gone through and taken out all the prompts, or followup questions. I'll take out client names, if the client has instructed us to do so. Or I'll outline the topics that we're going to talk about. I don't like sending someone a full discussion guide unless I have to.

When you call someone, do you find that they usually want to know who the ultimate client is? Is that a major sticking point?

It can be. I just say, "We have a company policy that I'm not allowed to give out the client's name unless I'm specifically directed to. I haven't been, but if it's important to you, I'll ask the client if I can give out their name." Then I get back to the client and they have to decide.

I always ask a client why they want the information, and I try to find out if what I'm doing is competitive or not, because it's so much easier if it's not competitive. I can at least give someone that information.

Anything else you'd like to mention?

I have a tip on competitive intelligence: In competitive intelligence, protect the name of your information source. You can get somebody fired. We have a policy that, unless it's something like a benchmarking project where everybody is going to get a copy of the results, which is rare, we do not give out the names of people that we've talked to. It could get back to their employer and they could be fired. In some instances, of course, you do identify the respondent—for example, when they're going to get a business advantage from it, or when you're putting people together.

What do you think are the characteristics of a good primary researcher?

Be really interested in people, and like people, and be flexible. Value your respondents and let them know it. We tend to treat people as if they're adjuncts to equipment. Remember that you're dealing with interesting human beings. That's why I do this, and I think it comes across. Let them hear your interest. The truth is, if you really listen, you can get great insights from anybody. That's why I love doing this.

I've done, I would say, more than five thousand interviews; I've stopped counting. When you have the experience of working in a lot of different subject areas and with a lot of different people, you bring from one to the other. It's really nice to be able to do that in an interview.

Now I've given away all my secrets—everyone can do it.

To that I respond "fat chance." As you would say, is it all right if I call you back if I have other questions, or if I need to check anything?

Absolutely. It's been a pleasure.

Super Searcher Tips

➤ In international interviewing, you have to be very careful of the phrasing, particularly in Asia. You shouldn't ask questions that can be answered "yes" or "no" because people will tend to answer "yes." You have to be very careful about your slang, because Americans tend to use a lot of sports slang, like an "end run" around something.

➤ Té's taping tips: The absolute first thing is to test your tape recorder. In an important interview, use new batteries. Test it with your voicemail or call someone and record yourself to make sure it's working. Check your tape every few seconds during the interviewing process, but never trust your tape. Always take detailed backup notes as if you did not have the tape on. And always ask your interviewee's permission to tape.

➤ *Chain Store Guides* are great sources in the retailing area. There's a chain store guide for the automotive aftermarket, for apparel stores, the supermarket industry, and so on. They list all the buyers and lots and lots of names.

➤ The *Carroll's Directories* are very good sources for government personnel. I can usually find the right person within three phone calls using their federal government directory.

➤ When writing up notes, figure it's a three-to-one factor. Every minute of interview will take three minutes to write up. The time spent preparing the report should be almost equal to the time spent getting the interviews. People always underestimate the time it's going to take. Ordinarily, it should be about fifty percent of your project.

➤ If the company has multiple branches, try to get one that's outside of New York City; people in New York are always too busy.

➤ I may actually preface sensitive issues by saying, "This may be proprietary but I'd like to ask this question." If they don't want to talk about it, I say, "You have an absolute right not to."

➤ You'll know you need primary research when the client has asked you to talk to people; when it's a best practices or competitive intelligence project; when the individual questions are detailed and specific; when the subject is brand-new.

➤ I rarely leave more than two or three messages in the same week, although I may call six or eight times a day until I finally get them. I'll also ask, "What's the best time to call back?" because I hate to throw somebody into telephone tag. I call that "dancing tape to tape."

➤ If you haven't heard back or been able to get somebody in a week or so, contact someone else in the office to find out what has happened to them. They may no longer work for the company, or may be out on leave.

Robin Yarmovsky

Renaissance Researcher, Corporate Setting

Robin Yarmovsky is the Market Research and Business Services Manager at Sun Microsystem's corporate library, SunLibrary. In addition to providing business, competitive, and market research services to Sun employees, she manages the contract negotiations for the business resources purchased by SunLibrary.

robin.yarmovsky@sun.com
www.sun.com

Tell me a bit about your background and how you ended up where you are today. It's such an interesting progression.

I started off going to school in Washington, D.C., in journalism. That was the beginning, I think, of my love for information and of my learning about interviewing people and utilizing primary as well as secondary resources. All of the skills that I would practice in various other jobs, including in corporate libraries, began there with my training in journalism. They included research, finding information, interviewing people, going beyond the secondary research, learning how to "do my homework," and then being able to write up and summarize, synthesize, and analyze the information that I found, so that other people can learn from that information.

One of the things I was trained to do was to utilize more than one resource. For validation, if possible, to find at least three sources on the same topic. That taught me several things. One, not to believe just one person or one fact that I've read. To see what other people are saying. It also taught me to recognize that the same information can be viewed by different people through different filters. It's not that it's not true, or it's not factual, but you have to factor in who said it, what filter they're seeing it through.

If, for example, I'm doing research on the progression of the Internet, and I interview a market research analyst, and then a top technology CIO, then a user, and then Al Gore, I might get four very different points of view, all true, on the state of the Internet and emerging technologies today. The idea is that, depending on who I talk to, I get a wider view of a particular topic. Limiting it to one person doesn't give you the ability to really understand the complexity of an issue. It's not always possible to talk to multiple sources, and it's not really necessary in every research project, but it's a guideline that I was taught, and that I try to carry on when I do research today and to pass on to other people that I'm working with.

This is beautiful stuff, keep going.

Last night while I was driving home, I was pulling together the different parts of my background that got me to where I am, in terms of doing primary research and the belief in doing primary research and how important it is. The next step, after completing school, was working for a journalist for three years doing research in Washington, D.C. We monitored Capitol Hill and the regulatory agencies. I was either attending meetings or following legislation and regulations, and then doing background research on those laws. Then I moved to a special library, doing primary and secondary research for the lobbying arm of one of the zillion associations based in D.C.

That added another layer to my primary research experience, because I learned the U.S. government very well. Working with the bureaucracy was another level in learning not only how to mine expertise from written material, which was very important to the legislation, but above and beyond that, to get interpretation by talking to people who were actually putting out those laws. Trying to find the right person in the bureaucracy was a challenge, and exciting. I also learned, at that stage, how to let somebody talk, and how to listen. How not to give up when you're not finding exactly the right person, because the government was so huge. And, using lots of different secondary resources, how to home in on who the gurus were and who the experts were. I learned the tenacity to find the right person, to be able to look at a really large organization and narrow it down. That's a classic scenario, someone sitting behind a desk and feeling flattered, or else upset, that someone is calling and asking for his or her specialized information.

That was the start of combining some of my skills. To show the progression, I also worked, for a short period of time after that, for a private investigative company.

Okay, tell me about the PI thing.

I worked for private investigators that did corporate investigation. I did secondary and primary research for them. It was around the time of the first big wave of mergers and acquisitions, and that's primarily what they did—big corporate investigations. They were frequently hired by law firms during hostile or non-hostile takeovers, to look at the companies and people involved.

Did you do a fair amount of public records searching in that capacity?

I did. Looking into who companies were, what made them run, what they were doing, and then getting interested in people and locating people became very attractive. I utilized lots of public resources. At that time, even though there were resources online through LexisNexis [80, see Appendix], Dialog [39], and other database services, it was much different from the way it is now with the Web. A lot of the research we did was actually on foot. It was very close to investigative journalism, utilizing all those skills to interview, locate information, and understand what you were seeing. I find those skills very, very similar to what librarians do, if you decide to use that part of your knowledge.

I want to describe how a building of learning occurred. Public records searching added a whole new level, because you can interview people, and you can also understand their backgrounds in another kind of way. Learning to use public records to find out more information about people was very powerful. It added to my level of understanding how information can be used. It also taught me about the ethics of information, which is really important when you're doing primary research.

The ethics issue is so important. Since you brought it up, let's talk about it now.

I'll start with the technique and then move into the philosophy. Usually when I do primary research, less is more for me. I've held conversations with people and gotten incredible interviews where they never even knew my name, let alone where I work and what it's for. It's absolutely amazing to me that somebody would give me all this information and forget to ask, "Who are you? Who am I talking to?"

I've been able to ask questions and make them feel at ease, or I push the right button, or they were just ready to talk to anybody, anyway. I've gotten gold, and I've hung up the phone and they've never known who I am. If they'd asked me I would have told them, but they chose not to ask me. Other times, I'll give information about who I am right up front, without someone asking me, if I can tell that I have to or that doing so will benefit me.

So, technique leads into ethics, because you can use a variety of techniques when talking to someone and still be ethical. If someone asks you who you are, don't misrepresent yourself. If they ask who you are and where you work, I feel you're always required to be honest. If they then choose not to provide you with information, then that's what happens. You figure out another place to go to get that information.

While it's important not to misrepresent who you are, on the other hand, you do not have to say everything. You don't have to give up information right up front. It becomes a dance just like other dynamics in relationships, where one person steps back and one person steps forward. When do you come forward, when do you step back? Whatever you do, it's important to maintain integrity in terms of how you get information because of both legal and personal implications.

You're always evaluating; it's not black-and-white. In each situation, you're constantly monitoring: Okay, do I feel all right about this? Can I do it this way? Can I do it that way?

That's true, but you also have a gut-level instinct. If you start off with integrity and ethics, when you hit that case-by-case scenario, it's just like anything else in life; you have choices that you can make, and your gut sort of lets you know, "Uh-oh, I might be treading down the wrong path."

Talk to me about the ethics of confidentiality— protecting the identity of the people that you talk to, and also the identity of your clients.

Confidentiality works both ways—talking to people internally within your organization, and external to your organization. Here at Sun, for example, when we work with our internal clients we protect their confidentiality. In some cases we do so because we're working on very confidential areas. We could be working with the legal department, or the strategic planning or business development groups. They might be looking at where Sun is investing, where they're strategically planning to go, or the next acquisition they might do. We keep all that information between us and the person that we're working for.

So you would keep confidentiality even from other people in Sun?

Exactly. We're able to work with those people, help those people, and provide them with the confidentiality they need to get their job done. The SunLibrary information specialists provide that same confidentiality in another way. We connect people within the company; we network people, which is another way to do primary research. We can tap into what we know about projects that we've worked on, so when we come across another project that might be similar, part of our job is being able to connect those people. What we don't do is do it without asking them. We protect their confidentiality by first going to that other person and saying, "We know someone else is working on this. Would you want to talk to them, would it be okay if they talked to you?"

Providing that internal confidentiality is really important, because if people know that you work that way, they feel comfortable about working with you. They understand that your job is to share information, and they are willing to tell you more about what they're doing.

It's important when you talk with external sources to be able to be up-front with them. It goes back to journalism: When are you talking off the record and when are you talking on the record? It allows for a freer conversation. People have said to me, "I'm going to tell you this, but you can only utilize it under these circumstances ..." It's important to respect your sources and to utilize their information accordingly.

Is there anything else you want to talk about on the ethics side right now? Otherwise we might go back to how your career evolved.

Nothing else on ethics right now; we might go back to that. Career-wise, I've worked in both library and nonlibrary positions. It just depended on where the research was. That's how I chose the positions—what was fun, what was exciting, and where I could do research. At that time it was a primary pull; it was my passion. After working for the PIs, I left Washington, came to California, and worked for about a year for an executive recruiter.

You are the renaissance researcher. Go ahead.

That was a perfect way to get a crash course in Silicon Valley. I helped generate candidates for the recruiters. I used secondary research for this, but I also used primary research to find out who does what inside companies, and to create a sense of companies' organizations and how they're set up. I got to learn quickly what Silicon Valley was, who the top players were, what they did, what the industries were, about biotech and high tech, what the hot companies were.

Although I thought I was tenacious before, and I was, this added another layer of thick skin that I thought I already had, but didn't. Doing primary research for candidate generation is a really tough job, a whole other level of getting people to talk to you. That job definitely created another level of thick skin in terms of not giving up.

How would you approach generating the candidates?

We utilized an internal database, but we had to verify that people were still in the same positions and figure out who reported to whom. We got that information in a variety of ways, using both primary and secondary research, and we used it to create organizational charts. We picked target companies, figured out the best candidates by job functions, then identified the people that were actually doing those functions, and selected candidates from that.

And after the recruiting firm?

I joined Failure Analysis, an engineering consulting firm that looks at why things fail—disasters such as buildings falling down or planes falling out of the sky, toxic spills, medical devices that don't work correctly, car crashes. It's a unique company and I found it a fascinating place to work.

I thought Failure Analysis was a fascinating company as well. I visited years ago, and I thought I had gone to research heaven— wonderful resources, supportive atmosphere, interesting topics.

It was very, very cool, because Failure covered all different engineering disciplines. It had chemical engineers, people with medical backgrounds, electrical engineers, mechanical engineers. It had a human factors department that looked at human error. We might be doing very technical searches on the corrosion of steel in order to determine when the plane's propeller failed, but it was always connected to human beings because something had happened to them. It was the human element that, I think, drove all of us.

At that time, we were very fortunate to have incredibly rich resources. We were doing state-of-the-art research. We needed to be very, very comprehensive. Often, we were studying accidents that had happened several years before; it could be ten years prior. Talking to people was as important as looking at documents, because we had to recreate the state-of-the-art of the industry or the technology at that earlier time.

Did you find that, if it was too old, it didn't appear online, that you had to go to primary sources to go further back in time?

Yes, certain things weren't online, if you were searching before a certain year. We put disclaimers on our online searches indicating the year the databases stopped, and that the next step might be a manual search. We might also interview people. At Failure, we interviewed people on an ongoing basis as part of what we did.

How did projects or requests come in to you at Failure?

They came in mostly via the phone, or requestors would come to the library. We did a lot of interactive searching, where people would actually sit with us while we ran the secondary online search. We trained them to search cooperatively, along with the research staff, because it helped us. We did a lot of scientific and technical searches, medical searches, chemical searches. Ideally, the requestor could have done this from their desktop, but at that point the technology was such that it was hard to do that. So they would sit with us for an hour or whatever it took, and we would do online searching together.

Did they tend to know exactly what they wanted? Or did you have to help them formulate what they really needed, as opposed to what they thought they needed?

In terms of getting information, the research interview is always really important. I place extremely high value on doing the research interview because I learn so much from it. Also, it gives the person I'm working with—whom I consider my research partner, not necessarily just my client or my customer—a vested interest. When I begin to talk to someone and get to know them, I get involved in what they're looking for and what their needs are. It makes me vested, too, in a way, and then I can strategize with them, which is exciting. It's always fascinating to see how the project looked on paper, and how it changes after you actually talk with somebody and strategize together.

As the research profession has known for a long time, you're not only interviewing experts to get information, you're also interviewing the person that you're doing the research for.

I love your term "research partner." I think I'm going to adopt that. Did people at Failure have

a sense of when they needed primary research and when they needed secondary, or is that something that you brought to the process?

It worked both ways. We had an extensive education system for the engineers at Failure. We taught them the capabilities of the research staff and how to work with us. It was a smaller company at that time, somewhere between three and five hundred people. We educated them so that they knew what our capabilities were and what the resources were. We did traditional primary research, and we also acquired unusual and bizarre things. We didn't just acquire documents; we acquired things like tires and trucks, so that when they were investigating an accident, they could rebuild the accident scenario. They knew we were fast and comprehensive, and that we were really passionate and dedicated.

Some projects were unbelievably comprehensive. For example, once we called all fifty states and talked to people in the state governments about a certain transportation issue. Then we compared each state to what was happening federally. We needed to find the right person in the right place, for each of those states, that handled that topic area. We had to find the information and analyze and distill what people said. Then we organized it in such a way that the engineers could utilize it for their investigation, and often for a trial as well, because in some cases the engineers were expert witnesses.

Did you have a project budget, or would you just use whatever resources were necessary to meet the need?

It was a consulting firm, and we worked really closely with the engineers, who were working closely with their clients at each stage of the project. We worked within budgets, and gave time and cost estimates to the engineers so that they could fit that into their project budget for their ultimate client.

If you had to estimate the cost of a project, what factors would you take into consideration?

We had to determine what resources we were going to use, guesstimate a general cost average for online resources, and then how many hours it would take to do that search, plus primary research, plus pull everything together.

You say you've done a lot of research partner education. Are there any misconceptions related to primary research that people commonly have?

People who haven't done primary research don't understand the fine tuning that it sometimes takes to find both the right person and the person who will talk to you. You might have a ten-minute conversation with someone, but it could take you two hours to find that person, get to that person, and actually have that conversation. That's hard for people who haven't done it to understand. When you estimate your hours to do a project, you don't factor in ten minutes for primary research; you factor in the couple of hours that it might take. It averages out. Some people you can reach right away, some people take longer.

We have other constraints at Sun in terms of the time we can spend making inquiries with market research analysts. Sun purchases blocks of analyst hours, and the time we use talking with the analysts is debited against those pre-purchased blocks. If we go over the alloted amounts of time, we incur additional costs. It's an education process for our client base to realize that, while we do have access to some of the analysts, it's not limitless and there is a cost associated with it. We can't just call the analyst and ask them in-depth questions, unless someone is willing to pay for it.

Have you learned any major lessons about primary research?

It is integral, an extremely important part of what we do.

Even if you don't know the topic, it's still important to plot out your questions and your strategy the best you can. Even if you haven't read reams and reams, have at least three to ten questions prepared. Hopefully you can squeeze in that many, if they give you the time. Then narrow them down to "If I only had five minutes with this person, what are the two main questions that I really need to know?" Having a strategy is really important.

If I have time, and I do not want to be so obvious about why I'm calling and what I'm calling about, I use another strategy. I may ask several different kinds of questions to camouflage the real question, because when you ask questions you might also be giving away competitive information. People know "Ah ha, your company is now looking at this topic." They can learn what you're interested in by the very questions you ask. So it's important to remember that not only do you learn when you interview but, depending upon what you say and what you ask, you can also reveal.

Let's go back to Sun for a few minutes. How do requests come in there? How does that process work?

Requests come in all different kinds of ways. Some we get by phone, some by email—we're a very email-driven society here—some via our corporate intranet. We have request forms for all of our services on our intranet, including research request forms.

How many researchers are there at Sun? And how many people are you serving?

We have four SunLibrary information specialists who conduct research. Right now Sun has about forty thousand employees.

Talk about Super Searchers—four of you handling forty thousand!

Potentially, they are all our clients, but the percentage of the people we actually work for is much smaller. We do have a very strong customer base, which is continually growing as new people come on board, as more people find out about us, and as we actively market our services.

Because of the company's size, we educate a larger audience in a different kind of way. We are currently looking at how we can scale our research services as Sun grows, including providing more value-added Web products created by the research team.

When requests come in, does somebody look at them and say, "Okay, you take this one, you take that one"? Or does it just go to whoever happens to be the next one up?

We have a process where two of us do the initial cut. We break out the information roughly into scientific and technical information on the one hand, and market and business information on the other. The researcher who's primarily responsible for scientific and technical usually picks up those requests. Percentage-wise, we get more market and business-type questions, so more of us concentrate on that area. Right now it's about three to one.

Then we work together and assign the rest of the requests. Inquiries are assigned by looking at several factors: people's timetables or schedules, what they're already working on, or if they're interested in a certain topic. If they've just worked on a topic and they're not deathly sick of it yet, they can pick up the next one and probably do that fairly easily because they're already knowledgeable. We try not to get one person stuck in a certain area—just because you did the wireless market, you always have to do the wireless market—for several reasons. If someone wants to specialize in a specific area, that's fine, but we don't want them to get tired of a certain topic or feel that, just because they picked up a project once, it has to be something they always work on. Having diversity is not only important to keep the interest level high, but it also allows us to meet other people, to work on other projects, and to grow our expertise.

Also, when you've done a topic for a while, you tend to grow your own filters. Not only are you getting information from your sources through their filters, you have to remember your own as well. Now let me ask about your range of turnaround times. How long do your projects tend to take?

They could be anywhere from a couple of hours to a couple of weeks. The average is two to three days. In those cases, the day they give it to you is the first day, regardless of what time they give it to you. Then you have the day in between, and then the next day it's due.

At Sun are the projects charged back in some way? Do you work within a budget?

We don't charge for our time at Sun. We do charge for online searches that come directly out of our budget. There are some resources that SunLibrary funds to people within Sun, some resources that are co-funded by different groups, and some resources, like fee-based online databases, that we search and charge back online costs. But in a lot of instances there's no up-front cost at all to the user. This fits into the culture at Sun. Other groups in Sun that do research, for example people doing competitive intelligence, don't charge back either.

So there's another whole center at Sun that does competitive intelligence?

Various people around Sun do competitive intelligence. The competitive intelligence analysts don't all work for the same people, but they've come together as a formalized group in an alliance. The SunLibrary information specialists have been active members from the inception of the alliance. We do competitive intelligence projects for clients within Sun, plus we work with and provide research to the competitive intelligence analysts.

What kinds of formats do you present your results in?

We work with our clients to determine what they want, and then provide it to them in whatever format they prefer. Ninety-five percent of the time, unless they just need something faxed to them quickly, we'll do a summary memo where we talk about what the project was, what we did, our search techniques, where we searched, what we found, what we didn't find, and other possible resources if they want to do next steps. We pull out key pieces of that information and organize it so that they can read the memo readily, look at the information, and figure out the relevant parts without having to sort through too much. We organize and synthesize and, in some cases, put value-added analyses on top of the information we deliver.

Do you find that you're providing more value-added material now?

It's a goal, and we're growing to be able to do that. The more resources we have that enable people to do some searching on their own, the more it frees us up. We handle pretty complex questions now. Over the years that I've been here, I've seen this happening more and more. At Sun, because the Internet is a prime business and we have such a strong intranet, some people are very accustomed to using online resources and finding information on their own. A lot of times they come to SunLibrary for those next-level searches. Some people don't know that certain resources are available to them, and we educate them. Other people send us requests and tell us, "I already checked all the resources on your page on the intranet." That's when primary research, and/or the next level of resources in our stable, kicks in. We start thinking about "Who else can I talk to?"

When you do a research interview what kinds of questions do you ask?

We try to do a research interview ninety-nine percent of the time, so that we have a personal connection with our clients. Our goal is to help better define their original request and to understand what they are really after. We ask all kinds of questions. We ask them if there are any resources that they have already checked and what those are. Are there other people, internal and external, they've already contacted and can they tell us who they are? I may even ask, "Where are you thinking of having us look?" Occasionally people find this uncomfortable, because they're afraid that they're supposed to know. But often, they have already thought about certain resources and don't say anything because they figure we're going to search them anyway. I like to get that information from them. Many times the resources are ones we would have searched anyway, but that way we get confirmation that they also think those resources will be good for the information they need. We also talk about deadlines. Negotiating deadlines is a constant, just part of what we do.

We ask them if they can tell us how they're using the information, so we understand the context and background. When we search, this helps us think, "They're doing it for this purpose, maybe they might need this also." The more we know about the request, the better. Also, if we think that it's a good candidate for primary versus secondary research, we'll ask them if it's okay for us to talk with someone outside of Sun. We work in a highly competitive environment so that's a very important question.

Do you also ask them how much you can reveal, when you're interviewing, about the client and the reason for the research?

Yes. It's important to check that with the person you're working for. As I mentioned before, when you interview external sources, not only do you get information but, by the very questions you ask, you *give* information—and it can be competitive information that you don't want known outside of your company.

Let's talk about favorite resources, and then you can talk about how you decide which ones to use when.

When I think about all the different types of research that I did in various jobs, it really comes down to knowing the resources for any specific question you get. At Sun we get human resource-related questions, legal questions … but a lot of the questions are technology-based and we look at certain common resources around that area.

At SunLibrary we have a wide variety of market research databases as a core resource. Other resources that we utilize include Dow Jones [41], InSite 2 [73], and Computer Select [32]. We have a whole stable of resources for market and business information as well as scientific and technical information. We've selected the ones that currently meet our needs.

We've just gotten Hoover's [65] for business information. Technical databases we use include ACM [3], and ILI [68] for standards. The Web is at our feet, and all of us have our own favorite search engines. The key in deciding what to use is knowing what is in each resource and how it might help you.

Another favorite resource is the people I interview when I'm doing primary research. I look at every source I interview not only as someone who can provide me with information on a specific topic, but also as a lead. It's really important not to just hang up the phone: "Okay, you won't talk to me," or "You don't know about this, well, thank you." Rather, my next question is, "Thank you very much for your time. Do you know anyone else I can talk to about it? What's the key professional association? Are there any trade journals that you can recommend?" I always try to ask who they think the experts are, or if they can connect me with someone else who might help me get the information.

You mentioned some good resources—key associations, trade journals, other experts, general leads. Any others?

Securities analysts, the government—both U.S. and international—newsletters, authors. Frequently I'll call leading journals and speak to the editors.

The basic idea is, who cares about this topic? That's pretty much the way I approach all research and determine which resources to use. I don't really break it down into online versus primary. Each is good for what it can offer. Online is good because it's noninvasive. You can find things out and no one knows about it. But there are times where online doesn't help. The way I've always looked at questions is not "Where is the information?" in terms of online or primary. It's "What is the answer to my question?" There may be a variety of ways of getting that answer. The whole reason for research is to find the answer to a question, so I use different strategies and techniques to get to my end goal. You learn to hone all your research skills so that you can meet that end goal. If the answer is in a file drawer, on a shelf, online, or in someone's brain, it really doesn't make a difference as long as you achieve the goal.

I understand completely. Online and offline work synergistically, interactively. Each one helps the other. The point is to use the appropriate one, the best tool at the time, to get the most complete answer.

At Sun, when we're researching emerging technologies, many times the information isn't yet in print. If you're ahead of the curve in what you're looking for, you can't rely upon what's been published. We find that, two to three months after we've called the market research analysts to talk to them about a question we're working on, it starts showing up in the published material.

Are there other clues that say to you, "Ah, for this part I need primary research. For this I'll go secondary?" Knowing that you're ahead of the curve is one. Are there any others that come to mind?

Yes. For example, when someone asks me for a very specific cut of market research. No one cares about that cut except the person who's asking the question. The analysts are not writing about it that way, because it's not important to them, or to the overall industry. When I find that, I'll talk to the analysts and say, "I see you're writing about this area but you're not coming at it from this angle. Why aren't you?"

If I talk to three sources that are not cutting the information the way my client wants and they all give me similar reasons, I can then go back to my client and say, "The key experts are not looking at the information this way, for this reason. What other data can you use, cut in a different way, that might meet your needs?" It verifies why I'm not finding the answer in printed resources. It helps me help my client develop another strategy: "What other set of data can we manipulate or look at that might get you to the same point? Can we shift our position and look at it another way?"

For other kinds of questions, after I look at secondary information, I will do primary research to round out the information. Let's say a report came out six months ago. What happened in the last six months that hasn't yet showed up online? What can I add that will make my results a little bit richer? In many cases, interviewing people who have knowledge about a topic area provides another level of richness.

In terms of getting the right cut, my feeling is that in online you're finding the answers to questions that someone else has chosen to write about, but with primary research you can

get the answer to the specific question that you want.

Yes, they're addressing your exact concerns. Also, when you talk to someone, you may find out about areas that you had not thought about. It may be something that you hadn't even considered, and they're willing to offer it up as a pearl. It may be another way of looking at the issue that's very important and strategic, and it's something that hadn't even occurred to you or the client. Basically, you get a scoop.

Let's go back to online sources for a minute and look at what you use the Web for, and how the Web has changed the way you do primary research.

The Web offers me more places to go. I have access to information now that, competitively speaking, was not available before—for example, government information. When I worked in Washington for the PI firm, I did the legwork. I went down to the agencies and courthouses and physically went through the records to dig out information. As the years went on, I used fee-based commercial online databases. Now, on the Internet, I have free access to government documents and can do some public records searching in a whole other way.

On the Web, international audiences are talking to each other and you're getting hits from all around the world, so the Internet can provide a "globalness" to your research. It brings into play an international aspect that was harder to access before. I can find leads to experts in more obscure places, see their biographies, and read their research reports online. There's a wealth of information on the Internet, especially for leads and clues.

Do you use discussion groups or email lists at all?

I monitor some; all the SunLibrary information specialists have their own lists they monitor. We follow Buslib-L [19], Web4Lib [138], and Free Pint Bar [54], among others. We have internal mailing lists within Sun covering specific topics, such as e-commerce, the Web, telecommunications, ASPs, and competitive intelligence. We're careful about what kinds of questions we put out on the Internet; that goes back to the issue of confidentiality and of keeping our competitive edge. But we do respond; if we see somebody who's in need of information, we will, when we can, try to help them.

Do you get a sense of who might be a good contact, when you see someone on a list who's made helpful comments in a particular area?

Oh, sure. I have information that I've saved not only for its content but as a record of who sent it. I've collected my own personal files of information resources from some of the key mailing lists. If I consider their resources valuable, I'll consider them as knowledgeable sources to tap into. For example on Buslib, I've seen excellent postings on business searching topics by Amelia Kassel [77], so I consider her a very knowledgeable source on business information. Gary Price [105] is another example of a good source whom I discovered through his postings.

How about company Web sites?

That's a given. There's a wealth of information there that you were never able to get before. Getting an annual report now is so easy. Some private companies even post them on the Web, even though they're not required to file with the SEC. When we're doing competitive research, typical questions are "What is the industry like? Who are the top players? Where is the market going? Where has it been? What are the trends, and how do we fit into that competitive landscape?" The Web is invaluable for that—for competitors' Web sites plus overall industry information.

How has the Web changed over the past years?

The search engines are getting better. I like HotBot [66] because I can use Boolean language, and I also use some of the search engines that operate on natural language. Some of them, like Google [58], are becoming more precise. There's one in Canada called Albert [7]. I've been able to play with it and find things that I couldn't find in other places. It's nice to be able to experiment to see what neat things come out. The Web allows you a quick first stab.

But I'm still a big proponent of calling Directory Assistance for phone numbers, because they can check multiple areas for me, and I can get immediate verification that the number is correct. In some ways, actually talking to the official phone company source seems more reliable to me than finding a phone number online. So often the online listing has been disconnected or the area codes have changed.

What resources do you use if you need to find a particular government office or source?

For years I used the *Yellow Books* [145]. Those were my little bibles. I could open up any federal or state *Yellow Book* or executive *Yellow Book* and quickly find key government officials.

I used those for years because it was a very clear way of looking at the government. Now I use the Web. I think that the U.S. government's presence on the Web is laid out really clearly. For example I use the Bureau of Labor Statistics [16], which is part of the U.S. Department of Labor, to look up employment statistics in a particular field for indications of employee shortages. You might not get phone numbers directly but you can call in to the government to ask the right questions to get to the right people.

Also, so much government information is now published online. You don't even have to talk to people to get to the right report; the right report is on the Web. Census data and government policies are available online. For government information, the Web is a gold mine.

It sounds as though you usually do start with secondary sources to do some preliminary research.

Yes, although sometimes I can tell by the question, and from my past research, that the answer is not going to be published. So it doesn't always behoove me to start that way. Sometimes it's not either/or. Many times I'll do a multi-pronged search where I place my phone calls and then go online. While I'm waiting for my contacts to call me back, I do my online searching, because getting people to call or email you back takes longer. Now that email is so prevalent, I also do interviews via email. That's a whole other technique.

What differences do you find among telephone interviewing, interviewing in person, and email interviewing or having an email interchange?

Interviewing people in person can be harder and it can be easier. There's a mystery about interviewing somebody on the phone. If you've never met that person, you can't visualize them. In some ways you have to work harder than if you were actually in front of them, because you don't have their body language to help you. You can't gauge as easily when they're pulling back, or when they're not going to talk to you, or when they're hesitant, or when they're ready to gush.

With phone interviews, you have the ability to be somebody else, and I don't mean in an unethical way. You can temper who you are in a different way. Because someone can't see you, you learn to express yourself. You have to be even more articulate, because you can't rely upon your body language. Every word is important, the way you ask a question is important, your tone of voice is important, and listening becomes really important. Someone can't see you nod your head and say, "Yes, yes, I understand," or "Wait, I'm confused about what you're saying." You have to use your words and your voice to work with them, to get to know somebody.

I think email is very different. It can be prohibitive, or it can be more expressive. Sometimes people will go into more detail about an issue than they would if they were talking to you. They can reflect on their answer first, so when they start writing they don't hold back. But then there's the flip side: "I'm writing it, it's documented, I'm not going to put that down on paper."

There are pros and cons to each type of interview. Knowing the differences helps you to choose which kind you should be doing, or at least be aware of the strengths and weaknesses.

And to try to play off the strengths and minimize the weaknesses. If you make calls before doing online research, how do you figure out who you're going to call?

At Sun, we have a ready stable of market research analysts. We work with eight to ten large market research firms and, with some of those firms, we have analyst access. So we can contact them first; that's a pretty easy decision. Then we do the next level, and that's where the secondary research comes in. We look for what other experts are out there. Are there firms that we don't usually work with that might be able to help us? If we've looked at a subject area before, there are the usual suspects—the government, associations, trade journals—that we already know about. You know that this is the right association or the key magazine for that area because you've been covering it long enough, so you just call.

When you've identified the five or ten people that you want to talk to most, how do you decide whom to call first?

It all depends on your strategy. Sometimes not calling the top person first can be useful. Doing the less important interviews helps when I get to that key one, because I have developed some background. If my key source mentions other people, I know who they are since I've already talked to them. The earlier interviews can be like doing informational interviewing when you're looking for a job. If you blow the interview, it's not as important.

So you're building up knowledge about your topic to get to the person that you really want to talk to, the interview that you're most concerned about or that you think will be a more difficult interview, or that—if you blow it—might be your last chance to talk to that person.

On the other hand, sometimes you need to be bold. Why mess around with talking to all those other people? There are times when you look at your list and just do it, just call. Your experience might be a very positive one.

It frequently is. The really top people, in my experience, tend to be wonderful. It's the middle-level or lower-echelon ones who sometimes stand on their dignity. Do you find that there are best or worst days or hours to call?

Normal business hours are best in most cases. On the other hand, a lot of us at Sun work long hours, ranging from people who come in early in the morning to those who stay really late. People in the outside world also work varying hours. I had a great interview with an analyst that happened at nine o'clock at night. She thought she was calling to leave me voicemail, but I was there. I was tired and she was tired, and we'd known each other for several years, so our guards were down in a different kind of way. I pushed a little more boldly in the types of questions I asked. She answered me because we were off-hours. We weren't off the record, but we were off-hours, and it felt like off the record. It was a very informative interview for me, and I think it happened because of that off-hours scenario.

Has email changed the timing factor?

Yes, because you can email anyone anytime, any day, and their feeling is usually "I have to get back to them sometime fairly soon." Either that or they ignore you totally. Email changes the equation slightly because of its immediacy.

I'll email people and then, if I haven't heard back from them, I'll call and say, "I'm not sure if my email got through." Blame it on technology. That gives them another way to get back to me, and takes them off the hook.

Do you have any techniques that you use to get through the gatekeepers, to get to the people you want to talk to?

It's easy to get lost, especially in larger organizations like government or big companies. You need to be tenacious. Before someone transfers me, I ask them who they're transferring me to, and what that person does. I ask, "Is there a direct number or an extension, so I can call them directly?" I can usually figure out whether they're about to transfer me to the right person or the wrong person. So, before they transfer me and I get into some bizarre loop, I can say, "No, I don't want to talk to his administrative assistant. I want to talk to an executive in the communications department."

I can't believe how many times I have forgotten to ask, "What's the number of the extension you're transferring me to?" And boom, they hit the button and—you're disconnected. And you've just spent twenty minutes in phone-loop hell getting to that point to begin with. Okay, any other gatekeeper thoughts?

Know the departments that you really want to talk to. Think about how that organization is set up and who you want to talk to, as opposed to saying, "I have this question," and letting the receptionist throw you around at will.

Another tactic is to say, "I want to talk to this department," because you know that this department is set up to talk to people on the outside. Even if they're Press Relations and you're not the press, they understand your question and know the organization, and you can talk to them on a higher level. I've had wonderful conversations with receptionists where I have learned a lot and they've been incredibly helpful. But if you're talking to someone initially and they're not helpful, having in mind some key departments that are oriented to the public—they're pretty much the same across all organizations—can be very useful.

If it's a government agency, there usually is a document division, or a library, or a technology office, or someone who handles outside relations. If it's a reasonably sized public or private company, then you know that there is somebody who does investor relations, or press, or PR, and those are good places to start. Go in there and say, "Well, if you can't help me, can you put me through to here?" That way you're not at the mercy of someone else's decision making.

I think you need to be bold about going for the top, if the top is the right place to go. Sometimes working your way up is better, and the top isn't where you want to go, anyway. But if it is, feel comfortable about seeing if you can make that interview with the president of the company.

Once you've gotten through to the person you want to talk to, what approaches do you use?

As I mentioned earlier, the kind of information I give out depends upon who I'm talking to and what I'm hearing from them. Many times I give less to begin with, because that allows me to listen, and then I'll answer questions. Other times, giving out information makes somebody feel at ease and, as long as it's okay to give out certain pieces of information, I do.

It's important to figure out who the person is that you're talking to, where they work, and what kind of information you want from them. Then set up some of your strategic questions around that. As I said: If you only had five minutes, what would be the one key piece of information you would want?

Let's talk about comfort levels and what you learn from silence.

So much of primary research, especially when you're on the telephone, is being able to really listen. Not only are you listening to someone's tone of voice and what they say, and then putting yourself in their shoes about who they are and what they do, but you're also listening to silence. The silence can tell you a lot about why someone is talking or not talking. When you know they feel at ease, it helps you decide what question to ask next. When they feel uncomfortable, you know you need to make the next statement. It helps you decide when not to ask another question, and when to ask.

Sometimes when I hear a silence, I don't say anything, and they start talking. But I have to gauge it. I wait and see. Sometimes I know that now it's time for me to come forward and take it to the next level, where they find out more about me. Especially if I've not said much up front, now it's my time to say a little bit more, to make them feel more at ease. Sometimes more information from me will help my cause in the end. Or I'll ask them the question in a different way to figure out what's happening. Why are they no longer talking?

So when they're shutting up because they're outside their comfort level, you can help them feel more comfortable by rephrasing the question, or by coming forth with information yourself.

Occasionally I ask them about the discomfort level. I think, okay, this is what's happening, they're withholding; I'm just going to be up-front and ask, "Is there something that you would prefer not to talk about?" Everybody's different; that's where that dance analogy comes in. You dance differently with different people, and part of it is being attuned to human nature. It sounds very psychological, but I think it is.

How do you handle sensitive issues? Much of what you're saying applies to that. But are there any other approaches that come to mind?

It helps to take the pressure off someone. To figure out a way to make them feel relaxed, not suspicious, not threatened by your asking for information. Part of that is your persona; it must be clear to them that you respect them for who they are and what they do.

There are all different kinds of ways to interview people. I can be pushy, and sometimes that works. "Well, what do you mean by that? I don't understand. What I really want to know is this; how does that work?" Or "What do you think about this? Can you tell me more about that?"

I judge when I can push and, if I make a mistake, I learn pretty quickly that I'm not going to do that the next time. It's part of learning to work with different personalities.

Some things never work. Yelling at somebody is never good. Tactics that don't work in your normal communications are not going to work when you're asking someone to do you a favor and talk to you. A lot has to do with intuition. That's the part I get jazzed about. "I just learned this, and had this whole dynamic happen between us. That was so incredible."

How do you evaluate the credibility or reliability of your sources?

Evaluating credibility is really important with secondary as well as primary information. With both I always look at the source. That's when looking at more than one source becomes important, because I might come up with conflicting numbers or conflicting data. I look at who that source is, and why and how they're putting information out. If I talk about gun control with someone from the Democratic Party and someone from the NRA, I'm going to get different information. Both are valid resources for different reasons. Attributing the information to a source is really important, so you're working with the information in context.

It is also important to document people who refused to talk to you. The very fact that they wouldn't talk says something. You should document that you contacted that person and what happened.

Once in a while, somebody has a reaction that seems way out of line compared to how anybody else has reacted. You say, "hmm, something's going on there." We don't know what, exactly, but again, that's important to document. Now let me ask you: Are there different characteristics for a good primary researcher as opposed to a good secondary researcher?

That's hard for me to answer, because I've always seen them so integrally combined. I think the curiosity level is the same, and the end goal is the same, but you use different techniques to come up with the answer.

The medium is less important than choosing the right tool to use. If you can go online and get the answer to your question, and it meets your needs, that's perfect. But rather than being a primary researcher or a secondary researcher, be a whole person who's doing research. Why cut off one arm when you can use both of them?

Some people may have a proclivity for one or the other. I think all the traits to do either primary or secondary research can be learned. I've worked with people who are dynamite online searchers, but interviews are more difficult for them. I think it's the fear factor. Primary phone research is difficult and frightening to some people because you can't see, and you have to use your intuition.

Speaking of fear, what else keeps people from doing primary research?

One thing that holds some people back is that they feel they can't call someone unless they've learned all about the topic. That's not uncommon. Sometimes I'll do my homework before I call someone, but other times I can't. Either the deadline is too short or the topic is so technical that there's no way I'm going to learn it.

I think people feel intimidated by the prospect of primary research: "I don't know about this subject, so I can't call anybody." "They know more than I do." "I'm going to appear stupid. Before I call them I'd better know as much as I can." You need to be willing to call someone and not be afraid or feel silly. You position yourself so that you can ask intelligent questions even though you don't know the topic area, and still get gems. Some people feel exposed when they talk to someone about subjects they don't know, and that's why online or published documents feel safer to them. Instead, why not look at it as "I'm not expected to know; that's why I'm calling the expert."

I know a fabulous secondary researcher who doesn't have the patience for sitting on the phone, especially dealing with people that she finds stupid. So for her, it's the frustration factor. Speaking of that, how do you handle

rejection or frustration? Are there times when you just lose it?

Honestly, I handle it better some times than others. Blind alleys are sources of frustration in both secondary and primary research. You just learn to keep going, you learn to take another tack.

Rejection is a huge part of doing telephone research. By the time I finished my stint doing executive recruiting, I could handle rejection pretty well. But it's still hard. I just pick myself up and figure out where I want to go next. I have a vision of a dog, a terrier with its bone, not letting go.

I've had some really bad conversations with people. I've had people who wouldn't give any information: "I'm not talking to you, goodbye." It has little if anything to do with what I said; they just don't want to talk, or they don't want to talk about the issues that I'm calling about.

Do you have any tricks or techniques you use if you just had a really bad phone call?

It's important to think about what happened and why. I don't dwell on it or make myself feel bad, but it's important to recognize what happened so I can work at not having it happen again.

If I've been rejected, I'm not afraid of asking again. Thinking of the person as a lead really helps. I go into most phone calls thinking, "I may not get what I want, but maybe they'll tell me about somebody else." Going into it with that second-level strategy helps me handle rejection better.

Do you see any changes in technology that are altering the way we do primary research?

Voicemail has already changed it. Caller ID is a big one for competitive information, because you can't call into companies in quite the same way. You can't just not say who you are, because they can tell who you are.

Email changes the way you can do primary research. Chat and instant messaging allow you to do immediate interviewing, and it's documented right away. Email is not just a private conversation between two people anymore. Anybody else can access it, depending upon the security of your system. It also can become a court document. There have always been legal ramifications to taping, but email has legal implications now as well.

With videoconferencing you can do conference calls in a whole other way, so it's not just a one-on-one interview. You can do multiple interviews and you can share information.

Is there anything else you'd like to talk about?

I do want to mention SCIP's [114] annual international conference in Atlanta, Georgia, a couple of years ago. I found it fascinating that there were several presentations focusing on primary research and telephone interviewing. Many people in their twenties were asking a lot of questions on techniques for getting competitive information on the phone. They were calling it "human collection skills"—the latest catchphrase for doing telephone, email, or primary research.

It was fascinating to me because, for a period of time, there wasn't much access to online information, so primary was what you had to do. As times changed, the move to using online resources grew, and people began to rely on those resources. It's really interesting to see these sessions taking place now that reconfirm the importance of primary research.

It's come full circle, in a way. I wonder if the Internet brought the sense of community and human connection more to the fore in people's minds?

The development of the Internet allowed people to connect with other people around the world. It is a very powerful concept. I think technology now helps that human connection.

There was a phase of online when it was all third-party resources and fee-based services. It wasn't interactive in the same way; you were interacting with data. This way you're interacting with data and with people. The Internet gives you that human connection. You not only get to look at data, but then you can email someone or connect with someone, or talk to somebody. It's like moving from getting no information online, to getting all of it online, to this place, now, where both genres are melding together. It's a wonderful time for people in the information and information technology world to be present. The opportunities that we have are incredible. And it's just the beginning, the tip of where the technology is going to take us in terms of communication.

And in terms of the real integration of knowledge from all those different sources.

Yes, that's the next step. How do you take all that data and manage it so that people can leverage it and use it and share it? I think it's a really exciting time for information professionals.

In the setting where I work, not only at Sun but in the SunLibrary itself, a lot has to do, I think, with the vision that my manager, Cindy Hill, helped to create—using the technology we have available to us, and the technology we're developing, together with the information itself to create knowledge-sharing systems to better leverage intelligence throughout Sun.

Cindy is wonderful—going back to her role in developing the research environment at Failure, and now at Sun. I've always been so impressed with her ability to articulate and educate and bring converts to the world of information.

That's absolutely true. Within SunLibrary, we feel that we play a significant role in terms of providing information and helping

Sun keep its competitive advantage. The resources we have, our experience and skills, and how we use them all come into play, helping us get the answers to the questions and turning questions into meaningful information and knowledge.

Super Searcher Tips

➤ Try to find at least three sources on the same topic. Don't believe just one person or one fact. It's not that it's not factual, but you have to factor in what filter they're seeing it through. Limiting it to one person doesn't give you the ability to understand the complexity of an issue.

➤ When providing information about myself, less is more. I'll provide information about who I am right up front if I can tell that I need to, or that it will benefit me.

➤ I look at every source that I talk to as a lead. I always ask, "Is there anyone else that you know that I can talk to about it? What's the key professional association? Are there any trade journals, security analysts, government agencies, newsletters, other experts and gurus, or authors you can recommend?"

➤ The whole reason for doing this is to find the answer to a question. Use different strategies and techniques and learn to hone all your skills so that you can meet that end goal. Whether it's in a file drawer, on a shelf, online, in someone's brain, it really doesn't matter.

➤ Good times to use primary research include when some-one's asking you for a certain cut on the information and you're not finding it online, to round out or update online information, when you're ahead of the curve on the topic, or when the information you need is too old to be covered online.

➤ You not only interview experts to get information, but you also interview the person you're doing research for—your research partner—to better define the original request. Ask what resources they have already checked. Are there other people they've contacted or considered? Where are they thinking of having you look?

➤ When you call into an organization, have some key out-side-oriented departments in mind. A document division, a library, a technology office, investor relations, or press or public relations are good places to start.

Photo by Pam Siela

Jeanne Tessier Barone

Teaching the Art and Skill of Interviewing

Jeanne Tessier Barone teaches full-time in the Department of Communication at Indiana University Purdue University–Fort Wayne. She is co-author of *Interviewing: Art and Skill*, and an award-winning teacher, writer, and artist.

barone@ipfw.edu
www.ipfw.edu/comm/

Why don't you start by telling me a little bit about your background and how you ended up doing what you're doing now.

I got my undergraduate degree in speech and taught for a year at a city college in Chicago. Then I did graduate work in sociology and worked in a mental health clinic for several years. Finally, I got a master's degree in communication and dropped out of the work force to raise my family. When we moved to Fort Wayne, I got back into teaching at Indiana Purdue–Fort Wayne and began teaching a course called Business and Professional Speaking that included some interviewing skills. I started teaching interviewing in a small segment in that class and then began teaching a semester-long course that looks at all different kinds of interview settings.

At that time, there weren't very many interviewing textbooks around. The one used at most places, *Interviewing: Principles and Practices* by Stewart and Cash [164, see Appendix], didn't offer enough information about interviewing to make a rich full semester. Jo Young Switzer, who is now a vice president of

Manchester College, was teaching the course here with me at that time. We were lamenting the fact that this best available text required so much supplementation, so we decided to write our own, *Interviewing: Art and Skill* [147].

How has the textbook situation changed over time?

Now there are quite a few interviewing texts out there, and in fact the Stewart and Cash text has been revised in ways which I think suggest that our book had some influence. They've added more kinds of interviewing and more depth to their treatment of interviewing. I like to hope that our text helped to stir that pot and that market.

Why do you think interviewing has become a much more prominent topic?

We have become such an information-centered culture, and interviewing is an important part of information gathering. There used to be relatively few communication departments that taught interviewing as a separate course, and that number has grown because of demand by people who want those skills. For a long time, people got hired into positions where they were given responsibility for interviewing, but it never occurred to anybody that you needed to learn how to do that. So there were, and probably still are, an awful lot of people conducting important interviews without a clue as to how to do it effectively.

What can you get from "going to the source" with interviewing that you can't get from secondary sources?

There is a quote by G.K. Chesterton, "The only two things that can satisfy a soul are a person and a story, and even the story has to be about a person." We learn best by connecting information to the individual lives and experiences of others. I think the fundamental gift of interviewing, of going to the sources, is that you get stories. It's one thing to interact with a machine and collect factual information and recommendations—about interviewing, for example. It's another thing to talk to someone who has used those skills and can tell you, out of their own experience, stories about when that set of skills worked or didn't work for them. And we remember the stories long after we've forgotten the formally presented information.

Well, here's a perfect chance for stories. The first thing I want to talk to you about is call reluctance. I think every one of us has times when the thought of picking up the phone and calling someone is just horrifying. You're one of the few people I know who talks about that issue. What do you see as some of the major causes of call reluctance?

I think they're very similar to the sets of feelings and responses, the doubts and concerns that we have when we walk for the first time into a party, for example. There is always a kind of vulnerability in meeting a new person. In a sense, every time we begin an interaction with another person we are opening ourselves to the risk of being rejected, of receiving messages that are going to damage our sense of ourselves or lay bare some piece of ourselves we don't want laid bare. I think it's every bit as anxiety producing for an interviewer as for the interviewee, because they take that initial risk of reaching out, attempting to make contact. The other person is always unknown until the conversation is well established, and most of us are afraid, in one way or another, of the unknown.

Is there a gender factor? Do men and women have different reasons for being reluctant to do an interview?

I think so. It has been my anecdotal experience, gathered over the years of teaching and working with people, that men in general are more reluctant to make calls, and especially those initial kinds of calls. Deborah Tannen [165] has a set of books written for lay audiences that all deal with gender issues. One of them is focused on work; it's called *Talking from 9 to 5*. Another one, *That's Not What I Meant*, is about differences in male/female communication, and a third one is *You Just Don't Understand.*

On the basis of her research and the compiled research of others, she talks about male and female communication as having different motivations. For example, according to Tannen, communication is about competition for a man, but about revelation for a woman. Men have an ongoing desire, in interaction, to maintain a one-up position. So men are more reluctant to enter into an interaction in which they don't know whether they'll wind up one-up or one-down. Tannen talks about, for example, men's reluctance to stop and ask for directions as being a one-down kind of thing, because that means admitting you don't know something to another person. Interviewers, because there's something they don't know and want to learn, are automatically in a one-down situation.

So what do we do with this? How can you overcome call reluctance?

If you're a person who perceives "not knowing" as a one-down situation, I think first you have to recognize that that is what's going on. What's involved in that, just like in lots of therapeutic changes, is reframing how we see that event. For example, rather than seeing an interview as a one-down situation, try to reframe it as information gathering, or as information sharing. While interviewers need what the other has, at the same time, through the collection of that information, they're going to have some kind of impact, which will give back to the other person.

In your book, you mention reimaging the caller and the called. What do you mean by that?

I think we need to see both caller and called as having power. The power is different, but there's kind of a power exchange. The interviewer, in creation and use of the questions, has a structural power in the conversation. At the same time, it is the stories and answers of the other person that are going to move the conversation along from one topic to another, one theme to another. Reconsidering the caller and called as a shared power situation could eliminate some of the call reluctance that people experience.

As long as we're talking about what people experience when calling, how about handling frustration or rejection?

That's a hard one we all struggle with every day. Reframing rejection in a way that depersonalizes it is really important and helpful. Right now, so many people are asking for and/or collecting information about other people. It's understandable that some of those called are going to feel suspicious, angry, or just fearful about what this person's motives are, about whether the motives given are the true motives, about how you extend trust to someone you know only by voice.

It's very hard for most of us not to take rejection personally. If somebody's yelling at me, I tend to feel a personal reaction. But if we can keep in mind that this is a very understandable set of responses, we can anticipate it and try to make room for it in the call. We can try to find as many honest ways as possible to say to the other, "You have understandable concerns about sharing some of who you are with me. Let me try to allay those concerns." Giving information, and allowing an opportunity to check back on whether I am who I say I am, may help. But none of that might be convincing to some people who will still be fearful and suspicious. You don't know who the last person was who called them, and how that person made them feel.

What major differences do you see between telephone and in-person interviewing?

I see immense differences. Within the field of communication, most research says the majority of the meanings of a message are carried on nonverbal channels. We make judgments about the words that a person is sharing on the basis of the expressions that are passing over their face, what they're doing with their eyes, skin tone, gestures, how connected they are to us, all of those things that are blocked when we're doing telephone interviewing.

Suddenly all the various ways in which we use nonverbal messages to test the truth telling of the other person are lost to us, and we are reliant only on the words themselves and whatever judgments we can make on the basis of the tone of voice, the pace of the communication, and those other cues that are also significant. It's like trying to tell what a television show is about with the mute button on, only in this case it's the image that's muted and we have only the sound. It increases the uncertainty of the communication incredibly to eliminate those other aspects. It surprises me that we have been so slow to develop the technology that would allow us to look at the person we're talking to, because that would be a very desirable thing. According to people in the discipline of communication, we would feel much more comfortable if we could see who it is we're talking to.

From the interviewer's side, I know a number of professional interviewers who've said that the day the video telephone comes, they're quitting, because we all go to work in our bathrobes and fuzzy slippers.

It will change things, that's for sure. But in some ways it will make the job much easier, because if I could see who it is I'm talking to, and know that I have a wider set of information on which to make my judgments, it would enhance my trust. We can still wear jeans and slippers from the waist down with the bunny slippers under the desk. Just make sure that from the shoulders up you look good, and don't put your feet on the desk!

I'd like to talk about designing your questions, and about types of questions—open and closed, and hook versus net.

The kinds of questions that you develop have to be based on what you need, what kind of research you're conducting. Closed questions are the most useful for compiling data fast. If I can answer with a yes or no or a specific number, you can collect and compile information quite quickly. However, that limits the kind of information that you're capable of obtaining. In evaluating the quality of service at a restaurant, if I make a series of statements to which I ask you to respond yes or no—"The service at the restaurant was acceptable," "The quality of the food was high"—I'll very quickly get a set of information from you, but I have framed all of the information. I have decided what needed to be asked. It might not be the thing that you most wanted to tell me, which was how you felt treated by the person who greeted you, and the impact that had on your whole experience. Sometimes, with telephone interviewing in particular, there's a desire to get through as many interviews as possible, get as much information as possible from a variety of people. There's a temptation then to go exclusively, or almost exclusively, with closed questions. On the other side, there's always the risk that we've lost the stories that needed to be told, that we didn't ask the right questions.

When you do in-depth interviews—which is really what I'd like to focus on here—as opposed to survey kinds of research, I imagine you still need to use a combination of questions.

You would use more open questions, though there's such a thing as a too-open question. You want to ask a question that clearly marks the specific terrain you want to visit, but then gives the person that you're interviewing as much room as possible to talk about all the aspects of that subject.

If you were interviewing an "expert," you would want to specify, as you have with me, the particular area of expertise that you're interested in. Then ask questions that really are open, but that stimulate their thinking in specific areas of that expertise, as you're doing here in terms of call reluctance and question design.

How about hook versus net questions?

These terms provide a way of talking about questions that look for a particular kind of response versus questions where you're more generally fishing. As a hook question, I might say, "I've been in that restaurant that I'm asking you to evaluate and I've found the service to be this. I had this experience with the chef. How does that compare to your own experience?" It's a question that shares something of yourself and invites them to compare their response. The risk there is that sometimes people try to please us by saying what they think we want them to say, to agree with us.

A net question would be more widely open-ended. "If I ask you to talk about your experience at this hotel, including the dining and the rooms, what would you say were the most important aspects of your experience?" It's a question that casts a wide net and lets them select and focus on what they think was really important. You see where this interview leads and follow it, in terms of what aspect of their experience to focus on.

With the hook question, you're actually baiting the hook with some indication of the response parameters or the responses you expect. And with the net, you're like a fisherman casting a wide net and seeing what you pull in. Looking at both—open or closed questions, and the

hook or the net—what are some situations where it's more appropriate to use one as opposed to another?

Closed questions are always useful to get very specific demographic information about the person, because that's the kind of data that you do want to be able to compile and compare quickly. Age, educational level, geographic location—that sort of raw demographic data helps us get a fix on who we're talking to.

Sometimes closed questions, Likert scale [83] kind of questions, can be useful to rate and qualify responses. I make a series of statements and you strongly agree, agree, disagree, strongly disagree, or have no opinion. It's one thing to ask me about my experience with that restaurant, and to ask somebody else the same. But if I want to know how I rate my experience compared to somebody else, then comparative questions, which limit my answer options, can be useful. They make it possible to collect information in a way that says sixty percent of the women loved this place, forty percent of the men hated it.

And open questions?

I have a great fondness for open questions; perhaps you have detected that already. I think that they are always useful in terms of allowing the person to tell you, for themselves, how they have experienced something, how this has impacted directly on their lives.

Open questions are what give us the individual stories and allow people to frame their experience in a particular way. In terms of research interviewing, my own preference as an interviewer was always for that qualitative research, the more open-ended interviews that give us one person's story deeply rather than a bunch of stories superficially. In addition to enjoying knowing other people's stories, I like the notion of myself as a storyteller. As a teacher, stories are the best way I know to convey information, so they are what I look for when I interview others. "Tell me about the time that you ..." Those are the kinds of questions that provide me with the information I'm usually seeking, that really get you the stories.

That leads me to the topic of probes. Could you talk a bit about the power of probes and what you'd use them for?

Probes are simply the ways in which, as communicators, we try to keep the information flowing. If I'm talking and not getting anything back, I'm going to run out of things to say, because communication is risky and always makes us vulnerable. If you're not telling me in one way or another how I'm doing, how you're receiving the message, I'm going to grow less and less comfortable, to the point where I don't want to share anything at all.

So, the heart of probes really is being an effective listener. It's important to have the questions that stimulate the conversation, but if I don't listen well, I'm not going to know what I've heard or be able to move things forward. Listening well involves giving ongoing feedback that conveys, "I hear what you're saying, and find it of interest. I want to know more about it. I appreciate your willingness to share your assessment of your experience."

Probing starts with just those kinds of sounds and responses that give ongoing affirmation to the other person. "Yup, uh-huh," those kinds of guttural responses that affirm our stance as a listener.

Beyond that, probing involves paying very close attention to the communication of the other so that we pick up the threads they might drop. We go back and say, "You mentioned this earlier. Tell me more about …," as you've done several times in this interview.

Sometimes when storytellers reach a place that may be a little less comfortable to talk about or that gives rise to emotions, they'll come close to a subject and then skirt away. The interviewer's task with probing questions is to gently say to the other person, "Can we go back and talk more about how you felt, or what that experience did for you?"

I think the greatest value of probing questions and being a skilled listener is that sometimes we find what we're not looking for. I value open-ended questions and probing because we might discover that, contrary to what we thought, a different set of factors, beliefs, or values is operating.

I think of that as the serendipity of interviewing, where all of a sudden you're getting answers to things you didn't even think to ask.

Exactly. I'll give you an example. As a rookie working in a mental health clinic, I got assigned to do group therapy at a nursing home where the staff wanted some help for their depressed patients. My experience with nursing homes was somewhere between slim and none, but I went with my own ideas of what to be concerned about with living in a nursing home. I met with this group of about fifteen people, in a very sterile, empty space that was called the recreation room. I asked them questions that I felt would be uppermost in these people's minds—about the food, their responses to the actual facilities, and "are the staff nice to you?" They answered me in monosyllables, or not at all. I'm thinking, "Boy, these people really are depressed. They're not talking at all."

All of a sudden one of them leaned forward—his name was Irving; he had emphysema and he had been sitting there just huffing beside me—and he looked me in the eye and he said, "Honey, this place is a morgue." I said, "What?" And he said, "This place is a morgue." Some of the other old people in the group said, "Irving, don't talk like that." And he said, "Well it is. It's not about the food, it's not about the staff, there's not a damn thing to do here. I can't drive my car anymore, I don't see anybody, we just sit around and talk ..." He just launched into this thing, which told me so much more about the depression that these people were dealing with than any of the very superficial ideas I had.

So you follow where your interviewee leads.

Exactly. When he said, "This place is a morgue," if I had said, "Well, that's a strange statement, does anybody else have any ideas?" I would not have heard any more about that. Or maybe I wouldn't have been able to shut him up anyway. But he really led the way, and that's what we have to leave ourselves open to as researchers.

Let's talk about specific kinds of probes. In your book, you mention accuracy probes for checking your perception.

That's so important, because sometimes we think we hear a person say something and we have heard it completely wrong. An accuracy probe involves paraphrasing back to them: "Did I hear correctly that you said this ...?" or "Let me make sure I understand. You think that ..."

We don't know what we don't know. We don't know what we haven't heard correctly, and unless we continually check our perceptions with the other person, we might come away with totally wrong conclusions about what they've been trying to share with us.

When we do that in conversation, when we say, "Did I hear you correctly, did you say this, this is what I think you said to me," it has such rapport-building power. It says to the person, "I really am listening, and I do want to understand, and I want you to keep clarifying for me until I'm sure I get what you're trying to say."

Another type of probe that might contribute to that rapport at the end of a conversation is the "clearinghouse probe." That's such a great term.

That's just one way to say, "Okay, last chance, what have I missed here? Is there anything important that I haven't thought to ask you?" Again, we don't know what we don't know. We only ask what we think matters, and it could be that something totally different matters a great deal, and we never got to it because our questions didn't lead there.

I generally ask as my last question, "Is there anything else you want to tell me, is there anything else I've missed, is there a black hole here?" That's produced some wonderful results. There's another probe with a wonderful name, the "nudging probe." I gather that it's a type of amplification probe for expanding or getting more information.

It's that verbal hand on the elbow that says "lead me a bit further." "Can you say a little more about that? Can you tell me more about how that felt? Can you explain what you mean when you use that word?" The little questions that try to push the conversation along.

Let's go back to how you would begin an interview and how that affects rapport-building.

I think that in the beginning, as the interviewer, you have to be able to share information about yourself. Within the discipline of communication, one of the basic lessons is that self-disclosure is reciprocal. If I want you to tell me about you, I have to be willing to tell you about me. Any two people continue to assess the depth of "my" disclosures measured against the depth of "your" disclosures, in judging whether to share more, to go deeper in a relationship. Interviewers obviously don't want to take up half the time talking about themselves, when it's really the other that they want to learn about. But at the outset, they have to be willing to share enough to encourage some sense of trust in the other person.

When I get those calls from telephone sales people at dinnertime, so often they call me by name, usually mispronounced, and without even having given a name of their own. "Hi, how you doing this evening?"—like I want to tell this voice that I don't even have a name for how I'm doing this evening. It's all I can do sometimes to not say, "Let me talk for a couple of hours about how you should have started this phone call. And then try your luck with somebody else."

We have to share enough of ourselves as interviewers that the other person feels they have some sense of who they're talking to, and some sense that we're trustworthy. From my own ethical viewpoint, that means that we have to be trustworthy. As interviewers, we can't misrepresent ourselves. Part of the reason that many people are reluctant to be interviewed and share information in research-gathering situations is because they have felt betrayed by past experiences. We do a disservice, not only to our own research but to everybody else's, if we're not trustworthy in the way that we present ourselves. First and foremost, we have to say enough, honestly, about who we are that the other person is willing to risk talking to us. The heart of rapport-building, really, is, "I'll go first. I'll show you mine." That's where it starts.

Are there other approaches or techniques to help build rapport as you go through the interview?

You start safe. You begin by asking about the kinds of things that the person is more likely to feel comfortable sharing in a new relationship. As a call goes on, as in this call, a sense of connection develops between the people, and by the end of the call I'm much more likely to tell you something that comes more deeply out of my experience than at the beginning. So the structure of the whole set of questions needs to be such that we lead from the more superficial, from the information that's easier to share.

Starting with the more general demographic information gives interviewees a chance to get a little comfortable in the situation, get a read on who it is that they're talking to, and then feel more comfortable sharing more.

In the early stages, we as interviewers have to work to establish our own credibility. We have to share enough about ourselves that the other person is willing to recognize something of our expert status. Not expert as in "I'm going to be intimidated by you," but expert as in "I can trust that this person knows what he or she is doing in interviewing me, and that their intentions are professional."

I find that it helps enormously here to do your homework first. Be prepared before you make that call. If it's a topic area like electron beam lithography, where I have to do a lot of preparation, I learn as much as I can so I can ask relatively intelligent questions.

You have to have a fair amount of information to ask a good question. But, even if you know the area, you can't ask your questions on the fly. I just don't think most of us are bright enough to do that. Ted Koppel's pretty good at it. Larry King's pretty good at it. But these are people with years of experience. Barbara Walters always has her scripted questions on her lap, even after all these years.

Part of it is learning enough about the topic to ask good, intelligent questions, but the order in which questions occur is very important too. You have to develop a flow to the information gathering. Balance what you think will be the safer, easier questions against the harder ones, and try to build that into the structure of the interviews so that people are moved in incremental stages into deeper levels of sharing.

To do a good interview takes a tremendous amount of preparation. You have to spend a lot of time getting ready. That's probably not what most people want to hear.

Maybe not, but it's the truth. And no matter how much you prepare, interviews take on a life of their own. You can watch them go in and out of deeper levels as you sense someone's

reluctance or nervousness or discomfort, and move back to build their comfort again.

Pulling back. Exactly. Any human interaction is such a living organism. Any encounter that we have takes on a life of its own, and you have to be ready to give up your script to follow where the interview's going. But, by the same token, you have to have at least started with a clear sense of what you want, and then be willing to adapt. I think it takes great flexibility to be a good interviewer.

How about dealing with the other person as an expert?

I think that's reciprocal too. If I'm an interviewer and I'm coming to you for information, I need to make you feel that I see you as someone with wisdom I need, and that I have chosen you, in a sense, to be the person who offers me that expertise. You use language that says to the other person, "In this particular area you are the expert, and I'm seeking your help."

Most of us like to be thought of as having expertise, and most of us like to be helpful. So we need to offer that to the person we're interviewing as well. My expertise is that I'm doing research on this topic. Your expertise is that you have the answers I need about this subject area, and I'm hoping that you'll be willing to share your wisdom with me.

That leads into my next question, which is how you motivate someone to participate, to be willing to talk to you.

Asking for help is one way to do that. Affirming that they have a kind of wisdom that is useful in some way, and also making them some commitment about how that wisdom is going to be used. If I'm doing research on family relations, for example, and asking members of families to talk to me, I can say to them, "Your own lived experience is where the truth is about families, and if you're willing to share it with me, I'll be able to collect information that leads to the truth." But we need to make a promise beyond that: "If you'll share this wisdom with me, I'm going to put it to use in a way that protects you." Whatever assurances of confidentiality are needed for certain kinds of interviews, or whatever acknowledgement is needed for other kinds of interviews, I'm going to respect you and your contributions. And you're not just helping me; I'm going to take your wisdom and make it of broader value.

In the case of our interview here, for example, you're helping other people who want to learn about interviewing. We all want to feel like we have contributed something in the time we spend on this planet. So if we can offer to the interviewee that their time will mean something, have some significance, that can be an important motivator.

Let's talk about difficult interview situations, which we've all had, starting with interviewees who are reticent.

This is a situation in which the more easy questions you start with, the better. Closed questions can be useful with reticent people. It might take tremendous effort on their part to frame a whole sentence, but they might be able to manage "yes" and "no" for starters. If I'm talking to someone who is reluctant to share with me, I am more likely to share—and better served by sharing—more about myself as a way of inviting that reestablishment of balance. Self-disclosure is reciprocal: "Okay, I've exposed myself to you in this regard; share back with me." The risk is that some people just want to please, and depending upon how or what we share, we could get answers that are not so much accurate as they are an attempt to mirror back what they thought we wanted.

With reticent people, probing questions are so important. If I ask you what your experience was at this hotel and you say to me through tightly clenched teeth, "I hated it," this is where probing questions come in. "Wow, you hated it. Boy, I'm really sorry to hear that you had that experience. Can you tell me more about it so I'll have more information to take back about that?" So then they say, "I hated all of it." "Well, let's start with one thing at a time. It would really help me if you would give me some of the details about it. Did you hate the service?" "Yes, I hated the service." "Can you tell me one thing you hated about the service?"

Keep developing probes that are very specific, and try to move the person from one thing to another, so they eventually get to the thing that bothered them the most but that they were reluctant to say. Maybe they felt belittled by the person who checked them in when they arrived. Sometimes, once they've said the part that was the hardest for them, the reticence disappears and they're willing to share more. Not always; some people are reticent from start to finish. Then we just keep gently probing, thanking them for whatever little we get, acknowledging that it matters, we're glad to have received it, and is there more?

Those interviews are like pulling teeth; there's no way around that. Some people find it very hard to trust. Even if that's not an issue, there are people who find it hard to express themselves, and who just struggle to find words.

In that little vignette, you used two techniques that are so classic: One, you showed empathy; you immediately said, "I'm so sorry to hear that you had that awful time." And the other was saying, "It would really help me."

Who doesn't respond to empathy? All of us want people to care about our experience. As for "help me," if in many human encounters people want to feel one-up, that's a perfect way to allow that. "Can you help me understand this better?" You're putting them one-up. If that's something that matters to many of us, and I suspect it is, then, as an interviewer, it's an easy gift to give.

How about the other extreme in interviews, the overly talkative ones where the person is just a motormouth?

An overly talkative person is a nightmare of another kind. With many overly talkative people, it's kind of stream-of-consciousness talking. They might start out answering your question, but in the course of that they take you on a journey that's so far from where you started that you don't even remember what you were talking about. This is a very delicate problem because, when a person talks very tangentially or circularly, we have to stay focused on our question in order to keep getting what we need. We need to be able to say, "Excuse me, I'm sorry to be interrupting, but could we go back to what you said a minute ago?" and draw them back to the subject matter.

This is harder than with a reticent person because it's so easy to offend. Sometimes overly talkative people don't pause long for breath, so we're forced to interrupt, and all we can do is try to do it as gently and as apologetically as possible. Do it in terms of "I'm interested in what you're saying now, but you said something earlier that I really want more know about," and try to draw them back to what is more nearly focused on the area you're working on.

The hardest part of that for interviewers is that it's very easy, in our own minds, to be led off track. If we find ourselves suddenly talking about something that has nothing to do with what we wanted, having a very specific structure in front of us can sometimes save us. Remaining focused is so important to the interviewer, and a stream-of-consciousness interviewee can lead us right out of the ballpark. With the overly talkative ones, you spend an hour, a day, and then you realize you didn't get what you needed.

You and Jo said something great in the book: "Listen for the tiniest pause when they catch their breath. You can't wait for a normal pause

with these people because they don't have one."

That's right. You have to look for micro-opportunities and leap in. Perhaps use a more closed question, or if it's open, make it a very narrowly defined open question. Not a net-type question, but "Could you speak specifically to how you deal with …", "… to how you felt about …," and keep narrowing the field.

How about someone who's evasive or deceptive?

If I were receiving indications that the person I was talking to wasn't telling me the truth, I would cut my losses, get out of that interview, and move on to another one. Because if you can't trust the information, what's the point of gathering it?

You need to make sure that you don't make a snap decision, though, because sometimes we're wrong. If I felt like I was being misled by an interviewee, I would try to use some accuracy probes—touch back to a story they've told me before to see if the story changes at all. There are ways in which we make judgments about whether our friends and relations are telling us the truth. The same kinds of tools apply here to test for ourselves our impression that we're getting deceitful information. No matter what kind of research you're doing, if they're lying to you, it's contaminating your results.

Although that in itself might be interesting information, I suppose. You spoke to so-and-so and what he said didn't seem to jibe with the rest of the world.

That's an ongoing problem for researchers who deal with taboo areas of human life, although there are fewer and fewer of those in U.S. culture. If you're trying to do research on sexual behavior or drug habits, people are very reluctant to tell the truth. So how do you conduct research in an area where the first impulse of everybody you approach is going to be to want to lie?

Well, how do you?

Use very careful self-revelation and give thorough explanations of the importance of the research for people who are dealing with difficulties in these areas. The Kinseys, in the research they did on human sexuality, convinced people who shared information with them that they were going to make life better for human beings, so people were more willing to share. They also made very, very complete and ongoing assurances of confidentiality that made the sharing feel safe. Those are the things you have to do.

How about if someone just doesn't want to talk to you?

Unless you need that particular person's expertise, I'd say cut your losses and go. But if it's that person you have to get information from, then you have to try to learn why they don't want to talk, and answer as many of those reservations and questions as possible. Suppose they say, "I think research is bunk." "I understand how you could believe that, because so often we see research in public media that's contradictory, and we see the same statistics used in different ways by different people. It's easy to get skeptical about research; I absolutely agree with you. But let me tell you more about my research and what I hope to do with it and how I intend to gather this information and where I intend to share it." If we can learn to address those questions and concerns, that's our best shot.

That's a great example of empathy: "I understand completely." "I understand how you would think that, and I agree with you." You're allying yourself with the interviewee.

That's right. We all know that bad research has been done. So if that's their objection, be up-front about it: "Absolutely, I agree with you. I don't want my research to fall into that category. If you help me by giving me the best information you can, I will promise you ..." Don't make promises you can't keep, but "I'll promise you that I'm going to use it in this way and share it in this forum"—that sort of thing.

The title of your book is *Interviewing: Art and Skill*. Do you want to talk about the art side of it versus the skill side of it?

The skill side involves many of the areas we've been talking about—doing your homework, learning as much as possible beforehand about the subject matter and the person you're talking to. I don't mean using subterfuge to gain information about them, but why are they there? What's their occupational status? What do they expect to obtain? That kind of thing; in a general way, gathering as much information as possible about the other person.

Or if you're calling an expert, knowing their work, what they've written, what honors they've had, who they've worked with.

You can affirm their expert status and at the same time affirm your own by demonstrating that you've done your homework. The skill part is in the preparation, the development of that clear sense of focus in advance: What exactly is it I want from these interviews? What do I hope to learn?—and keeping in mind that we have to be open to learning what we didn't expect, and then in the careful preparation of questions, of a script that will lead us and lead the other through the information. That's the part that we can learn best from books and secondary sources.

The art part comes from remaining really connected to our own human experiences, and connecting what we do as interviewers with what we do in all human relationships. Trying to keep in mind the humanity of the other person, the kinds of feelings and needs that motivate them in much the same way that they motivate me. Trying to find ways, not through manipulation but through honest empathy and compassion, of connecting my story to their story. And listening well.

I think listening actually is more of an art than a skill, because it takes an incredible amount of focus and willingness to set my own needs and thoughts aside in order to give my whole attention to you. The art part is what comes from practice and experience. It's really about keeping it connected to your more general knowledge about being human and about human relationships.

There is a tendency for new interviewers, in particular, to come on like gangbusters with all their skills and not leave enough room to hear and respond to the very particular human being that they're dealing with at any given moment. That's where the art comes in. You learn over time to read those pauses, to read those reluctances, to hear that sort of slight evasion that turned away from the subject at hand, and to be listening well enough to come back and say, "Can we go back there again?"

You get a sense that each interaction in the interview shapes how you go forward from there.

That's a good way to put it. Every step leads to the next step, and if I ask a question or make a statement that puts you off, the whole rest of the interview is going to be affected unless I fix that. The art part comes in as being sensitive enough to think, "Oh boy, I sense a difference here. Since I made that last statement this person is responding much more evasively," and then being able to go back and say to them, "I'm sorry, I'm afraid I may have made you uncomfortable when I said this a minute ago. I didn't want to do that, and I'd like to talk about it again and see if I can make that better."

Now, truth be told, most of us are always learners in human relationships. We fail as often as we succeed. And if divorce statistics are any indication, we fail at a more alarming rate these days than in the past. We need to approach interviewing as "my effort to be my best relational self in that particular place and time." My goal as an interviewer is to build and sustain this relationship successfully for this hour and a half or whatever it is, and to really understand the awesome power of being able to do that. If I can win your trust, then you'll tell me your truth, and if you tell me your truth, then my research is good. And if you don't, it isn't.

Similarly, when you pick up on someone's passion or their joy—what really turns on their lights—and you can go with that, it also seems to open wonderful doors.

Who doesn't like to talk about the things they love? Doing research, especially interviews that involve seeking out experts, should be golden, because experts usually do what they do because they love it. The cards are stacked in our favor as long as we don't blow it.

Speaking of not blowing it, let's talk about problem questions—questions that are not clear, that are double-barreled, that are too long or too short.

It's amazing how easy it is to write a bad question, even now, having worked at this for many years and with very careful attention. There are so many ways in which we reveal our prior biases or agendas without even knowing we're doing it, so many ways we muddy the data by phrasing questions poorly. With a double-barreled question, for example, if you ask a person essentially two questions at once, how do you know which one they've answered? "Did you like that hotel because the accommodations were pleasant, or because of the service?" I'm confusing my results and the odds are pretty good that I won't get answers to both parts of the question.

And you won't necessarily know which one they haven't answered.

We often run questions together in our own minds and ask them all at once while we're thinking of them. It makes it hard for the person we're interviewing to keep track of what we're really asking. This is one of my greatest weaknesses in interviews; I often ask two or three questions at once. One thing leads me to another thing, and it's, "Would you talk about this and then say something about that?" and the person goes, "What was the first one again?" Ask one question at a time and make sure that it *is* one question.

Also, scrutinize those questions to make sure they aren't leading, or boxing the person in: "Have you stopped beating your wife?" I think the greatest risk in all research is that we think we know what we're going to find, or what we want to find. In one way or another, that leaks into the questions we ask, into our means of research, and into the way we approach the subject.

Suppose I say to you, "You really didn't care for the food at that restaurant, did you?" That's a really obvious example, but it takes courage to disagree with whatever you read as the agenda in that question. It takes standing up to, and challenging, what we think is the point of view of someone we don't know well. The odds are that people are going to hedge their bets in situations like that and just go with what they think you want to hear.

Two others types of problem questions that you mentioned are questions that are too long or too short.

Again, that's where some art comes in. A question that takes a hundred words to describe requires a tremendous amount of focus on the part of the interviewee to hold all that clear and get to the heart of what you're really asking. The best gift I can give as an interviewer is to ask a question that is as succinct as possible, but shares enough information to identify the topic area I'm exploring, or the particular story or experience I want to hear.

There was a good example in your book of a question that's too short. Instead of asking, "What about income?" a social worker might have to say, "I need to know what your income was last year."

In that example, if I ask, "What about income?" and the person answers, "$24,000," I'm not absolutely sure that what they're telling me is what I think I'm asking. Is $24,000 what they hope to be earning next year, what they know they will earn this year, or what they hope to earn in a month? If the question doesn't delineate the parameters sufficiently, then I can't evaluate the data in a meaningful way.

Is there anything else you'd like to add, or any other recommendations you'd like to make to people going into interviewing?

I would like to emphasize again that listening is the most vital skill, even more important than what you say. We all tend to think we listen well, but we don't. We don't know when we don't listen well. When my son was in fourth grade he attended a school where they wrote lengthy evaluations of a child's performance instead of report cards. He came home with his first evaluative report, and I started to read it to him. The whole time I'm reading it to him, he's playing with a pile of paper clips and filling a little Hot Wheels truck. This evaluation has all these positive things about him and then it says, "However, Ben doesn't listen well." I keep reading and he's playing with the paper clips and finally I said, "Did you hear that part now?" and he said, "What?" And I said, "Did you hear the part where your teacher said you don't listen well?" And he said, "I don't know what she's talking about. I pay attention all the time."

If there's an area that an interviewer wants to hone as a skill, listening is a great place to begin. It's ironic that we teach all kinds of speaking skills but we seldom teach listening skills with the same intensity. There are very few courses offered on listening. Our communication department doesn't offer one. Go figure. We have all these courses on speaking but not one on listening. There are a few good books about it, and some private courses offered through seminar companies, as well as in-house in a few corporations. But the best way to know where we stand as a listener is to ask the people who know us well, and be willing to hear the feedback: How would you evaluate me as a listener? What kind of a listener do you think I am? What do you think I should do to get better as a listener? Start with that and see what information you can gain. Anything that you can do to improve your skill as a listener will serve you well as an interviewer.

Super Searcher Tips

➤ Rather than seeing an interview as a one-down situation, try to reframe it as information-gathering or information-sharing.

➤ Saying, "Can you help me to understand this better?" puts the interviewee one-up. As an interviewer, it's an easy gift to give.

➤ Reconsidering the interview as a shared power situation could eliminate some call reluctance.

➤ You want to ask a question that clearly marks the specific terrain you want to visit, but then gives the person you're interviewing as much room as possible to talk about all the aspects.

➤ Closed questions are useful to get very specific demographic information about the person. Sometimes closed questions can be useful to rate and qualify responses. I make a series of statements and you strongly agree, agree, disagree, strongly disagree, or have no opinion.

➤ Open questions are what give us the individual stories and allow people to frame their experience in a particular way.

➤ Sometimes we think we hear something and we have heard it completely wrong. An accuracy probe involves paraphrasing back: "Did I hear correctly that you said this? Let me make sure that I understand." Unless we continually check our perceptions, we might come away with totally wrong conclusions.

➤ You have to develop a flow to the information gathering. Balance safer, easier questions against the harder ones so that people are moved in incremental stages into deeper levels of sharing.

➤ With an over-talkative interviewee, listen for the tiniest pause, for micro-opportunities when they catch their breath, and leap in. Don't wait for a normal pause with these people because they don't have one.

➤ To know where you stand as a listener, ask people who know you well, and be willing to hear the feedback. Anything you can do to improve your skill as a listener will serve you well as an interviewer.

Photo by S&S Photography

John Nolan

Elicitor Extraordinaire

John A. Nolan, III is Chairman of Phoenix Consulting Group in Huntsville, AL. Phoenix provides competitive intelligence and competitive assurance services and training to clients in a broad range of industries. He is a frequent presenter at national and international conferences and is the author of *CONFIDENTIAL: Uncover Your Competitors' Top Business Secrets Legally and Quickly—and Protect Your Own* [158, see Appendix].

jnolan@intellpros.com
www.intellpros.com

Can you tell me just a bit about your background and how you to came to do all the things you're doing now?

I was honored to have served in the intelligence community for twenty-two years, both in the United States and overseas, in a variety of intelligence collection as well as counterintelligence assignments. That shaped my view of the way intelligence is conducted. My undergraduate and graduate degrees were in international relations. I decided when I was about to get out of the government that I would get a Ph.D. in international relations and then get a job at some small college or university as an international relations professor. My wife said that she was not going to trade the genteel poverty of government service for the genteel poverty of academia, and pointed out that, since I had helped her so much with her business courses when we were undergraduates, I seemed to have a natural affinity for it. So I wound up going back for an MBA.

The first two courses that I took were an international marketing management course and a strategic planning course. And I was slapped right in the middle of my forehead by the very, very close relationship between what I had been doing in the intelligence community and what people needed in the business community, particularly in marketing management and strategic planning. I realized they could use the intelligence process in order to accomplish their responsibilities a lot better.

That was in the middle part of the 1980s, which happily coincided with the growth of the competitive intelligence field, and with the formation of SCIP (the Society of Competitive Intelligence Professionals) [114] in 1986. When I left the government in 1988, I went to work for a management consulting firm, and then two years later formed Phoenix Consulting Group with four of my colleagues from that other firm.

Our focus was, and remains, on transferring the techniques, tools, skills, orientations, and attitudes common to the international intelligence community to the business intelligence community. We're not talking about assassinations or putting exploding cigars in the opposing CEO's humidor or overthrowing governments or businesses—any of the more nefarious aspects of the intelligence community. But fundamentally there are elements that are common to both communities, and each has an opportunity to learn from the other. Our experience is that many companies are at a significant advantage if they employ both sides of the intelligence process: collection and protection.

Today I'd like to focus on the collection side. I'd actually like to jump right into elicitation, because that seems to be one of your most popular seminars and one of your key sets of concepts.

We always work on the basis of articulated client needs, as opposed to wandering about and gathering information and hoping someday somebody will need it.

People obtain information from other people through a variety of means. One of those means is interrogation, which is the preferred form for law enforcement types. For example, you can picture Andy Sipowicz from NYPD Blue saying, "Hey, bozo, it's my turn to ask the questions. It's your job to answer. You don't get to ask any questions."

That's not going to get you very far in business.

That's pretty adversarial, and problematic because the questions very often indicate where someone's interest really lies. Interrogation often has a dampening, even a chilling, effect on the course of a conversation. Sometimes it requires greater deftness or subtlety before you can be really explicit about what you're interested in. That's where people go from interrogation into an interviewing mode.

A person who is engaged in interrogation has authority that derives from the institution he or she represents, like the FBI or whoever. That means you *will* cooperate with this set of questions. In the case of an interview, the authority of the interviewer derives from, perhaps, the ostensible purity of his or her motives—for example, a journalist whose brief is provided by the people's need and right to know. Or the interviewer might be a therapist, dealing with a molested child or an abused spouse. Or they might be a researcher. Typically they're less adversarial in their question format—though if you get an interview from Mike Wallace, who's standing in front of you with a tape recorder and a video crew from *60 Minutes*, you might consider that pretty adversarial.

But, by and large, the interviewer is less demanding than the interrogator. And depending upon the skills of the interviewer, people lapse into normalcy after a certain period. They lapse into greater comfort in an interview than in an interrogation. But common to both is the nature of asking direct questions, which are, themselves, problematic from a variety of perspectives.

For example, I do this in seminars very frequently: I pick out a man and say, "How's your sex life, Fred?" And Fred generally pales, or he gets a big grin, or he drums his fingers, or he stares at his shoes. Everybody else in the class laughs. Then I tell them, Fred had a couple of options here. Two kinds of things can happen when I ask him a question like this. Either he can give me an answer, which is the data response, or he can give me a process response, which is really an unarticulated process with Fred asking himself a bunch of questions like "Who is this bozo? Why is he asking such a loaded question in an environment like this, with a mixed population of men and women, younger, older ... What's he going to do with this information if I give him an accurate response? How will it appear if I give him inaccurate information? Who is going to be impressed positively or negatively with whatever my response is?" and so on.

What I have done by asking such a direct and pointed question is focus on what I'm actually interested in. If I were really interested in Fred's sex life, the worst possible thing I could do is ask him a direct question in front of all those people. Believe me, I'm never interested in Fred's sex life—but if I ever were, what I should do is spend some time with Fred, construct the setting in such a way that it is relaxing and nonthreatening. I might go out with him and play racquetball, for example, and afterwards have a couple of adult beverages to cool off. Or I might arrange to meet somebody at a trade show or at a conference, instead of calling him in the middle of his performance review interview and trying to get him to answer questions then. That's the wrong time, the wrong place, and the wrong circumstances.

And this brings us to elicitation?

What we will do in elicitations is get what somebody has without asking them direct questions, using techniques that we've honed over a couple thousand years in the intelligence community. These techniques follow a fairly rigorous process. The process begins with the recognition of the downsides of questions. That doesn't mean that we don't ask questions, however, because, indeed, we do. We'll ask questions at the beginning of a conversation and at the end of a conversation. But they will be at a macro level, of a general character, that is usually pretty much of a tangent away from what we're really after.

We do this because cognitive psychologists have reported on the basis of their research that people tend to remember questions a lot longer than they remember the conversational elements of an interaction. And they will remember the front and the back of the conversation much longer than they'll remember the muddle in the middle. So we specifically get somebody to respond to a generalized question at the beginning of our interaction with them, and we gradually guide that conversation, in an organized way, down to the kinds of things we're interested in. By "gradually" I don't mean it's going to take two hours; sometimes it takes four or five minutes.

Once we've gotten what we're interested in, we don't just close the door and say, "Thank you very much," so that the person walks away feeling abused or used. We don't want the conversation to end at that point, lest they focus so much on the last element in that conversation that they're a problem the next time we want to talk to them. So we close the conversation by moving it away from that topic that we were most specifically interested in and have just gotten information about, and back out to a more generalized, more macro subject. We'll ask questions associated with that, so that at the end of the conversation, the person does not feel threatened, has been asked certain questions, has given their opinions about matters of a generalized nature, and walks away feeling comfortable, not used.

Could you give me an example of some questions of a generalized nature that you might start with?

I might be dealing with a retired military officer who is a program manager for a defense contractor. He has information that would be useful to us as we gather information on behalf of a client in the defense or aerospace industry. If I'm going to ask him questions that are directly related to the kind of work he does, the kind of activities that his company is engaged in, it would be foolish of me to ask him those questions directly, because he's going to be very much on the alert in a conversation like that. In this particular case, I have a military background. I know that I've got certain things going for me already, and I know some things about him already. I know that he's probably got some opinions. So I might ask the question, "Remember when the Clinton administration was attempting to install a nationalized health-care system? What did you think of that? Was that a good idea or a bad idea?" At that point he might spend three or four minutes giving his opinion. Frankly, I don't care what his opinion is, as long as I've gotten him talking, because I want to be able to guide the conversation. Now, you might ask, "What does guiding the conversation mean?"

Sure, let's go on to some of the elicitation techniques that you would use.

That's the elicitation. We'll hear him talk about how he disagrees with nationalized health care, and then I might say, "Obviously you've had some experience with socialized medicine during the time you were in the military." That's when he launches into more of his thoughts. "… if the government can't be trusted to provide it to the military people, who think they've got an actual contract to do that, then they certainly can't be trusted to do …" and so on. At that point, after listening to him talk about his military experience in relation to a couple of questions, it might be useful for me to say, "You know, it's at times like this that I wonder why I ever bothered to make the military a career."

And that's the first elicitation technique, which is what we call a provocative statement. A statement designed to get him to ask the question "Well, why *did* you make the military a career?" That gives him a sense of control of the conversation, because he's now asking the questions. Remember, of course, the people who are asking the questions are always in control. It's also, at the same time, setting up another technique. When he asks me, "Why did you?" then I can say, "It's kind of a family deal, a generational thing. My second great-grandfather fought with the Irish brigade in the Civil War, my first great-grandfather, in the Spanish-American War with Teddy Roosevelt and the Rough Riders. Then both my grandfathers and my dad, so when it was my time to go, I went."

I offer that as the quid pro quo, something about myself. The more truthful information I give him about myself, the more trust there is on the part of the other person. So I've built trust with him, built some confidence, and he's got some degree of control of the conversation. Then, knowing what little I've already learned about him based on how he's articulated his beliefs and clues like where he's from in the country, I know that if I offer him something about myself, he's going to respond with information about himself. And from that point on, I know that a variety of techniques are going to work with him.

Some examples are word repetition or mild flattery or mild criticism of some organization or institution in which he has a share or an interest. I might use disbelief or I might use naiveté— all mixed together, not one after another, lest they become so apparent that it becomes problematic. Gradually, we will go through each of the topical areas that I'm interested in. As the conversation develops, I will pick and choose which of these techniques yield the best results. Sometimes they don't work, but most of the time, as you become more skilled in using them, and as you stack these various techniques on top of each other, you get the responses that you want.

Then, at a certain point, you feel that you've gotten enough for today, or for this conversation. That's one of those instinctive feelings that come to you over time, both in your general experience and with that particular individual. You then ask another question that derives from the last thing that he talked about, that takes you back out into a more generalized topical area.

Is that what you mean when you talk about the conversation hourglass—that you handle broad topics at both ends and get to the specifics that you really want in that middle section?

Exactly. Say, for example, we want to know about his family, priorities, values, and so on. He talks about his wife, his kids, how proud he is of them, all except for one kid who's got a drug problem. After we've spoken about his kid, we then go on to talk for a while about federal drug interdiction or education or health care or incarceration policies, so he thinks, again, that I'm really interested in national issues. When he leaves, the questions that I've asked related to health care and the drug interdiction policy are the ones that we know will stay with him. We use questions to obtain his ideas about national drug policies so that when he leaves, his focus and recollection will largely be on that macro issue. If we don't, if we stop with the discussion about the son, he'll remember that far too long; he'll see that we attached significance to it and wonder why. The upshot of this would be suspicion on his part about our motives—and we want him to be as cooperative as possible on future contacts, not suspicious.

Let's talk about some of these elicitation techniques in a little more depth if possible. For example, you talked about word repetition.

That's similar to what you might get out of an active listening course where people are told that they should repeat a key word or the last phrase that an individual has used. We approach it just a little differently. We try to reframe things. For example, if someone starts talking to me about his educational background and his advanced degrees, instead of asking questions such as: "Where did you go to graduate school?" or "Where did you get your advanced degree?" or even repeating back the words "advanced degrees," I would change it to a statement. Like "Ah, graduate school, a good time was had by all." If I know the guy I am talking to is an extrovert, I'll just leave it hanging there. Because I know extroverts hate silence as much as nature hates a vacuum. So I can almost count one one-thousand, two one-thousand, before he'll start talking about where he went to graduate school. And I have not used the specific phrase or words but I have reframed them into a conversational mode that is less threatening and less obvious than word repetition.

If he's been around the business or military or government worlds very long, he may have taken an active listening course and would recognize word repetition for what it is. I change it around a little from the classical style that most people recognize as word repetition in an active listening format. And I would very rarely use word repetition with an introvert. Because, an introvert is going to be comfortable with that silence. I know an extrovert is not.

Okay. How do you use mild flattery?

The fellow I was just talking about in the previous example might respond well to flattery. I might say something like, "Well, it was obviously a lot more than a couple of graduate degrees that got you where you are." What's he going to say? How is he going to respond? With information about his degree field, most likely. If he responds with one of those self-effacing "aw, shucks" comments, we simply don't accept that. One or two "Ah, come on …" prompts usually will yield what we're after. In today's workplace, most guys will say, "I couldn't possibly use flattery in a business setting." But that's not true. I might be in trouble if I said, "Oh, Risa, I really like your dress, it shows off your figure." But I can say, "Risa, terrific job on the XYZ project." And it's my experience, and that of my colleagues, that women can get away with a great deal more flattery than men can.

It works beautifully. But I usually do think the people I flatter are wonderful. I honestly do think, "That was just great, what you told me" or whatever it is I happen to say.

That degree of sincerity that you put out along with your message is a key factor. I think it was George Burns who said, "Acting is all about sincerity. When you can fake that, you've got it made."

I love it! How about using mild criticism?

That involves criticizing an institution or belief system or an organization in which an individual may have a vested interest. It is not criticizing the individual: "Oh, you're stupid! How could anybody believe that?" You are criticizing with a certain degree of deftness as opposed to emotion. For example, dealing with someone in the cable industry, you might say, "For such a high-tech operation as this, the cable service seems to be pretty lousy." If you're talking to the vice president of operations of that cable company, the chances are that he's going to be pretty defensive about that. In defending the quality, he is going to talk not only about how good it is now, but how we're going to love it even more when we see the improved programming.

Then all you have to do is criticize the potential for better programming: "What are you talking about, five more violence channels? Three more Simpsons channels? Two more sex channels?" And he'll say, "Oh, no, no," and go on to explain what changes are on the horizon, which may well be competitively valuable. Especially if his business rival does not yet know what deals he's working up with which networks and which broadcasters.

So criticism is directed more toward the institution, where flattery is directed toward the person. How do you use disbelief?

You could actually flatter a person on the basis of his or her participation in an organization. But you're right, criticism isn't personal.

We use disbelief almost everywhere, from a kind of awestruck reaction to utter and complete disbelief. Very often you say, "I can't believe ..." when it's simply a device to get somebody to explain something to you.

There are various human characteristics associated with elicitation, and one of them is a desire to correct, or substantiate, or further explain, or defend. All of those reactions will pop up on an elicitor's radar. And it's an active radar, not passive. We're actually and deliberately pinging for the kinds of responses we need in order to understand that person better. So, the radar analogy really goes quite far in this case.

There has to be a certain amount of flexibility and imagination on the part of the elicitor during a conversation, paying attention not only to the words that are being spoken, but also to those opportunities that are presented during the conversation. He or she is going to use those opportunities to cause that person to say more about the topic than they might otherwise say in response to a direct question.

For example, I might perceive somebody to be a frustrated teacher, or somebody who likes to be a mentor, or the company know-it-all. In that case, it's very easy for me, as an elicitor, to suspend my ego and all its component parts—my education, my experience, what little intellect I might have, my knowledge of a topical area. I can suspend all those things in the interest of having someone who is a natural-born teacher tell me more things.

The same thing goes for disbelief: "I can't believe that a factory like yours could put out more than a thousand widgets a month." "Yeah, well, let me tell you, Fred, we not only did a thousand widgets last month, we did eighteen hundred. And when we get finished with this re-engineering project that I happen to be in charge of, we'll be pumping out three thousand widgets a month." That's the kind of thing that disbelief allows you the opportunity to capitalize upon in a nonthreatening way. Not by saying, "You're a liar," but rather, "I really find it hard to believe that anybody could do this."

"I really find it hard to believe ..." is a wonderful lead-in. How does that compare to naiveté?

Naiveté is structured essentially the same way. Fundamentally, you've got to be able to suspend your ego and say, "I really don't understand this. It all seems like black magic to me." The use of naiveté capitalizes on someone's desire to correct you, to substantiate whatever it is that you are working on, to supplement your knowledge. It doesn't mean that I'm stupid, because you won't talk to me if I'm a stupid person. But if I can ensure to your satisfaction that I'm (a) interested, and (b) undereducated in your discipline, and (c) a dedicated student, and you happen to be the grand master, then I can be naive for as long as it takes while letting somebody teach me. Naiveté means you've got to have a certain amount of humility, because if you say, "I already know all that," that's not useful, it will shut somebody down. "Well, if you already know all that, then I'm not going to tell you anything more."

Frequently, you really do go to people because they are the experts, and you do want their help in understanding something. You've also talked about "pleas for guidance," which seems to go along with that.

Pleas for guidance can range anywhere from helping you learn more about a particular topic to "Where else can I go to find this out?" At the opening of the conversation, it might be capitalizing on somebody's characteristic helpfulness. It's different in Europe. In my experience, going up to a German and expecting him to be as helpful as an American is a fool's mission. But if you're dealing with someone who answers the phone, you might say, "You know, I'm really under the gun. Can you help me with this one thing—or put me in touch with someone who really does know? Because I've been told you're the smartest person that ever wore hair when it comes to x or y or z." That's a plea for guidance.

Or at the end of the conversation, "Is there anybody else who knows anything more about this?" At that point they'll respond with, "Yeah, there's Fred and Mary and Joe," or else they might respond, "Look, maybe you didn't get the message, but I really am the best there is. And let me give you another example of why I am the best there is." And then they go on and tell us more. When they get finished with that, you can try again: "So, who else can tell me more?"

Are there other elicitation techniques we should talk about?

Bracketing is one. Virtually anything that is quantifiable is susceptible to the use of bracketing. In bracketing we set a floor, which is typically a pretty realistic one, and then a fairly wide range up to an unrealistic level. For example, if I wanted to talk to somebody about the price of an expected new product, I've got a choice. I could say, "Well, I guess this is going to cost five or six bucks?" The guy will respond, "Well, yeah," and I'm lost. I have no way of really knowing whether five or six bucks is accurate or not. I know that five bucks is probably the absolute minimum, but I have no idea what the real range might be. I need to bracket that down, so I'll say, "What's it gonna be, five bucks or thirty-five bucks?" Typically, the guy will respond with something like, "Closer to the lower end of that."

If I say, "You mean like six or seven?" and he agrees, I still don't know for sure, because I've put those words in his mouth. So I'll say, "You mean like fifteen." He'll say, "No, no, no, maybe more like ten or eleven." Now, I've been looking at his clothes. He may be dressed like I am sometimes—those times when my kids say that I am living proof that 7-Eleven has a men's department. So, if I see this guy has polyester pants, a polyester tie, you know a million baby polyesters gave their life for his wardrobe, then, I make the judgment that this guy is pretty cheap. So I say, "If it's more than ten or eleven, then I can come to you for the difference every time I need to buy it?" And he'll say, "Well, I don't know, maybe thirteen, thirteen-fifty."

So I've moved from a floor to what I already know to be an unrealistic ceiling, and we're narrowing it and narrowing it and narrowing it. Then, for the *coup de gras*, to get him to be explicit, you offer him some kind of personal buy-in. The personal buy-in was when I said, "If it's more than you said, then you will pick up the difference?" Effectively, I want to get him to say, "You're not getting into my wallet, Jack. And I'll give you the right answer before I let you into my wallet." The subtle and not-so-subtle psychological aspects and presenting characteristics of the individual really shape the selection of which technique you are going to use.

I do want to get into that in a lot more depth. But before we do, that example of bracketing was great. Are there any other really top techniques that you can tell me about?

We use oblique references a lot. Let me start off with a psychological principle first: If I'm having a hard time understanding something, the most effective way for you to describe it to me is not in abstract terms, but with as concrete an example as possible. I'll give you a for-instance here. If I'm dealing with a production engineer who works in a manufacturing environment, he probably knows what OSHA (Occupational Safety and Health Administration) [101] is, and he probably hates OSHA because it's an impediment to their productivity. You have to wear eye protection in order to go into the men's room, that kind of thing. So if I'm interested in what's going on in a manufacturing environment, then I'm going to talk to him about OSHA and the impact that it has on American business. The only place that he connects with that in reality is in his own facility. So he's going to say, "Oh yeah, they're really a pain in the butt."

"So you know quite a bit about OSHA then, if you know that they're a pain in the butt?"

"Oh yeah, they come into our place all the time with these unannounced inspections. As a matter of fact, they just shut down this production line because we were using some stuff that they thought was unsafe. And we've got to reengineer the whole production line and that's probably going to mean three weeks of down time. We got people sitting around that can't work. But we've got to pay them anyway while we retool and redesign and get this whole new process in place that's acceptable to those pettifogging weenie bureaucrats in OSHA."

"Oh, so you've got to do that or what? They close down your plant?"

"Either that or they fine us."

"Sometimes those fines are pretty hefty."

"Well, look, when we got shut down the last time, it cost us $350,000."

If you're selling against that particular manufacturer, you now know that they can't keep up with demand because they've got a production line that's shut down, and so forth.

But the oblique reference comes in where? Is that when you introduce a broader topic, but you know that he's going to respond from where he's standing?

Right. The oblique reference is to OSHA, and the only place that it makes any sense is inside his plant. This guy is not an OSHA regulator, he's not somebody who has worked on Capitol Hill. He's a guy down in the bowels of some manufacturing plant who has to put up with the pain and suffering that OSHA causes. The only place that OSHA has any meaning, in his mind, is inside his plant. And that's the only perspective he can clearly articulate to someone who is preternaturally stupid, which is what I am.

He's explaining it to me, and the more interested I am in what he's telling me, the more he's going to tell me about it.

This is on a practical, down-to-earth, real-life level, and not some general abstraction or concept that doesn't provide the kind of detail that I need from him. The longer he persists—if in fact he does, and that's a rarity—in staying in the abstract, the more I'll remain purposely confused or obtuse. Or I'll simply go on to another technique.

Are there any other major techniques that you want to talk about?

I've probably covered the major ones. We've got about forty that we teach people, but these are the ones that people mostly identify with. There is one we call confidential bait, which is like the quid pro quo that I alluded to earlier, but at a higher level. It's like "Well, I really shouldn't be telling you this …" You begin exchanging a confidence with this person and they reciprocate at the same level of confidentiality. It's a quid pro quo taken to the next level.

There's partial disagreement, where you can disagree with somebody and, either out of pride or defensiveness or whatever, they correct you or they tell you why they believe something or why the company did this. It's called partial disagreement because you are not directly in their face. It's not "You people are too stupid to walk upright without a wheelbarrow." You might couch it in qualifying terms such as, "Well, somehow that doesn't always seem to be the case." You can hear the qualification in my voice with "somehow" and "always seem." You are disagreeing, but not smacking them in the face with your disagreement.

So that's different from mild criticism.

Exactly. You're just being mildly disagreeable. The purpose of elicitation is to maintain as much of an even keel, rapport-wise, as possible. That's not always possible in an interview, and certainly not always possible in an interrogation, because those have usually begun in an adversarial way.

Each time I think we're done in this area, you mention another great technique. Any others?

If I were giving a seminar right now, I'd have thirty or so that I'd be able to talk about or demonstrate. These are just off the top of my head. Sometimes people will listen to me in a conversation and they'll say, "Oh, that was really neat, the way you did such-and-such." I don't even think about it, because once you internalize something, you tend not to think about what it is that you're doing.

It's like learning to drive a car with a stick shift. After you've been driving a car for five years, you don't think about shifting. But the first time you shifted gears, boy, that was a traumatic experience. That's what I was getting at earlier when I said that we don't really apply these techniques in a rote way; rather, we get that instinctive, gut reaction that this is going to work with this kind of person, or this other approach will work with those kinds of people. You internalize the process to the extent that you don't really think about which technique you are going to use at any one moment.

That's so true about the gut instinct that develops with experience. But when you're first learning this on a conscious level, how do you decide which techniques to use on which people and in which circumstances? What are the tip-offs?

Part of it is knowing the type of person you're dealing with, and what techniques you have used successfully with this kind of person in the past. For example, I alluded earlier to using disbelief or naiveté with the person who is a teacher or an instructor by nature, because that allows them to be the superior who is teaching you. I know there's a 95.5 percent chance that that person's going to respond affirmatively to those techniques. If I'm dealing with an extrovert I am going to use word repetition combined with silence. It all depends on his or her presenting characteristics, and on how I've seen other people with those same characteristics respond to these particular techniques, which I have gained mastery over during the course of my lifetime.

This is not to say that all of this is rocket science. Many of the people who come to our seminars and workshops already use some of these techniques, but they don't use them consciously. As a result, they don't have an organized process. Bringing it up to consciousness allows them to be much more effective with a diverse population.

Say somebody is accustomed to always getting a lot of information by using word repetition. They're really good working with extroverts, but then they bump into the introvert and it doesn't work. And they wonder, "Why didn't I get anything out of him?" Well, because that's not a technique that works well with introverts. You've got to see what the presenting characteristics are, and then match the arrows in your elicitation quiver with the techniques that you know he will be responsive to.

What would work with an introvert?

Naiveté. Particularly with an introvert who is in a technical discipline. Say I'm dealing with an accountant. What do we generally know about accountants? They hate imprecision. They have chosen a life that revolves around numbers and accuracy. The balance sheet has to balance. They'll spend hours looking for that odd penny. So what am I going to purposely do? I am going to purposely make an erroneous statement, which is another technique that I didn't cover because it just didn't come to the top of my mind. But it did now. Okay—a purposely erroneous statement is offered for the express purpose of having someone correct me.

You've mentioned that executives and lawyers, for example, might need to show how clever they are. Are there certain techniques that you might use with people in positions of authority?

Sure. People who are in positions of authority are extremely susceptible to flattery. Very often people in positions of authority take the success of the organization as the result of their personal brilliance. You can't be unctuous or oily or greasy in your flattery, and you can't use it until it becomes saccharine sweet, like listening to a Karen Carpenter song. You have to avoid that.

But there are different categories, different types, different typologies. Are you at all familiar with the Myers-Briggs Type Indicator, the MBTI [87]? It would probably help for me to mention that, throughout the business and government communities, the use of psychological profiling is pretty common. As a result, I've spent much of my life dealing with the operational aspects of the MBTI.

Do you want to go into the MBTI a little bit, and how it relates to choosing elicitation techniques?

What elicitation techniques you choose will depend partly on what you personally have learned over time, and partly on certain constructs. A construct, like the Myers-Briggs, for example, is an artificial framework that allows you to be more organized. The MBTI has four continuums—Extroversion/Introversion, Sensing/Intuition, Thinking/Feeling, and Judging/ Perceiving. When we first deal with people, we try to develop whether they're an ENTP or an ISTJ, so we'll know what elicitation techniques will work with them.

Can you explain that a little more?

ISTJ stands for an Introverted, Sensing, Thinking, and Judging personality. The first one, extroversion versus introversion, doesn't just mean that somebody is an extrovert in the sense of loud and boisterous. Rather it's somebody who gets support and energy from external as opposed to internal sources. An introverted personality is the opposite. I'll take you through an exercise. Is Bill Clinton an extrovert or an introvert?

Extrovert.

On the next level, is Bill Clinton a sensing guy or an intuitive guy? That is, is he somebody who loves to dig down into the details of something, or is he interested in grand global strategies and legacies and that kind of stuff?

My sense of him is that he goes both ways.

Actually, he has been forced into a mode of understanding and capturing the details in order to be effective. But his preferred modality is to operate in the grand strategy realm.

Then the next level is thinking versus feeling. What motivates him more, logic or emotion?

Feelings.

Absolutely. "I feel your pain!" I don't mean that disparagingly; that is just an accurate characterization.

The last level is judging or perceiving, which in the simplest way describes whether people have a real high need for closure, keeping to timetables, making sure that everything is done within established parameters, and making decisions quickly. Or would they prefer to keep their options open, with more dialogue and more information gathering, thinking more along the lines of "the decision can wait" and "I'll get there when I get there."

For example, the ISTJ is your quintessential engineering/accounting type guy. He's introverted and likes to deal with detail. He's motivated by and makes decisions on the basis of thoughtfully reasoned logic, and he has a high need for closure. That means that, if I want to provoke him, I am going to make purposefully erroneous statements about those things that he treasures as detail.

So one way of using a construct like this would be employing silence, as you said, with people you perceive as extroverts, because they hate silence. What else could you use?

You could use disbelief, or a mild criticism of something in which he has an important investment. We were talking about the cable industry earlier. If I'm dealing with someone who, as a cable guy, is really interested in programming, it's not going to do me any good to criticize the cretins who come around to do installations because they never get there on time. Or that they have outages, that every now and again the cable goes south. That doesn't bother them. If you were a telephone company executive, that would bother the heck out of you. Because that's what teleco guys do, they live and breathe reliability, and courteous employees who get there on time, do their job, and so on. But cable guys don't care about that. Cable guys only care about programming. So, if I'm dealing with a cable guy, I'm going to criticize his programming, because he could care less about the other things.

So, for example, mild criticism doesn't necessarily tie to whether somebody is an introvert or an extrovert?

No, not necessarily. Some elicitation techniques apply to introvert versus extrovert, some apply to thinking versus feeling. For example, using naiveté or disbelief or partial disagreement with somebody who loves details is probably going to present you with a lot more response. We're operating now on the second dimension of sensing—loving facts and details—versus intuition. Irrespective of whether they are extroverts or introverts, they're going to correct us if they have a high degree of respect for accuracy.

So you're saying that, as you talk to the person, you're constantly feeling out who they are, what's important to them, how they're responding. And, based on all that input you're getting and maybe viewing through organizing constructs like the MBTI, you determine which techniques to use with them. Are there other useful constructs?

The conversational hourglass is a construct. What I call the four corners of elicitation is another construct. Say you've got a horizontal and a vertical line intersecting. That gives you four quadrants. The left-hand quadrant might be quadrant number one. In that one, I would place outcomes and objectives. Never go into a conversation without having an outcome or objectives in mind. It's amazing how many people start off a conversation without an outcome. What is it that I hope to achieve during this conversation? Most people are just kind of hanging out at the mall most of their life, conversationally speaking.

The next quadrant is history and presenting characteristics. Are there certain things that I know about someone because of their personal history? If I know that they went to Notre Dame, I know that they are going to view the world slightly differently from somebody who went to Harvard, or who was an Ag major at Iowa State. Those are characteristics that I have identified over the years as distinguishing those kinds of people. It doesn't mean that they had to go to those particular schools, necessarily, but rather that they have certain presenting characteristics that are common to many people that I've met and observed over time, and I've seen what made those other people tick.

When I find those same characteristics or personal history experiences in the person I'm about to talk to, or am talking to at that moment, I'm going to have a foundation of generalizations upon which to proceed. And if I am wrong, there isn't any third-grade Mrs. O'Toole standing over me with a ruler, ready to smack my knuckles. There's nobody watching, so if this particular technique doesn't work, that's okay, because I have another twenty-five or thirty techniques that I can use.

And you've learned something. You put that in your data bank.

Exactly. And our database of sources contains precisely those kinds of information. The third quadrant of this framework is techniques. Techniques that have worked well for this kind of individual in the past, and the kind of techniques that I have mastered and feel comfortable with. We encounter many people who, when they're first learning these things, try to use all of them. Instead, we say to use one or two or three, in a practice sense, all the time. Then, when you are really comfortable with a particular technique as an organized process, add another one that you haven't used before. Pretty soon you'll be up to twenty or thirty techniques and you'll not even think about using them; you'll use them naturally. That's when you'll know that you've got good command of them. It's a matter of marrying techniques that you know will work well with this kind of person, with the kind of techniques that have worked well for you in the past.

The fourth quadrant is watching for the changes that occur in somebody as you are talking to them. For example, I'm sitting on a bench with a guy who is shorter than I am. The conversation gets around to personal finances. He's demonstrating character-istics that I recognize as those of somebody who is nervous talk-ing about this kind of thing. He might feel, here's this big, ugly, dumb guy talking to him and he is uncomfortable talking about dollars. By the time we've finished talking about dollars—and believe me, I'll get a lot of information about his personal finances, if that's what I'm after—by the time that portion of the conversation is over, I will have slumped down to the point where I am actually shorter than he is.

I am paying attention to those behavioral changes, those messages he's sending that say, "I'm uncomfortable." If I wish to continue that conversation, then I'll make physical changes that will allow him to feel that he's more in control and less threatened. Or, if I get the impression that we have now gone as far as we can possibly go without wrecking our rapport, then I'll just guide the conversation on to another topic where he is more comfortable. Otherwise, you risk your entire relationship with that person if you insist on beating him over and over with the same hammer.

What are some of the clues that let you know when someone's feeling uncomfortable?

Changes in their breathing, changes in their physical posture, changes in their mannerisms, like a facial tic that appears when they get nervous. Or if they blanch suddenly and all the blood drains out of their face. Those are what we call macrobehaviors. We are always looking for macrobehaviors and microbehaviors that indicate that somebody is uncomfortable. It may be yawning or tapping their foot as if to say, "I'm out of time, hurry up, get on with it." There are lots of behaviors that send messages saying that whatever you happen to be doing, you are doing it wrong. They're not as comfortable as they had been, they're not as cooperative, they're less interested.

What would you do to bring it back to a more comfortable level? You mentioned changing your physical posture.

Another is to mirror their breathing. If you know anything about group dynamics, you've heard of mass hysteria, which is said to account for Hitler's success, for example, in captivating the German people. Some of that had to do with their singing and shouting "Sieg Heil" all together. What that did was cause them to all breathe together. People who study communication suggest that one of the most profound ways to establish rapport is to breathe at the same rate, pace and depth as the person with whom you are interacting.

So I always monitor breathing, and there are lots of ways to do it. People think that to monitor somebody else's breathing, you've got to stare at their chest. Actually, I'd be paying attention to your shoulders, because your shoulders move the same way your chest does. If your hair hangs down onto your shoulders, I'll watch the movement of your hair. And/or I'll pay attention to the tonality of your voice and whether that bespeaks shallowness or depth in your breathing. Your voice will change according to your breathing pattern. And your breathing pattern will change according to external stimuli. These things sound like common sense when you point them out, but they take on real profundity when you examine them and begin to apply them.

What else might you do to restore someone's comfort level?

Change my body posture in other than macro terms. You know we send messages to other people constantly. Just nodding your head is very useful. Or becoming more expansive. People tend to follow the behaviors of other people. I just alluded to the mirroring behavior associated with breathing. If you look at three guys sitting on a couch watching a football game, they'll all reach for their beer at the same time, all slug it down, put it back down on the coffee table, recross their legs—all three of them at the same time. It's because they're in a profoundly developed state of rapport.

That's what we call mirroring, or matching, and you can do it either consciously or unconsciously. It's interesting when you pay attention to people doing it. The reason it works is that people tend to want to seem like the other person. We attempt to develop these fairly profound states of rapport. When the other person begins to become agitated, for example, we modify our behavior. If you and I get into a discussion that leads to a disagreement, which leads to an argument, suddenly you are screaming at the top of your lungs at me. The typical response might be "Slow down. Come on, stop being so emotional." Well, that's the last thing you want to hear at that point—"Don't you tell *me* I'm being too emotional!"—and the screaming goes even higher. The best thing for me to do is raise my voice level congruent with that of yours, and then begin to slow down.

So you match the other person's state and then modify yours, and hope that they will mirror yours in modifying theirs. You mirror their breathing, mirror their posture.

Yes. You mirror or match their language, too. If, for example, you are much more visually oriented than auditorily oriented, I am going to change my linguistic pattern to be more consistent and congruent with yours than with my own.

Would you do that initially, or only to bring someone back to a comfort level?

I do it throughout. But I particularly emphasize it when the conversation has gotten to a tight level. You have to be paying attention, so that long before it gets to a place where it's almost unmanageable, you have already taken these steps to guide it back to a level of normalcy.

I am wondering what differences you see between doing this in person and doing it, for example, over the telephone.

Ah yes, excellent question; I was wondering when that was going to come in. This has to do with the value of hallucination.

Let's talk about the value of hallucination. Are you're saying that when you don't see someone

in person, you automatically create a hallucination of them in your mind?

Yes, and I have never in my life been right. When I actually meet the person or visit their office, I always discover that I'm wrong. But that doesn't matter, because from then on I know what they look like, how they react to various kinds of stimuli, and what their office looks like. The next time I talk to them, I have a perfect mental image, as if I were there talking to them. In effect, I am not talking to them on the phone anymore, I am talking to them face-to-face. Either way, I am always talking to people face-to-face.

Even when you haven't met them, when they're only a voice on the phone, you create a picture in your mind?

You know what the picture is that I have of you right now? You are wearing a bathrobe, big bunny slippers, you have a tape recorder, and you've got a big stack of 5x8 cards with questions on them, based on the research that you did in preparation for this interview.

You're not exactly right, but close enough! I don't happen to be wearing my bathrobe and bunny slippers today, but they're certainly part of my interviewing wardrobe, and the cards are absolutely right. But what's the value of having these hallucinations, of having a vision of the other person in your mind?

I'm exceptionally comfortable in this conversation. The more comfortable I am, the more confident I am, and the more I can accomplish in a conversation. Comfort is really important. I am not uptight, I'm not worried, I'm not bothered. The more comfortable I am in this environment, the more I am ultimately going to be able to control the course of this conversation.

And having this picture helps you develop that level of comfort?

Absolutely. Think about being in a dark room. There are no lights, you feel a presence, and suddenly Darth Vader is in the room with you. How do you feel? Real comfortable? Of course not. But if you picture yourself in a bright sunshiny office, and you are sitting next to a potted plant and there're 6,000 books and 400 pictures of my kids and grandkids, you just think, "I feel really comfortable." Now, which of those two interview situations are you more comfortable performing in? Even if I am Darth Vader, which one are you more comfortable in? Where do you feel more in control, where do you feel more relaxed and more confident?

In the lovely office, of course. But are you saying that you try to create a picture of who that person really is, or do you try to create a picture that will make you feel comfortable with that person?

I am going to create a picture of who I think that person really is, and then I am going to put them into an imaginary situation where I feel the most comfortable. Hopefully it will come across in my voice to that other person that he or she can be that comfortable, and they're going to become more relaxed. Maybe you hear it consciously, maybe unconsciously. At that point, you lean back in your chair and think, "Ahh, we're comfortable together."

So you are using auditory clues, plus you're using your mind to create a visual environment that you don't have on the telephone. Do you

find that you're getting more body language clues and so on when you interact in person?

It's immeasurably easier in person because you are getting all kinds of clues all the time. You're getting visual clues, you're getting auditory clues, you're getting kinesthetic clues. Simply the way somebody shakes hands with you is a clue. I can use a handshake for comfort, or I can use it for power. I can send all kinds of messages just by a handshake. I can communicate to you comfort and sincerity and warmth and gentleness and all that other stuff, even though I've got these giant hands. Or I can communicate a bunch of other things to you. If I want to be much more domineering, I can do that, just by the way I shake your hand. I don't have that opportunity over the phone, so I have to make up for it with outrageous behavior at the beginning of the conversation to try to put you more at ease.

Let's go on to a totally different topic. How do you go about finding your sources, the experts or the people that you want to speak with?

That's a great question, particularly in today's information-rich environment. Most of the time we are talking about external sources of information. Over the course of the last ten years we've been developing this database of sources that we've already talked to. We have seventy-nine thousand people in our database and, within that group, we usually can find people in most industries. A friend of mine uses the phrase "used to was," so I use it. Used to was, it would take us weeks to find fifty people to serve as sources on a project. Now we'll find fifty people in an hour and a half. And that's if we don't know anybody in that industry to begin with.

Let's start with a field that you don't know anything about. How would you find those sources?

If the client says, "We want you to look at the electro-optics division of company X and find out about their new pulsed laser activity," the first thing we'd do is go to the Net. We would use a variety of search engines. Every day the people in our research organization find imaginative new ways. They might say, "AltaVista's [8] got this new thing which has really been giving me some joy."

They might look, for example, at what kind of words appear on a resumé. We go to various posting services for resumés, so they'll get twelve resumés, maybe. And we find ten guys who claim to have Ph.D.s in electro-optics, and to have some pulsed laser technology experience. Then we look at their companies; maybe they used to work at the company we're interested in.

If it's someone who's posted stuff on the Web, we might communicate with them, but we might not communicate with them directly at their place of employment. We might use Web-Ferret [137] for example, or search.com [118], to get a cross-reference to the guy's various email addresses. We might find him in the alt.naked.backpacking forum. We might not approach him as J.Jones@XYZ.com, where he works, but we also know him as JSquared@aol.com, so we might write to him there and strike up a conversation that relates to naked backpacking, or go to the discussion forum or chat room there. We might refer to him by virtue of the Web posting for his resume, and say, "We understand you used to work at such-and-such a company. We searched on the Web for people who know about these kinds of things, and your name came up as someone who is an expert in electro-optics." We'd send him email, preferably at his home, or at night so that he gets it at home. And we say, "We've been told that you are the smartest person ever when it comes to blah-blah-blah." The next thing you know he's written ten email pages back to you, along with three attachments showing you how brilliant he is.

Are there print resources that you like a lot?

When we go into a company, we do an assessment of what they already know in the particular topical area that they want us to inquire about. Let's use the electro-optics area again. We'll go in and visit with ten of their Ph.D.s. Each one of them has the conference proceedings from the last ten years of the IEEE (Institute of Electrical and Electronics Engineers) electro-optics sessions. We'll borrow those conference proceedings, and our person will take our little hand-held scanner and scan in the abstract and the name and company or university affiliation of everybody who's written in the proceedings.

You also mentioned trade shows.

We'll go to those conferences, meet people, develop relationships with them, and get them to introduce us to other people. The best relationships we have are developed from in-person contacts. We have a whole team of people who do nothing more than trade shows, and they're there to gather information and to develop new sources of information. They can assess those people in terms of where they went to school, what they like to talk about, how many kids they have, what kind of neighborhood they live in, what kind of sports or hobbies they have. So you have all these ways to develop common ground with them.

Any other sources that you use?

One of the other things we do is make a lot of telephone calls at night. Why would we call a company at night? We have university kids who work for us as researchers at night and their whole purpose in life is to develop a pool of people to talk to inside a particular company. The easiest way to do that is to call at night and get their automatic switchboard that says, "We're closed right now. If you know the extension of the person you want to talk to, dial it now. If you want our names directory, press 1."

So you press 1 and it says, "Enter the first three letters of the person's last name." So you punch in 2-2-2 and you get Anna Aber. A-b-e-r. And then it says, "Is this the person you want to talk to? Press 1 for yes." And then Anna Aber's recording comes on and says, "This is Anna Aber at extension 3456 in the marketing department of XYZ company. I can't take your call right now, but if you leave a message I'll get back to you quickly." The option is to leave a message or return to the main menu. You write down "Anna Aber, ext. 3456, marketing dept." You continue the process, staying inside that menu until you have everybody's name in that company. You've created a directory of that company.

How about experts, if you're trying to find experts in a particular area?

There are lots of places on the Web that list expert consultants or expert witnesses, people who are self-described experts. One good example is the Sources and Experts list [120] compiled by *St. Petersburg Times* news researcher Kitty Bennett. People have written articles that appear on the Web. You can go to professional societies. For example, if you go to the Society for Competitive Intelligence Professionals Web page, they've got a peer help section [116]. So, if you want help on a particular topic, like benchmarking, financial analysis, or online information sources, they've got members of the society who have listed themselves as experts or as resources. That's always an option; we use those very frequently. We do secondary research as much to identify the authors of articles and to find sources named in the articles, as to gather information on the actual topic.

Once you've got your sources, either on the phone or in person, how do you introduce yourself?

We follow the SCIP ethical guidelines [115]. One says that we'll always comply with applicable laws. Another says that we always identify ourselves by our true names and organization prior to the initiation of any information-gathering contact. What that means is that we don't do rusing. Insurance salespeople do rusing; telemarketing people especially use ruses.

So you'd say, "I'm John Nolan with Phoenix Consulting." But then you'd stop? You wouldn't say anything more than that?

Actually, we would say a little bit more than that. We'd say, "We're working on a project and we were told that you were the smartest person in America when it comes to XYZ."

Let me just quickly share with you the statistics that derive from our contact base. After every contact our researchers render a two-part report. One is the contact report itself, the information portion. The other is what we call the Basic Source Data report, or BSD, where we put in things like the number of kids and the person's hobbies and all that stuff I alluded to earlier.

There is a pair of questions that deals with how the person reacted to the opening of the conversation. It has remained pretty consistent across time that, out of every hundred people that our researchers call—they will always start by saying, "Hi, my name is such-and-such, Phoenix Consulting Group. I'm working on a project and I've been told you are smart in this area. Is this a good time?"—fifty people out of that one hundred will either say, "Yeah, this is as good a time as any" or "Call me back when I've finished this little project I'm working on now." So, fifty people out of a hundred are willing to talk to us at the beginning of a conversation. For our purposes, the beginning of a conversation is not the beginning of the elicitation section, as we discussed earlier.

The other fifty are a little bit more suspicious. They'll say, "What's this Phoenix Consulting Group and what does it do? And what are *you* doing?" And we'll say, "We're a research firm in Huntsville, Alabama, and we are working on a research project on behalf of a client." Almost all of these people ask, "Who is your client?" And we say, "Unfortunately, we are bound by confidentiality terms in all of our research projects, so we can't disclose the name of the client." You'd think anybody would say, "If you're not going to tell me who your client is, then I'm not going to have anything more to do with you"—click—and hang up.

And indeed, that happens with fifteen out of the remaining fifty people. The other thirty-five people say something like, "Oh yeah, we've got to put up with that confidentiality garbage at our place, too. What can I do for you?"

So, in our experience, eighty-five people out of a hundred are willing to talk to us at the beginning. And if we get them to talk to us in the beginning, that's when we begin directing the conversation, guiding it to the things that we're interested in. We scan the BSDs every year to see if there are any substantive changes in the overall responses of people we've interviewed, compared to the previous years. The bottom line is that the numbers stay roughly the same year after year, for the most part, geography and industry notwithstanding.

People who don't do this for a living are always amazed. "Why do people talk to you? How do you get them to talk to you?" And my response is, "People just like to; they are willing to." In my experience, many more people than you might imagine are willing to talk to you.

I get maybe five or six interview requests in a ten-day period, and most of the time I try to take them. Journalists are never surprised when I share that with them, because they get the same kinds of responses and more. I asked somebody from *The Wall Street Journal* their hit rate, and first he said it's amazing that you asked, because nobody ever asked that question. Then he said, "Almost everybody I call is willing to talk to me." And I said, "That's not surprising; it just means that you've picked the right people to talk to." You don't waste your time calling people that you know won't be willing to talk to you in the first place.

Once you've talked to someone, how do you evaluate the accuracy and the validity of the information they've given you?

We evaluate both the reliability of the sources themselves and the reliability of the information they provide. With sources who have provided information in the past, we ask, "Was that information accurate? Has their information been confirmed by other sources?" Sometimes we factor in their qualifications or background. Say, for example, this is the marketing director for this company and he is in a position to know. We won't mention his name, but we will describe his position and the fact that he's inside that company, which allows the reader to know that the information did not come from the janitor of the company next door.

And the reliability of the information, you said, is based partly on external corroboration. Any other factors come to mind?

Sometimes it's timeliness. If we have a source who repeatedly has provided us with information only after the event has occurred, then we know that that's all he's ever going to tell us— things that are more or less considered to be in the public domain. Some people just want to maintain a relationship for whatever reasons, for whatever the future might hold. If you ask them to let you know if anything is happening, they will call you periodically to give you an update, but it's always old information. So you keep their motivation in mind and you know that you're not going to be expecting any rocket science from them.

Do you present these evaluations to your clients in some formal way?

We have a scale that speaks to the source as well as to his or her information. That scale runs from A all the way down to F with regard to the source. "A" is a source of known reliability based on our previous experience with them. "F" is a source whose credibility cannot be determined at this time. In the middle are people who have provided us with false or inaccurate information in the past.

The other part of the scale has to do with the information itself. It ranges from 1 to 6. "1" is information that's been corroborated by other sources. "6" is "cannot be verified." In-between includes evaluations such as "we know this to be false."

The value of this scale is that we can ascribe a parenthetical notation, like A1 or F6 or B3, to virtually every paragraph in a report. A reader can look across the footer of our report and see what that matrix means, and then immediately see the validity of each paragraph's information for his or her purposes. That's one of the ways we help our clients—by delivering not just data, but information they can apply immediately to help answer their questions.

Super Searcher Tips

➤ People remember questions a lot longer than they do the conversational elements of an interaction. And they remember the front and the back of the conversation longer than the muddle in the middle. We get what they have without asking direct questions, and we bury it in the middle of a conversation.

➤ Using "naiveté" as an elicitation technique, you suspend your ego and say, "I really don't understand this." That capitalizes on someone's desire to correct you, to substantiate, to supplement your knowledge.

➤ A "plea for guidance" can range from "Where else can I go to find this out?" to "I'm really under the gun. Can you help me with this one thing, or put me in touch with someone who does know?"

➤ Virtually anything that is quantifiable is susceptible to the use of "bracketing." In bracketing we set a floor value, which is typically pretty realistic, and then a fairly wide range up to an unrealistic level. And through successive questioning, we narrow it and narrow it.

➤ The four corners of elicitation are having an outcome or objectives in mind, knowing the person's history and presenting characteristics, marrying techniques that have worked well on this kind of individual in the past with the techniques that I have mastered and feel comfortable with, and watching for those changes that occur in somebody as you are talking to them.

➤ People who study communication suggest that one of the most profound ways to establish rapport is to breathe at the same rate, pace, and depth as the person with whom you are interacting. Mirror their breathing, their posture, and their language.

➤ Interacting in person you get visual, auditory, and kinesthetic clues all the time. Just by a handshake I can send all kinds of messages. I can communicate to you comfort, sincerity, warmth, gentleness, or power.

Lynn Peterson

Public Records "To the Ends of the Earth"

Lynn Peterson is president of PFC Information Services, Inc., a public records research firm in Oakland, California. PFC Information Services provides public records research for law firms, corporations, lenders, venture capitalists, employers, the media, and other information research firms. Lynn has been quoted on public records research in a variety of sources including *The Wall Street Journal*, *Kiplinger's Personal Finance Magazine*, and *The Information Broker's Handbook*.

lpeterson@pfcinformation.com
www.pfcinformation.com

Tell me something about your background, and how you ended up where you are today.

It's been basically a series of accidents. My background for the first ten years following college was as an industrial engineer, doing time-and-motion studies, boring stopwatch work. I was in charge of the development of procedure manuals. Then my job went to southern California, and I decided, "No way." So I started thinking about what I could do. I had three little kids, twins and a three-year-old, and I didn't want to commute. I started an employment agency called Prairie Home Companions, bringing caregivers from the Midwest out to families in California. I did that for five years. It was a very good business, and a very difficult business dealing so intensively with people.

Part of that process involved doing background checks on the applicants that we were placing. Families were taking a leap of faith in bringing someone out from a different state, and we had to turn these people inside out. I was paying a private investigator to do those background checks. My husband happened to have a conversation with a friend who was a retired investigator from the District Attorney's office and a private investigator. He said, "Oh, Lynn could do this herself, she doesn't have to pay somebody else. She's good with computers." He took me under his wing. Under his tutelage I became aware of not only what we could do in terms of background checks on individuals, but the enormity of the amount of data available online and elsewhere.

I got an offer I couldn't refuse, sold the caregiver business, retained the information business, and decided that I would try to learn all I could about information. I had two mentors, Sue Rugge [113, see Appendix] and Jack Fink, who was a wonderful private investigator. They're both deceased now.

Public records research is not a profession. It's really a craft that you can only learn through experience. Jack marched me down to the courthouse and said, "This is how you do this, this is how you do that." I've been doing public records searching since 1989. By a series of accidents, I found something that I really enjoy and that's challenging, because it's always different due to legislative and technological changes.

What kind of clients do you have?

I've got a variety of clients. My bread and butter is law firms. Large law firms, particularly, do a lot of outsourcing. While law librarians do know something about public records, they tend not to be specialists. So, frequently, if it's a really nasty one they give it to me.

What would be a really nasty assignment that a law firm would give you?

I had one yesterday where the name was equivalent to John Smith, and all they knew was that he was old and he once lived in Brooklyn. I'm supposed to find out all I can. Often they don't want to mess with obtaining hard-to-get documents, so they outsource a lot of that kind of research. I'm involved in high-profile cases. I worked on the O.J. Simpson case for months and months obtaining hard-to-get documents, and it was ridiculous, just living hell. I also work for venture capital companies, for lenders, corporations, large accounting firms.

What would you do for venture capitalists?

If they're considering making an investment, they would want me to check out the company and perhaps the board of directors as well. It depends on the nature of the company. If a company is involved with hazardous substances, they may want me to check the environmental records and make sure there are no problems there.

On occasion, I used to do work for the entertainment industry, writers and the media and so on. I don't do much of that anymore because I feel a little uncomfortable with that kind of research. I think celebrities also have privacy rights and, even if it's legal, it isn't within my comfort level. I've got more work than I can handle anyway, and I just don't want to do that.

Each of us has activities that we're really comfortable with, and others where we think, well, this may be okay, but it's not okay for me. What kinds of projects do you do?

The most frequent is due diligence research, usually within the context of a pending merger-and-acquisitions situation. In those scenarios, they want me to go to the ends of the earth to find out anything in the public record pertaining to the company and, usually, to the members of its board. We're looking for things like litigation, tax liens, assets, and, if it's a manufacturing company, maybe environmental issues. With board members we look for the same kinds of records, including criminal records—everything imaginable.

When I say due diligence, it's really a matter of how much budget the client has. If they have a small budget, we're usually very limited in terms of what we're able to accomplish. If they have a larger budget, we can go on endlessly looking at the records.

I've got one client with a venture capital firm who calls me up and says, "I'd like the five-hundred-dollar 'peek in the shorts' on this company." I know exactly what that means, and I do as much as I can within that five hundred dollar limit. Then he might call me and say, "This one's really important. I'd like a thousand-dollar peek in the shorts."

How do your requests come in? Do people phone or do they email you? Are most of them repeat clients?

Usually they're established clients, and often it's a phone call. Sometimes they email their requests. With any kind of research project, the first step is helping the client determine what it is that they really want to know. The reference interview is the beginning. They know they want information. There's always a problem that needs to be solved. They don't know exactly what's out there or what might answer the question. Sometimes the client will call and say, "I want a real property search, I want this search, I want that search," and it may not get at what they really want to know. That may be something else entirely. We discuss what their needs are, what the case involves, and then we mutually decide upon the approach and the budget. My job is to use my expertise to determine what we can accomplish within that budget. What would make the most sense? Given the budget, what kinds of research would yield the answer to the question?

When you're asked to estimate budget, how do you do that?

I have a Ouija board. Seriously, it's often really difficult to estimate. These are not flat-rate searches. It's not like "$29.95 for this and you get what you get." It's a function of how far we're going to go, how much we find, how much time is involved, and then how many records we may go out and retrieve manually. It's often a multi-step process where maybe the client gives me an $800 budget to begin with, and I do all I can within that budget. Then we see that there are additional issues that perhaps should be examined, that we were not able to take care of within that budget. They may authorize more budget. Sometimes it's many steps.

What kind of deadlines do you generally have? And how long do your projects tend to take?

Just about every project is urgent, rush, do-or-die. Rarely do they say, "Take your time, a couple weeks will be fine." Online searching you can bang out very quickly, but when you are talking about retrieving information manually, human beings are injected into the process. Depending upon how old the records are, and whether or not they're available without going through some horrendous process to get them out of storage, the timing can be all over the map.

A project can take months, it can take an hour. It's highly variable.

How do you present your results?

I present a report defining what we've searched. If it's online searching, I paste in the information under each type of search that was conducted. If there are manually retrieved records, they accompany the report, or they might be sent later, when they're available. Depending upon the client, there is often an executive summary. You tell them what you searched, over what period of time, what the findings are, what was included in the search, what wasn't included, here's your data, and then what it all means.

It sounds like you actually do quite a lot of value-added work in terms of interpreting the data for the clients.

Absolutely. It depends on the client. If it's a law firm, they might want to do their own interpretation, which is just fine, but certainly we'd include some kind of summary pointing out those things that I think are most interesting and probably most revealing.

While we're talking about clients, are there any major client misconceptions about public records searching?

"Just go to the Internet." I could scream when people say that. There's a lot of information on the Internet, but it's a situation where you get what you pay for, too. There are numerous public record sites available. The BRB Publications site [15] lists all the free public record sites out there, and it's great.

But frequently I save my clients money by using a commercial vendor instead of a bunch of Web sites. Instead of going piecemeal and taking much longer, I can get it all. I can swoop through the database and harvest the data instead of picking little pieces here and there. Also, I have found that there's very little historical information available in free public records sites on the Web.

How far back do the online records tend to go?

It's variable. For example, for corporate records, I'm always retrieving Secretary of State records on the Web, and it's usually current information. If you want to obtain historical records, you've got to go to a commercial vendor or search manually.

Can you give me a sense of how you approach a project? How you integrate your online and offline searching?

Usually I start with online searching. Even though only twenty percent of public records are available online, it's useful to rule out certain kinds of records, and find out where we need to search manually. Maybe we want to know if somebody in New

York City has any lawsuits filed against them, so we start there. But if we do find stuff, then we send someone out to do manual research and retrieve records. Sometimes, too, I do newspaper searching or some other Web searching preliminary to the actual public records research, because it might point me in the direction of records that I might have overlooked otherwise.

If we find a situation where there are lawsuits, for example, then it's up to the client as to whether or not we want to get copies from the case files. That's really my bread-and-butter work.

The information that you can get online, with court records for example, is very cursory if available at all. In most jurisdictions, when you find a lawsuit, what you're going to get with the online search is the date it was filed, the case number, the plaintiff, the defendant, maybe the attorneys of record, and maybe some notation like "contracts" so you know what kind of case it is, versus, say, "divorce." And that's it. It doesn't tell you what the case is about. So then we have to send someone out to get copies of documents from the case file. That's where the real information is. It's not always easy. Case files are often in storage, and it can be a lengthy and involved process, because you've got to go and make an appointment to have them brought out from storage, and then come back to review the records.

Sometimes, even when you go to the primary documents, there are additional steps to take. For example, with civil litigation pertaining to an individual with a relatively common name, it's often very, very difficult, even when you have the primary documents, to know if it's your person. This happens all the time, because often civil court documents don't contain any identifiers at all, just the name of the plaintiff or the defendant, as the case may be.

If I can find notarized documents in the case file itself, I call the notary who notarized the documents and ask for a copy of the notary log. Most notaries that I've spoken to are absolutely appalled. They have no idea that they have to provide that, although they're informed of it when they get their notary commission. Sometimes they have to go dig things out of storage, and they act like you shot them in the groin when you ask them for that information.

The notary log contains information like date of birth, driver's license number, and address. So that's a way to discern whether or not the plaintiff or defendant is the person on whom you're conducting your research. Just calling the notary is sometimes a whole project in itself because, particularly if it's an older document, the notary may be difficult to locate. In California, at least, notaries are commissioned by the Secretary of State, and the Secretary of State would have information about where they are. That information is also recorded at the county level. If a notary dies, their records have to be turned over and they're stored at the county, so that's another example of where primary research can come in.

Sometimes nothing at all is available online and manual research is your only option.

Can you give me an example where that was the case?

I had a top-secret investigation involving an educational nonprofit organization. The clients were considering making a large donation, but first they wanted to know all they could about this nonprofit.

A 990 is the form that nonprofit organizations have to submit to the IRS, like a nonprofit tax return. There are places on the Internet where you can get 990 information. If you go to the Guidestar site [60], you'll find a lot of 990s there. However, if you want to go back to previous years, or you want to get their form 1023, which is essentially the form that provides them with nonprofit status with the IRS, that information is not online at all.

So I hired a college student with a clipboard and a business card. I didn't even want her to know what was going on, because this was so sensitive. I sent her out to five different nonprofit organizations, and I told her we were conducting a survey of compliance by nonprofit organizations with the IRS regulations pertaining to public inspection of documents. They're supposed to have this stuff available to the public for anybody to walk in off the street to look at. Most of these places had never had anybody ask, and they were very, very shocked when someone actually came in and wanted to see it. But she got the information. She was able to get not only their 990s going back several years, but also exhibits and attachments to the documents. She was also able to get their 1023s. It was beautiful. That's something you could not get online at all.

So manual research helps when you're going for completeness, and when you need historical records.

Right. There's another good example that comes up frequently. In environmental cases, they're always looking for what they call PRPs, potentially responsible parties. If there's a toxic site, they want to find out who was there before, where the deep pockets are, who's going to have to pay for remediation of the site. We may have to go way back in time. I had one case that was a horrible toxic nightmare in New Jersey. Why are they always in New Jersey? This site had been heavy industrial since the industrial revolution—it had originally been a woolen mill with huge vats of dye and, at one point, they manufactured fluorescent lights there. Obviously there was nothing much to be found in terms of historical information online. This was an obscure little borough, and I ended up sending somebody out to the borough hall. They spent a month down in the basement, where nobody had ever been before, digging through old records to find out what companies had occupied that site.

How do you ensure and evaluate the credibility of information?

If it's truly due diligence research, where they want every possible base covered, I would tend to use multiple online vendors because there are data holes; it's amazing what you might miss on one database versus another. The producers may tell you that this database includes all liens and judgments, but then you find out that the judgments included are only those from municipal courts under $25,000. Another source might give you everything. You have to really be aware of what's included in any particular database. For extra security, I often reiterate the same search using multiple vendors.

In terms of sending retrievers out to obtain documents, I have my own network of people that I rely upon on a regular basis. I've used these providers for years and have good rapport with and trust in them. But sometimes we need something from some podunk place in North Carolina where I may not have my own retriever. When that happens, you've got to find somebody with whom you can have some reasonable expectation, one, that they're going to know what to do once they get to the courthouse or wherever you're sending them, and two, that you're going to get the information in a time frame that you can live with.

The BRB publications site has something called PRRN, Public Records Retrievers Network [110]. I would go to that site and find someone who covers that specific geographic location. Then I'd go to one of the BRB's source books of public records like *The Sourcebook to Public Record Information* and do a little prep work to find out about, say, court records.

When I call the retrievers, I ask some questions to see if they know their stuff: "If it's civil litigation and I expect the amount to be over $100,000, where would that case be?" I pre-screen them. I think that's very important, because there are a lot of Tom, Dick, and Harrys out there who really don't know what they're doing, and how would you know? They might come back and say, "I didn't find anything," and how do you know they even went?

I had a case where I was digging through EPA records for some obscure mining corporations. Every set of records that I pulled out, I noticed the same name above mine on the sign-in

sheet, and realized that this person was pulling these exact same records. When I gave the client the information he wanted, I mentioned that this other person had been looking, too. It turns out that this was someone that they had sent to get those records, who'd come back with nothing. He'd looked at the same records but not with the right kind of eyes.

That happens a lot. You make an interesting point, too—that, particularly under FOIA, requestor information becomes part of the public record. That could be very, very important to a client. Do you want to talk for a minute about FOIA?

Sure, tell me about FOIA.

FOIA is the Freedom of Information Act [53], which was enacted in 1966 under Title 5 of the U.S. Code. FOIA applies only to federal records. States have their own versions of FOIA, and it's essentially the same process. For example, in California, we have the California Public Records Act. Under FOIA you can request documents and you can also request information about who else has previously requested the documents you are asking for. It's often very interesting to find out who else has been looking at the records.

I had an extremely involved case dealing with bidding for a water district contract. One party alleged that the other party had a less competitive bid, yet they won the contract because there was undue outside influence by a high-level governmental official. There were allegations about this, but no concrete proof. I sent the director of this water district a request under the California Public Records Act asking for copies of everything pertaining to the bidding on that project, including the bids and all correspondence. I was flatly turned down.

Some of these places that I'm obtaining records from are pretty darn obscure and they don't exactly have an FOIA officer.

They may have Betty, and a couple of other staff, if that. When my request was turned down I asked, "Who is your district's counsel?" I sent him my Public Records Act request, and voila! Suddenly the records were available. It was not like Erin Brockovich—I did not have to flash my boobs, all I had to do was flash my FOIA before their counsel.

They had no staff, so I got my own person in with a portable photocopier and copied literally hundreds of pounds of paper. I told her to get everything, and when I got this whole mess of paper back, my job was to sort and catalogue it. They were in no order whatsoever. In the midst of all these hundreds of pounds of paper I found the smoking gun: I found a memo from this governmental official endorsing this particular company. And on top of that, the only other party who had ever requested anything from these files was the person who had sent the memo—because they wanted to know whether or not it was really in the file.

And they also had wanted to know if anybody else had wanted to know!

So that was very cool. I want to stress that FOIA requests require a great deal of persistence. In that particular case, I was told flatly at the outset, "No, you're out of your mind. We're not going to give you that."

Here's another example: I've had to obtain a lot of information from the SEC. We know how to search Edgar [46] and find a lot online, but there are little things like staff comment letters that you're not going to find on Edgar.

When a company submits a filing to the SEC and the SEC wants further clarification on something, they send a staff comment letter. Those are regarded as nonpublic information but available under FOIA. If the filer of that information has requested confidential treatment, then you have to fight and appeal when they say, "No, this is subject to confidential treatment." They have to justify that it indeed does contain trade secrets or whatever FOIA exemptions would preclude them from providing that information. There have been scenarios where I have said, "You can't tell me that all twenty-three pages of this document are trade secrets," because maybe they will redact sections, so you then get part of it and may be able to find something that might be relevant.

Sometimes FOIA is incredibly easy. They copy it, they send it to you, they don't even charge you. You just never know.

Are there certain approaches that you've found tend to work when you're dealing with these keepers of the information?

It depends on who I'm talking to. I try to use persuasion. I try to be sympathetic. Sometimes I'll say, "My boss is going to kill me if I don't get this information." Other times I may take a more officious attitude, like "What do you mean? This is available under the Public Records Act. You have to provide it to me. Who is your corporate counsel, or your county counsel?" It's just like phone research; you have to somehow assess the nuances and decide what approach to take—coaxing, cajoling, whatever will work—to get some bureaucrat to give you what you want.

When you go there in person, how you dress matters, too. I don't usually do courthouse running myself. I send people out, unless it's something really special or in-depth, in which case I don't go down there in jeans; I go in there looking like an attorney because I tend to get better cooperation that way.

Let's go to the major resources you use. What are your favorite print resources?

I've alluded to the BRB source books. I could not begin to do what I do without those wonderful books. It's the most up-to-date information, and they're priced right. In California there's a really great book that I use on a daily basis, called *Paper Trails* by Stephen Levine and Barbara Newcombe [155], published by the Center for Investigative Reporting. It is like the bible in terms of

California public records. It's absolutely the best of the best, and I only wish that there were similar books available for every state.

That's about it, in terms of the actual nuts and bolts of the work that I do. I have a lot of other books on my shelf—*You, Too, Can Find Anybody* [150], and *Don't Hire A Crook* [151], and *Checking Out Lawyers* [161], but as far as the day-to-day nitty-gritty is concerned, *Paper Trails* and the BRB books are really the best.

How about CD-ROMs? Do you use those anymore?

The only CD-ROM that I use is another BRB publication, *Public Record Research System CD-ROM Annual Disk*. It's a compilation of everything in their books, pretty much. It has an "Add Page Notes" capability right on the screen that lets you add your own notes to the material, like if a phone number has changed or if you have a specific contact person at a courthouse. The notes show up on the screen for the entry where you added them. It's very convenient; I just never use it. I still like books; I can just write in them.

I keep track of who I know at what agency, and that makes a huge difference. If I have found contacts in a particular governmental agency or court or whatever who have been particularly helpful, I always write down their names. I often send a letter. Sometimes, if they really go above and beyond, I may send them a box of chocolates to thank them, and that goes a long way toward building rapport.

Merlin [85] has some excellent CD-ROMs that everybody raves about. That sort of thing, like a CD-ROM of real property, tends to be more useful for companies that do a lot of the same kind of repeat work. It's not as useful to me because my work is totally different every day.

How about favorite online vendors?

I have a whole host of online vendors that I use. I don't often use LexisNexis [80] for public records, because it's expensive, and there are other, more competitive online vendors available. They all seem to be pretty much consolidated now under ChoicePoint [27] who's buying out the industry. They very recently bought CDB Infotek [24], they bought DBT [36], they bought IRSC [76]. They own all these companies now. Information America [71] was owned by West until recently when ChoicePoint bought them, and now Information America is going away and all the information that was in IA is supposed to be integrated into DBT's AutoTrackXP database [12].

In the past would you have used DBT for one type of thing and CDB for another?

Sure, and I might still do that, because it's not one single database. It's still information from different providers. I get billed separately for them, but they're all owned by ChoicePoint. Another vendor that I use that is very, very good is Superior Online [124]. They cover the mid-Atlantic states, and they offer a whole gamut of information. I might search CDB and Superior on the same subject to see if I get the same data, which I sometimes don't. It's odd, because they buy it from the same places. Another primary source that I use all the time is PACER, Public Access to Court Electronic Records [102]. The federal courts online—that's the best public records value in the universe. There's a charge for PACER, but it's really, really low, and it's great. So those are the big boys.

Do all the major public records database vendors cover the same types of records? Do some of them, like DBT, specialize?

They may cover some of the same types of records, but they may cover different things as well. DBT has many different kinds of public records, everything from real property to corporation to Dun and Bradstreet [42] records, all of which are available from some of the other vendors that we've mentioned as well. But, in addition, the primary reason I would use DBT would be for locating people.

Even if I know where somebody is currently, I may want their address history to find out where they have been. So I know then that I need to search in those other locations.

DBT has the best people-finding tool imaginable. It's called Faces of the Nation.

I may want to search criminal records, civil litigation, tax liens, bankruptcies, judgments, real property, you name it. Sometimes you find information in Faces of the Nation that you don't find elsewhere. They also have records from individual states that you may not be able to find through another vendor. Particularly Florida; they have vast coverage of Florida public records. Florida is a sunshine state in more ways than one, certainly as far as public records are concerned. It's a very, very open state. You can find everything from divorce records to permits to carry a concealed weapon. You name it and it's there.

How about Information America or CDB? What particular things would you use those for?

It's more a question of whether they cover a particular geographic area or, if more than one covers an area, then who has the strongest coverage. If it was Harris County, Texas, would I go to CDB Infotek? Would I go to Information America? You have to be so cautious with online records searching because they'll say it's statewide or nationwide, and it just isn't. You hear in the media all the time about these "big brother" databases. Well, I'm afraid, folks, it ain't quite the way it's portrayed to be. You have to see what's really, truly included in any particular database, and I don't think any of the vendors do a very good job of making that information available to subscribers online. You often have to call customer service and ask, "What exactly am I getting with this search, and what are the inclusion dates?"

How do you keep up with the ongoing changes in the different databases and commercial

vendors? Is there a good source for monitoring what's going on?

There is no good source. It's very hard. You have to keep your eyes open. I network with a lot of people and I interact online with others. That's the main way I keep up. It's very helpful in terms of learning about sources that are changing, coming down the pike, or that have gone away.

Are there types of sites that you tend to go to for additional background information when you begin a project?

Oh, yes. The online stuff is usually the preliminary research phase. I use a search engine like Google [58] to search a particular subject. If it's a company, I would crawl all over their Web site before I even get into the public records. I might also do some newspaper searching, and take a look at SEC filings, before I launch myself in a thousand different directions obtaining other kinds of public record information.

It depends on the budget. If it were a little project, I might just go to free sites if I could possibly do it that way. If it were a more in-depth project, I would use a commercial vendor to provide the information. I often work with colleagues, especially in AIIP [4], the Association of Independent Information Professionals. I might rely upon AIIP members to do periodical searching for me because that's not my forte. I often farm that out to somebody else because, frankly, they can do it better than I can. I digest the information that they provide, and that may point me in some directions I may not have even thought of.

I wouldn't dream of doing patent searching. I'll call an expert on that. It's just not what I do. I think it's important for people to know what they can do and do well. When I talk to other people who say, "Oh, I've got CDB Infotek, I can search public records," I often think to myself, "Well, okay, but it's very dangerous."

How has the Net changed the way you search?

I have so many sites bookmarked it's ridiculous. Besides the individual sites, there are a lot of others, like that BRB site I mentioned, that list tons of sources available for free. The specific sites I use a lot include Search Systems by Pacific Information Resources [117]. They've got over two thousand public record sites of all kinds, which I like very much. I can find information nationwide by state and, within states, by various counties and so on. Then there's U.S. Party/Case Index [132], which includes most U.S. District and Federal Courts. You can look up cases by the parties to the suits, or by case number, or even by Social Security or tax ID number of the parties involved. I also use the California Secretary of State [21], and the N.J. Division of Revenue [95], for example, with records available online. I've got sites that list registered sex offenders. There's a List of Defaulted Borrowers in the Health Education Assistance Loan (HEAL) Program for chiropractors, doctors, dentists, and so on; it's also known as "Defaulted docs" [63].

Defaulted docs, I love it. What a great name.

I do an awful lot of research on physicians and that can be very, very interesting. There are a lot of sites, like AIM DocFinder (Administrators in Medicine) [5], where you can find out about any kind of disciplinary actions against a physician. You can go to the American Board of Medical Specialties certified doctor home page [9] to find out if they're board-certified in a particular area of specialization.

One of my favorite sites in California is the California Docfinder [20]. This is produced by the California Medical Board, and it tells you things like where they went to school. It lists disciplinary actions, too.

I've got a lot of information pertaining to topics like elections and campaign contributions. Those are areas where the Web is very, very useful—California codes, California legislative information, legislative tracking.

Have you found that, over the years, you're using the Web more?

I'm using it quite a bit more and I'm certainly using it faster. There is a lot more information available, and it's getting more efficient to find and use. I don't have DSL. I want it, but I'm concerned about getting an adequate firewall installed, because of the sensitivity of the information that I access.

That brings us to legal and ethical aspects. Are there areas that you're particularly aware of, or about which you're particularly concerned?

There are lots of ethical issues involved in what I do, areas where you have to make some judgment calls. For example, I've done quite a bit of opposition research for political campaigns. I may not like the side that my client is taking on a particular issue, or I may not like the candidates, but I don't make judgments about those things. If it's a lawsuit and I'm doing some work for a law firm, I don't make judgments about the rightness or wrongness of my client's position.

I had one case, though, that just broke my heart. It was a woman who was suing a Fortune 100 company for racial discrimination, and they were trying to find out what her motivation was. Usually in these scenarios they tell me, "Find any dirt you can come up with, and I mean anything." I found a small claims case in someplace like Apache County, Colorado. Big deal, just a small claims judgment. The client wanted copies of everything, and it was the middle of the winter, so I sent this poor retriever off in a snowstorm to go get this information, because it had to be at my client's the next day. She went and copied the information, got back safe and sound, and faxed it to me. It turned out that this small claims judgment involved medical bills that had been unpaid to the subject's pediatrician for her child, but it was a superbill, which is a term used by the insurance industry, where the diagnosis is shown. The child had HIV, and I was really unhappy about finding that information.

The poor woman obviously needed the money. Even though medical records are private information, when they get entered into the public record they become public.

Where I do draw the line, however, has to do with work for individuals. I have a policy relating to finding people. I get calls, for example, where someone wants to find birth parents or a child that was put up for adoption. Usually those searches come to me through an attorney, but if they come from an individual, my policy is: I would be happy to do the research for you. However, if I find the person, I will not disclose their whereabouts unless they agree that they want to be in contact with you. And if they don't want to be, then you still have to pay me. And nine times out of ten they go away, which to me is not a good sign. I can't play God. When I don't know who I'm dealing with, I will not provide sensitive information to individuals.

How about liability issues and liability insurance?

I carry a million dollars worth of Errors and Omissions insurance. Also, with all the changes that have gone on in terms of laws pertaining to the retrieval of personal information, most notably FCRA [51], the Federal Fair Credit Reporting Act, which was revised in September of '97, I don't think I would sleep at night if I did not carry liability insurance.

Under FCRA there are certain "permissible" purposes for which you can obtain information, purposes like employment, issuance of insurance, issuance of credit. If a situation falls under FCRA, particularly employment, the applicant needs to give permission. I won't do anything unless I have the forms that we need in order to conduct that background check. Also, if we find something derogatory about the person, like a criminal record, it is essential that the client understand the procedures to be followed. These are adverse action procedures, where the applicant who is being denied employment must receive a copy of the report and be advised of their rights and given an opportunity to rebut the information.

I'm totally in favor of safeguards like that. Even though we put disclaimers on everything, information can be missed or be wrong. We try to take pains to advise people that this information can serve as a tool, but that's all it is.

Can we talk a bit about the four major categories of public records research that you describe in *The Information Broker's Handbook* [162]—preemployment, asset location, missing people, and CI?

Sure. Up until now, we've been talking more about esoteric types of research that don't come up all the time. They may never come up again, or the same issue might not come up for another ten years. On the other hand, some kinds of public records research do come up all the time. One is preemployment, which we've already touched upon. The kinds of things that we look at with preemployment are criminal records, civil litigation, workers' compensation claims, bankruptcies, liens and judgments, driving records, educational verifications, professional licenses, Social Security number verifications, and so on.

And you're pretty much able to do all of these online?

No. Except for the driving records, in fact, we are prevented. The vendors have joined together to form something called the IRSG, which is the Individual Reference Services Industry Group [69]. They have made certain decisions about who they're going to give access to and what kinds of information they're going to provide. While, for example, I could certainly go to CDB Infotek and get criminal records from, say, Los Angeles County, we are prevented from doing that for preemployment. The opening screen on the database advises you that you cannot use their data for any permissible purpose under FCRA.

I think it's a good thing because, if you're doing a preemployment check and you find a criminal record, how do you know that "Joe Blow" is your Joe Blow? There's no date of birth, there's nothing there to tell you. Furthermore, in many states we are precluded from disclosing information about criminal records that do not result in convictions, so how do you know the guy was convicted? Therefore, in situations involving civil or criminal records that are being researched for the purposes of a preemployment background check, we send someone out physically to search those records.

And you do that based on the history they've given you of where they've lived?

No, not exclusively. They do sign a release form. They do tell us information about other names they may have used and other addresses within the past seven or ten years. Then we obtain information, for example, from credit bureaus that would show different names or different addresses. If something shows up that they didn't list—a name, an address, a previous employer— that's a red flag. Also, people with derogatory information in their backgrounds may play little games with their Social Security number or their date of birth. By doing more than one kind of search—for example, obtaining a driving record where the date of birth is displayed—we're able to cross-check and verify that information.

How about asset searching?

Asset searching is something that I get involved in fairly frequently. I always find it ironic, kind of sad, actually, when attorneys come to me and say, "I want an asset search; I won a hundred-thousand-dollar judgment." Nine times out of ten, particularly if they have taken the case on contingency, if they had done the asset search first, they would know the person doesn't have any assets. I had one case like that where the attorney said, "We won a half-million dollar judgment." First, we couldn't even find the defendant, and when I did find him, it turned out he was incarcerated. The only asset he had was probably the money he earned making license plates.

We do not search bank accounts and things like that. People always say, "I want to know all their stocks and bonds and their bank accounts"—sorry, that's off-limits. That kind of information has traditionally been retrieved by PIs who either use pretexts or inside sources at banks or whatever to obtain that information. That is not part of an asset search. It's not legal, it's not something I do—unless, within the context of public records research, I find something in the public record.

Most often that happens on a divorce case where you find a whole listing of assets including what they've got in their bank accounts. We look more for things like real property records. That's usually the largest asset that any individual has. We may look for vehicles, we may look for business ownership.

We often look at UCC (Uniform Commercial Code) filings because, if we do find assets, it may be because they've been put up as collateral in transactions secured by that collateral. Just as a pink slip indicates ownership of an automobile, a UCC filing indicates ownership of a particular piece of equipment or some other asset that's been put up as collateral. In a lease situation, if a person or business is leasing a piece of equipment, it connotes that someone else owns the equipment. If you find out that the equipment had been used as collateral, guess what? That's not going to help you very much, because the actual owner has dibs on it.

On the other hand, if you find that your subject is the secured party in a UCC filing, if the person who had borrowed from your subject defaults, then things like trailers, yachts, and so on could potentially become assets. I would probably go to CDB Infotek for that kind of search.

And missing persons?

Missing persons is my favorite game. If I could just do one thing, I would want to do that because it's so much fun. One of the reasons I like it is that it's finite. You either find the person or you don't. You know when you've hit a home run.

Most often I'm looking for missing persons not for some glamorous reason, but for some really boring reason. Maybe it's a witness that I want to locate, or there's a patent issue where a missing inventor wrote something twenty years ago and my client wants to invalidate a patent position.

How would you start looking for a missing person?

It depends so much on what kind of information I have to go on. If it's just a name, it can be very, very difficult. If you have a Social Security number, a date of birth, a last known address, the name of a spouse, or if the name is really uncommon, you're much more likely to be able to find a person. I had an interesting case involving William Saroyan, the author. Stanford University wanted to acquire Saroyan's papers, and they hired me to track down his heirs. First I got his will from Fresno County. I think he had a son and a daughter; I remember there were two grand-daughters. I'll never forget this case, because their names were Strawberry and Cream Saroyan. How did those girls get those names? With females, too, it's more difficult because they often change their names. I don't think either of these women were still Saroyans. There were probably ten Strawberrys in the United States, and maybe three Creams. I found them. It was so easy because you can search just by first name if you want.

That was a case where I used DBT. I would generally not use the Web to find individuals. If their name is at all common, it can be just ridiculous, unless you have some other fact about them that you can plug in—for example, the companies that they're affiliated with or, if it's an inventor, the type of technology. You might start there and get lucky, but most of the time you won't.

I had a Catholic religious order that wanted to locate all of their ex-priests because they wanted to have a big reunion and start an online mailing list. I had five thousand ex-priests to locate. It was very challenging, because, one, they didn't have a whole lot of budget to work with. Two, for many of these people, all I had to go on was their birth dates, and for a lot of them, all I had was the Latin name that they had taken when they became priests. So it might be Father Veritas or maybe just the Latin version of their given name. That was mostly DBT again.

So you just tracked down various leads? You'd try these twelve that might be him, or find somebody who might know somebody who knows him?

Exactly. Then we sent out a mailing with the ones I'd found. It went on for months and months and months, but I got eighty percent of them.

If it's somebody who has not surfaced in some time, it will almost always involve manual research at some courthouse somewhere. It may involve marriage records. If I'm trying to find somebody and I know the name of the spouse but I can't find either one of them, I might pull their marriage record and find out who witnessed their wedding, and then find that person.

That's great. So you're always thinking outside the box. Which brings us to competitive intelligence or CI work.

I would rather call it company research. I think that's a better term, because the context within which that research might be done can vary. It could be some sort of litigation research, it could be CI, or it could be a venture capital situation. There could be a multitude of reasons why you're conducting that research. Depending upon the kind of company, you could go so many different places for information.

Typically, if it's a corporation, you search the corporate records. You want to know if they're in good standing with the Secretary of State. You want to know who the corporate officers are. I might get a Dun and Bradstreet BIR (Business Information Report), and that might point me toward other information. We search for litigation, we search UCCs. We might search environmental records or real property holdings. If the business is involved in retail, we might look at their sales and use tax permits.

Certainly, if it were a CI situation, I'd look at the company Web site. And frankly, a lot of the CI stuff, in my public records world, would reside in court records. I might find something juicy in a court file.

How about instances where phone research has been involved?

There are some cases where I've done extensive phone research. I'll tell you about one phone situation involving CI, because you won't generally find anything too revealing on their Web site or in the public records that are available online. You've got to go to the actual physical case files or whatever; you might find something good there. But usually these scenarios involve really talking to people.

I had one case where they wanted to find out who was working in the research and development department of a company that manufactured a particular type of watercraft. Through newspaper searching, I found an article about NOx and emissions and changes in EPA standards. So I called this guy who was head of their NOx R&D department, and I waltzed him around for half an hour about NOx, emissions, two-stroke engines, four-stroke engines, whatever. And at the end I said, "Oh, is there anybody else in your department I could talk to?" And he was so kind as to give me five or six different names. I talked to those guys and asked the same questions. When I was done, I had the whole organizational structure of the R&D department.

Another example dealt with solid waste baffle systems used in sewage treatment plants. It was a patent case, and my task was to find out what kind of baffle system each sewage plant in Connecticut had, and when it had been installed. So I had to talk with engineers at each sewage plant in Connecticut. It was absolutely horrifying when I started, with sewage tanks, sludge, pictures of floating turds. I thought, "How am I ever going to be able to talk to these people about solid waste?" But I really got into it and found that the people I talked to were the most wonderful, communicative group that I have ever had to interview. If I missed them they would even call me back. It was great.

What do you like best about public records research?

As I said, missing persons are my favorite. And, really, really juicy, difficult cases where budget is unlimited. The client gives me the problem, and it's up to me to figure out how we're going to find that information. I have done many projects with whole teams of people working on different elements, calling upon people with different areas of expertise or people in different geographic areas, all contributing to the project.

What do you like least?

Doing preemployment background checks, because it's very repetitive. However, it is really important. Employers have become sensitized to the need for this information, largely due to negligent hiring lawsuits. If an employee who's hired has a propensity for a particular type of criminal behavior, and the employer fails to ascertain that by doing a background check in the preemployment screening process, then when the person commits a crime in the context of their job, the employer can be liable. There is a famous case involving a repeat sex offender who learned TV repair in prison. He got out of prison and got hired by a TV repair company. They didn't do a background check on him, like most of these companies don't. They sent him out to some woman's home. He got the layout, figured out how to get in, came back that night and raped and beat her. He was not very swift and was caught, but the employer was sued for negligent hiring.

Employers have seen too many pictures of employees coming in and shooting up a building, so they are very concerned about this. There's a whole lot more preemployment background checking being done today than five years ago. But with that have come a lot of supposed background-checking companies that are less than professional, that charge rates that are completely unrealistic: For $29.95 you can get this, this, and this. It is impossible to do a good job at the rates they charge. My concern is that people will be lulled into a false sense of security. There will be some disasters, I think. These companies are all over the Internet, advertising that they can do anything for almost no money. Sorry, you get what you pay for.

There are companies out there that say they can do "nationwide" criminal records checks. There ain't no such thing. The only national criminal database is the FBI database, which I mentioned in an LLRX [84] article I wrote about criminal records called "Navigating the Maze of Criminal Records Retrieval" [103]. That's not public record. What these companies are actually doing is searching newspapers looking for any mention of a crime in connection with a particular name. The gaps are just absurd.

People say, "I see five sites right here in front of me on the Internet where I can get a national criminal record. Why can't you?" It drives me crazy. There are a lot of companies out there offering information they cannot provide, period, let alone at the cost they're saying they can do it.

What other changes have you seen over the last five or ten years?

This whole field has evolved radically over the past decade. I do many things differently than I did ten years ago. So much more information is available online. I'd say that fewer than ten percent of public records were available online ten years ago, and I'd double that number now. In that LLRX article, I talked about what's happening with information that's now becoming available online. We've always been able to get docket sheets from the federal court, for instance, but now you can get the actual documents. All you need is Adobe Acrobat and, voila, there they are. In the past, you had to—and I still do, every day of the week—send letters out to retrieve documents from those courts. Of course the older cases are not online, but the newer stuff, more and more of it, is available. That's changed things drastically.

Part of the reason why more and more information in this sphere is becoming available online is that various governmental agencies have seen the value in doing it. Rather than having to pay a bunch of clerks to sit there and provide copies, some agencies are even charging for the information online. There's a cost benefit involved, so that's one reason we're going to see more and more available online. I think we'll continue to see an explosion of information online, though it's not going to solve the problem of obtaining records that are historical.

We have an opposite trend occurring simultaneously. With growing concerns about privacy and personal data, information is becoming harder to retrieve, and can only be retrieved under very rigid guidelines.

What do you think will happen with this trend? How do you see things changing over the next five years?

There is pending legislation and litigation on curtailing access to what we've always called credit headers. That's the top part of the credit report, which contains the person's name and Social Security number and addresses, but no credit information. That identifying information is integral to much of the research I do. That's often the first step in doing legitimate research. Much of the research that I do also involves fraud investigation. Without access to that kind of information, I don't know how we're going to do it. With due diligence research, where I need to find any kind of civil litigation or tax liens or bankruptcies or judgments involving an individual, how am I to know where to begin looking without having that information available to me?

I think it's an over-reaction. Individual privacy needs to be protected, but I don't think the answer is to cut off access to professionals who are engaged in legitimate research for business reasons. Information should not be out there on the Internet for Joe Blow, who wants to be nosey, to grab. The IRSG has established a set of standards and controls. They're not going to let just anybody have access to their databases. They really check you out. I was shocked that I had to provide references when I signed up with DBT. They actually called them up, and their questions really pertained to the kind of research I do, my ethics, my professionalism, and so forth. So the vendors are taking seriously the threat to the availability of information.

A couple years ago I wrote a rather long article, "Online Personal Information: Access vs. Excess" [103]. I was on my soapbox about why I feel so strongly that this information must continue to be open. I can go to the Privacy Rights Clearinghouse [107] Web site and see all this stuff about identity theft. For the most part, this is anecdotal evidence. I do not think that identity theft is occurring wholesale across the nation because of people accessing online data. I think it's happening more as the result of low-tech crime, where people are throwing things like bank statements, credit card receipts, and documents containing their social security numbers out in their trash, or not being careful about revealing personal information. I think that there's far greater danger in that.

I support the IRSG principles that the vendors have put in place whereby they define the situations in which you can access information that they provide. As I said, they are very, very cautious about who they grant access to. I am very much opposed to sensitive personal information being available to anybody who can provide a credit card number over the Internet. I think information can do great harm or great good, depending on who uses it and how.

What changes in technology might affect public records searching?

Just as I mentioned, documents becoming available in federal courts, among others, private entrepreneurs out there are thinking along the same lines. They're thinking about taking portable scanners to courthouses and scanning records on demand, and then transmitting them via the Internet. So, rather than sending someone out to get the file, photocopy it, and FedEx it to me, I get instant transmission instead. I look at the documents I've gotten and say, "I think I also want this document and that document." They'll get those too, and boom, I've got it. That'd be way cool.

Do you anticipate an upsurge in the number of people at your level of public record searching? People who do really thorough, complex jobs?

I certainly hope so. I have kind of a special niche. I'm hoping that more and more law firms will see the benefit in outsourcing this kind of research rather than having their law librarians try to tackle it.

What qualities make a good public records researcher?

Detail orientation is absolutely essential. A person shouldn't even think about doing this kind of research unless they really love detail, unless they're anal about detail. They also need the ability to think both analytically and creatively.

It's very much like making a quilt. It's about taking lots of little bits of information and sifting through them, and finding a pattern so that a picture emerges, and then putting it all together so that it can warm you at night. You take the data, sift through it, figure out what it means, and then give that information back to the client, telling him, "This is what you've got."

There's a bit of intuition involved, too. Maybe that's part of creativity. A lot of this is about following hunches. But in order to have those hunches in the first place, you have to know what's possible and what kinds of records are out there.

So, having done your homework and having had the experience is what enables you to have the hunches. Your brain is back there processing without your knowing it, sifting things. Any other last comments to people who might be thinking about going into the field?

It's important to be an apprentice. I mentioned at the beginning that I view this not as a profession *per se*, but as more of a craft. I think you do need somebody to teach you. I have told most people whom I have advised in the last couple of years to join PRRN and learn how to be a public records retriever, before they even think about searching online for the records. That's often a good way to begin because there's very little overhead, much to be learned, and an immediate source of income.

I do consulting with aspiring public records researchers. I also consult with other kinds of researchers who want to know more about public records so they can utilize them more often or more efficiently in the context of the other research they do. I tell those people that they should start, not with learning how to search records online, but with getting down to the courthouse and digging through records. Use your neighbor's name, if you want to be nosey, and find out all you can. Actually learn what the records are like in their primary state, rather than in the abstract, because it will make a world of difference in your understanding of public records.

The gold nuggets are seeing the records in your hands, seeing all the information they contain. You can't get that from an online listing.

Super Searcher Tips

➤ Public records research is not a profession, but a craft that you can only learn through experience. It helps enormously to have a mentor who can march you down to the courthouse and say, "This is how you do this."

➤ In most places, an online search will tell you the date a lawsuit was filed, the case number, the plaintiff, the defendant, maybe the attorneys of record, and maybe some notation so you know what kind of case it is. It doesn't tell you what the case is about. The real information lies in the actual case files.

➤ When I call records retrievers, I ask some questions to prescreen them: "If it's civil litigation and I expect the amount to be over $100,000, where would that case be?" There are a lot of Tom, Dick, and Harrys out there who really don't know what they're doing.

➤ The primary reason I use DBT is for locating people. They have the best people-finding tool imaginable, called Faces of the Nation.

➤ You have to be cautious with online searching because vendors say "statewide" or "nationwide," but you have to call customer service and ask, "What exactly am I getting with this search and what are the inclusion dates?"

➤ If it's a company, before I launch myself in a thousand directions obtaining other kinds of public record information, I crawl all over their Web site, do newspaper searching, and look at SEC filings.

➤ In the preemployment context, people with derogatory information in their backgrounds may play games with their Social Security number or their date of birth. By doing more than one kind of search, for example, a driving record where their date of birth is displayed, we're able to cross-check and verify that information.

➤ People always say, "I want to know all their stocks and bonds and their bank accounts." That's not legal unless it's within the context of public records. Most often that happens when you find a divorce case with a whole listing of assets including what they've got in their bank accounts.

➤ If I'm trying to find somebody, know the name of their spouse, and can't find either one of them, I could pull their marriage record, find out who witnessed their wedding, and locate that person.

➤ Often civil court documents don't contain any identifiers at all, just the name of the plaintiff or the defendant. If I can find notarized documents in the case file itself, I call the notary and ask for a copy of the notary log, which contains things like date of birth, driver's license number, and address. That's a way to discern whether or not it's the person you want.

Alex Kramer

PI, CI, Public Records

Alex Kramer is the principal of Kramer Research, a Washington, D.C.-based information service specializing in private investigations, competitive intelligence, public records, film, literary, and media research. Kramer is a past president of the Association of Independent Information Professionals and is a licensed investigator in Washington, D.C. and Virginia.

Kramer@KramerResearch.com

For the record, I'm talking to Alex Kramer, and we're recording this interview. We will use an edited version for the book *Super Searchers Go to the Source*. Is that okay with you, Alex?

Yes, that's fine.

Can you start by telling me something about your background and how you ended up where you are today, doing CI and PI and public records?

I would like to say this was something I wanted to do all my life, but the truth is I never even knew this area existed when I was growing up. I just stumbled into it. I got out of college and took a job as a paralegal because a friend got me the job and I didn't have to think about it. While I was working there, a conversation came up between a friend of my family and my mother. This woman had to give up her job as a private investigator, and she and my mom decided I should take her job. I was young, didn't know anything, was intimidated by the whole process, and I finally got pushed into it. I called the investigating firm, and they said, "It's about time." They'd been waiting for me. It was a small two-person firm that did everything, and they basically needed another warm body there. I started telling everyone I was going to be a private investigator, and they kept asking me, "Are you going to carry a gun? Are you going to be following people?" And I said, "Oh my God, I didn't think about that. I don't know." Two days into the job I finally had enough nerve to ask, "Am I going to be carrying a gun?" And my boss just laughed and said, "You watch a lot of TV."

This was '88 or '89, and a lot of things weren't automated and weren't online. To get the information, you had to go out there, roll up your sleeves, and get it. They started by dropping me off at the courthouses and I would just sit there like a deer in the headlights, stunned, looking around, and after a while I was able to feel it out a little bit.

How did things work out? Where did you go from there?

I quit after three months. The firm was splitting up, and the woman I got along with best suggested I contact some of these other investigating firms. They hired me to subcontract on some projects. Then a position became available, and I broke into working with one of the international firms as a researcher. Later, the same woman was starting up another firm and asked me to come work with her and her partner. There I learned a lot about running a small business, about how to make money by doing research, and everything's that involved. After just over a year, when that firm split up, I started doing projects for the large investigating firm. I was always the one who was up for going out to the various courts and agencies and doing the manual research. So they started calling me more for that kind of work.

Were you starting your own business at that point and going from there?

I still thought I was looking for a job. I was freelancing to get some money. Then, I met the I-95ers [67, see Appendix], an informal group of independent information professionals in this area. They met every three months for networking, and some of them introduced me to AIIP, the Association of Independent Information Professionals [4]. I learned that people do this as a business, this isn't just freelancing, and my terminology changed. Instead of calling myself a freelancer, I called myself a business owner. A freelancer and an owner of a small business are basically the same thing. Yet there's a mindset that I think is different, and that's what steered me in the direction of running my own research firm.

In order to get a PI's license, do you have to work as an apprentice to another PI for a period of time?

Each jurisdiction has different requirements, and the jurisdictions are generally by state as opposed to county or region. I'm licensed in Washington, D.C. and Virginia, and the licensing requirements are very different. In D.C. it's a background check, license, and bond, and that's pretty much it. The Commonwealth of Virginia requires each firm to have a compliance agent who ensures that all of its PIs remain in compliance with its licensing requirements, such as insurance, continuing education, and so on. I had to complete a training course and, because I'm a one-person firm, to become my own compliance agent and get the agency license. I believe that in Maryland you may have to be affiliated with another firm. New York has a test. In Pennsylvania, you have to appear before a court. Unfortunately, at this point there really isn't any reciprocity between jurisdictions, and it's difficult because you have to build bridges to work in other jurisdictions.

How about liability and liability insurance?

For my licenses, I'm required to have liability insurance. I have Errors and Omissions insurance for my Virginia license and a surety bond for my D.C. license. Still, I tell my clients right off, I work to the "best of my ability." Public records are not an exact science. If something is written wrong, if something's misfiled … There are too many variables out there. You do the best you can. That's all I can try to do or guarantee to my clients.

What kind of clients do you have now? What kinds of projects do you do?

When I started doing this on my own, I made the decision not to do database work. I had some training when I worked with the other investigating firms, but it was an overwhelming concept for me to start getting subscriptions to all these services. So I decided not to get involved in that. Clients started calling me for fieldwork more and more, and suddenly people titled me a public records researcher. It wasn't something that I labeled myself, or started out trying to achieve. So now my clients are people who are looking for public records research.

Public records are anything available to the public. It's huge. That includes court records, agency records, Freedom of Information Act requests. It's kind of a generic term for everything out there. My clients now include a lot of the investigators I worked with in that large investigating firm. There's been growth in the industry and a lot of movement to different firms, so the majority of the clients I work for still are investigating firms.

But it's broader than that. I do some literary research. I've done some film and screenwriting research. I really enjoyed working with authors and screenwriters. The problem is they're not the bread and butter. The bigger businesses have more money to spend. Because of the location I'm in, Washington, D.C., and what's accessible here, I'm able to get a lot of different kinds of business. With the Library of Congress [82], National Archives [88], all the government agencies here, in addition to the metropolitan area with all the courts and business establishments, I have access to an overwhelming amount of public resources here.

Do clients just phone in with a request? How do projects come to you?

Fast! I've never advertised. I'm small, I work out of my home. I find that when I start telling people I'm a private investigator, they ask me to do things that I really don't want to do—domestic situations, things that are difficult for me to do as one person without a backup or a team. I get work by word of mouth—people I've worked with before, people who've joined other investigating firms, or law firms, or unions. My name gets passed along, and then they'll contact me.

Certainly you're known within the Association of Independent Information Professionals ...

The interesting thing about that is that a lot of the AIIP people aren't really knowledgeable about how public records can help them. My experience with AIIP has been totally rewarding. But as far as AIIP members calling on me is concerned, many don't have a clue about how I could help them or how useful public records really are. It's an untapped resource. People who sit in front of their computers all day don't look beyond it. I'm sure you get the same thing—many people have no idea how, as a telephone researcher, you can help them.

Part of what we want is for people in general to understand the range of resources that are out there, to go beyond online. You wrote an article for AIIP *Connections* [33] in 1998, that gives a wonderful quick view of some aspects of public information. It was titled "Public Information,

Private Companies." Would you read that into the record for me?

"Your client is a manufacturer of widgets. There have been rumors in the widget industry that a small up-and-coming manufacturer wants to take over your client's company. No one has ever heard of this new company. Naturally, your client is concerned and calls on you, the information professional, to help substantiate the rumors and find out everything you can about this company. Your client claims to have conducted preliminary research. They say they have checked local periodicals, the Internet, and trade publications. They also have obtained a Dun and Bradstreet [42] report. None of this research is producing the information that your client wants.

"The first thing you do is identify who this company is and who the key players are. Corporate documents will be a good start, and you're in luck if the annual report lists the names of the officers and directors. This helps, but what else should you do? You try court documents to attempt to locate litigation—besides the legal information, you will find more names and will gain insight into just what kind of company this is. You find a suit filed by an employee over breach of an employment contract. This information is invaluable! Try to get the disgruntled employee to talk to you. You also discover a divorce suit with a settlement agreement that lists the spouse's involvement in the company and the company assets. You now have your finger on previously unobtainable financial information on the company. Court records also list some judgments granted to the company from a patent dispute. The patent is key because some details of widget design and manufacturing are outlined. All this is great information, but your client wants more.

"The client knows from the assets discovered that the up-and-coming widget company has the financial resources to actually take over your client's company. Your client is now well informed about the money aspect, but wants to figure out how the competitor is doing business. This knowledge could help your client better position their company should they be approached.

"Since the widgets are manufactured with plastics and paints, you recognize that there could be environmental permits needed. Local, regional, and state environmental agencies have lists of permits for certain types of equipment—these offer more clues that can be tracked. Inspection reports indicate the number of employees at the manufacturing site. Land records give a history of the property so you can find out what other businesses occupied the location, which might in turn offer some clues about the physical layout.

"The day of reckoning approaches and your client receives a call from the head of the up-and-coming widget company. They wish to meet in person. Your client is apprehensive—the tone of the conversation is definitely 'takeover.' At the meeting your client plays his hand, revealing that he has information about their manufacturing processes, corporate structure, personnel, and finances. The other company has similar information pertaining to your client. Both company heads are impressed with the other's knowledge and resources, and they decide to work together and amicably merge to build a better company.

Your client thanks you for your hard work and offers you stock in the newly formed company. The two company heads ask you to evaluate the future of the widget industry, and you are off on another research project!"

That's such a nice look into public records searching.

It really kind of sums it up, tapping into all those resources. I understand that, for people who are not familiar with public records, that article may not do very much; I'm just throwing out terms. But I'd tell them to latch on to what they can. Most of us can understand corporate records or articles of incorporation. Break it down into individual parts and start with what you already know. With public records research, one thing leads to the next, and it's a matter of follow-through that gives you the complete scenario I described in that article.

When clients come to you, do they generally know what they need? Or do you have to do a reference interview to find out what they really need as opposed to what they think they need?

I do a lot of work for the larger investigating firms, and they come to me with tasks, with assignments. Generally, they've already isolated what type of work they're doing, whether it's an asset search or a due diligence background investigation on a company or an individual. They've already broken it down to "I need public records, I need an individual or a company checked in this region, or with this agency."

As the investigative business is developing and branching off into boutique or sole proprietor investigating firms, people are coming to me with projects more than with assignments. I'm now getting pulled in to do more of a research proposal. I'm trying to branch out to do more of that. But the investigating firms tend to act a little like lawyers, in the sense that they think they know everything and they don't need somebody to teach them what's out there. But they know public records in a limited sense. Even though they're knowledgeable about it, they're only tapping a small part.

I offer, as a service to my clients, to come in and tell them how to compose a research request and how to use a subcontractor. On the reverse side, I'll tell researchers or other people whom I train how to take an assignment, what questions to ask, and how to follow up.

Let's start on the client side. How do you tell them to best phrase a request when they talk with a subcontractor?

First you tell them not to say, "I need all public records." Which is what they want to tell you and will tell you. You assume that the person doling out the assignment has enough knowledge of what they really need and want. In due diligence, which is a background investigation, you're looking for anything on this person that will fill in where they were and what they were doing at various times, and give a picture of their background. In an asset search, you don't necessarily need to know if they had traffic violations, which you would in a background search, but you do need to know if they owed money and had financing statements or Uniform Commercial Code filings.

They need to tell me what type of case they're working on, so I'll know that it's a background investigation, it's an asset search, it's a competitive intelligence case. That gives me a framework for what I'm doing. And then, if we have three individuals, for example, that we're trying to find assets for, we'll break it down to the jurisdictions where they've lived the longest. If they've lived in more than one area, do we have a budget to go to more than one? If not, which one is the most critical?

Then, how specific do they want to be? Do they want to go down to the lowest court and look for small claims-type things, or does that not really matter? Are they just looking for the big bucks? The parameters of the research are defined by the end product they're searching for and by what the budget permits. Time also factors into budget; what's their deadline?

So you know what they want and you know the time and budget parameters. Then, within that, you prioritize in terms of where you're going to start?

Exactly. And, on a low-budget case, how to get the most bang for the buck. Know what you're looking for. I'm not saying you'll necessarily find it, but public records is definite in the sense that it's either there or it's not there. Maybe it wasn't recorded well, or the search wasn't done well, but there's really no gray in public records. It's black and white; information is there or not there. So you have to know what specific information you're going after.

What would you say to a public records searcher about the kinds of questions they need to ask the client?

I would say, "Be clear on what you're going after. What does your client want?" Then you can offer them options: "Did you consider checking this?" or "Maybe we ought to go to the SEC to see if they have any broker-dealer records." As somebody knowledgeable in this area, I can complement whatever they've already set up.

How do you estimate the cost of a project, when your projects are so varied?

It's a little difficult but it gets better over time. I charge by the hour. I'll talk to a client, we'll establish a budget, and I'll work within the budget. Dealing with public resources, there are so many factors that dictate how the project goes, and there are so many unknowns. We're sending somebody back out to the courts today because one county courthouse had their computers down for a week. You've promised a client results, and promised you'll do it that day, and it's totally out of your hands. So there's a lot of guesswork involved. But I try to negotiate what I think is a reasonable amount of time and budget. We keep them abreast of what's going on, tell them what we've done so far, alert them when we'll probably need more time.

What are some of the factors you need to take into consideration, or that end up affecting a project?

I'm laughing, because traffic and personalities are the biggest factors. The majority of the work I do is hands-on manual research, so we have to be in a lot of different places during a day.

As the D.C. area becomes more congested, it's getting more difficult to get around in a timely manner. I am pretty pleased with
the back roads and alternative routes I've learned in order to get
through. Also, with the volume of work that I do, I can piggyback
projects and work for more than one client in a day. That way,
you can diffuse some of the cost that it takes to just get places.

But the other major factor is personalities. Everywhere you go,
you're dealing with civil servants. They have their rules, they
have their moods, and you're at their whim. You can't say, "I want
to speak to a supervisor" all the time. It's crying wolf. You'll never
get anything that way, and sometimes even the supervisor can't
help you. They tell you that copying the documents will take
three to five days. Every one of my clients wants it that day, and
you have to alert them ahead of time. It's just part of the job.

What are some techniques you've found for dealing with those gatekeepers to the information?

Treat them like people. You're going to go back and see them
again, so treat them with respect. They're there every day, and
they have their good days and their bad days. I tell people I'm
training to work with me that the dress code for going into the
courthouse is "Don't look like a messenger and don't look like a
lawyer." There are attitudes and assumptions that go with each
of those extremes.

Just be friendly with these people, understand their limitations and that they're working with a gazillion other people every
day. That's my main technique. The payback is that I know a lot
of them now, by name or by face. Most are friendly to me; they
either roll their eyes when I come in or give me a big smile.
Sometimes I ask them for favors and to push it, and sometimes
they'll do that for me.

What kind of product do you deliver? How do you present your results?

My clients are generally looking for the hard-core research. I give them a cover page for the work I've done. If it's court research, I tell them specifically what indices were searched, what dates, what names we searched, and I attach a copy of the records. Sometimes we'll analyze the property records or the court cases, but my clients usually need the work too quickly for that, and they're willing to do it themselves. They just want the cold hard information. It's pretty much a very quick turnaround, and giving them the raw material.

Are there any ethical concerns in the kinds of cases you take?

If a person wants to find someone because they got cut off on the road and they want revenge, I won't touch it. I'll do almost anything for business where it makes sense, but I won't touch some things. I've been asked to work on adoption issues, or to find things about ex-spouses, that I won't touch.

How about any major client misconceptions?

They think I can go to these courthouses, because I'm so familiar with them, and get anything that I want immediately. They think that if the case is sealed, I can open it, that I can bribe someone to give them the information quicker. They think that there's got to be a way to get around the system because they're corporate America, and money talks. Money doesn't talk in courthouses; that's the biggest misconception.

How do you manage their expectations?

Brutal honesty. I try to tell them ahead of time. I feel like I'm always the naysayer, always being negative: "We'll do this today, but I'm not sure if I'll get the copies today." I try to give it to them up-front to set the level of expectation.

Then, as you said earlier, you keep them abreast as you're going along, so they know the

courthouse computer's down for a week or whatever.

That doesn't always make it easier. Nobody can understand how the whole court computer can be down and that there's no backup system. I don't understand it either. You check to see if there's hard copy available, or any other alternatives. My clients are comfortable that I've checked out other options and that I'm experienced enough to take the initiative on exploring other routes.

Can you share any great success or horror stories from your public records searching?

Bland, Virginia. It's really a place. I was sent down there. The first problem was that there was no place to eat because the county's so small. I had to go to the general store, buy sliced bread and American cheese, and eat in my car. Then, they really didn't have any court index, and the courtroom is so small that there's no way to shield what you're looking up. The clerks are right over your shoulder; you can't do any confidential work in there. There are no public phones. I had to call my client from the clerk's telephone. So, the horror story there is dealing with the lack of anonymity.

And the success story?

Bland, Virginia. The clerks knew what we were looking for and were able to give me the personal story on the CEO of the company we were looking into. They told us what they knew about him, down to his marital status and where he vacations. We were doing asset searches and we found out other places where he owned property because the clerk was able to rattle them off.

That's great. Any others?

I have a huge CI success story. We were looking into the manufacturing of certain types of large vehicles. First of all, the CI company I was working for took the time to educate me on parts of these vehicles. I learned their makeup so I'd understand the general process and know what to look for. The client's client wanted to know if they themselves were manufacturing in the most efficient way possible. So they wanted to get clues about their competitors' manufacturing processes. They were interested in questions like whether to paint before or after the assembly line pieces were assembled; whether to store everything on site or move it elsewhere.

I was sent to the towns where five or six manufacturing companies were based to do public records research. Because paint was involved in all this, I went to the environmental files. The very first company that we were looking at included a layout of the facility and the assembly line in its environmental report. And now my client would know exactly how the assembly line worked, which is incredible information. I broke the layout plan up into sections, photocopied it, and FedExed it to my client. They were meeting with the ultimate client the next day. My client opened the FedEx package not knowing what it was, because I hadn't really realized what a gold mine I'd found. The first thing they opened was the assembly line layout. I got a huge bonus on that one. It was the first thing I'd ever done for these people and their expectation level after that never went down.

The client goes, "How did you ever do this?" But you pull one rabbit out of the hat and the next thing they're saying is, "All right, where's your next miracle?" What kinds of things did you do for literary or film research?

For films, I did some wonderful costume research on masks from Elizabethan times. We had to get pictures so the costume designers knew what to use. We looked in books first, and there weren't many, so we had to tap into a lot of other resources. We went through the Library of Congress, and the library of the National Gallery [89] here in D.C. We went to F.I.T., the Fashion Institute of Technology [49].

We did a project for an overseas client who was working on a pre-Nazi period piece set in Hungary. They wanted pictures of what homes looked like back then, but since everything in their local libraries had been destroyed during the war, they needed the U.S. resources.

Another interesting client was a gentleman involved in selling reprints of photos, one of the store chains you see in malls. He wanted to access all the photos that Ansel Adams did when he worked for the Park Service. All those photographs were in the public domain. So we went to the photographic divisions of the National Archives and the Library of Congress and got copies of all these photos that were available to the public, to reprint and market.

In researching homes, masks, and photographs, did you locate experts in these areas who could steer you toward correct information and resources?

Sure. The wonderful thing about working in D.C. is that there are experts for everything. If you go to the Library of Congress, every division has its expert or resources. The photographic division is very separate, with all these people who know about the photos. When we were doing research on the homes in Hungary we'd go to the Hungarian reference librarians and talk to them.

Let's switch over to the area of direct observation and your experiences doing that kind of work.

First of all, I want to throw out a term we use that people seem to be uncomfortable with. We call them "drive-bys" a lot. Everybody thinks we're doing a drive-by killing. Actually, a drive-by is checking out a physical facility or something like that. For an example, you might have a Dun and Bradstreet report that says a company's dealing with government contracts, shipping a million dollars worth of construction equipment. You go to this facility and find it's an office building in Georgetown. Something's not matching up. There's no delivery dock, no storage area, nothing there that would indicate that this kind of business is going on. You would never have gotten that from the paperwork. Maybe you could have gone into the public records and looked at the size of the facility, but you really don't know until you see it for yourself.

Also, we're all "big business" now. You go by someone's "big business" and you realize they're working out of their house. There are a lot of shared office spaces or suites that people are using now. They used to use Mailboxes, Etc. You go by an address and you find out that Suite 2B is really mailbox 2B. That says a lot about the business.

If you're trying to investigate a client for a merger, you get a different feel when you look around. You can tell if they're in a residential area or a business area. You look at property values in the neighborhood, see what types of cars are parked in the driveway and around the house, things that indicate the economic status of the area. You can see if they haven't been there in a while, if their lawn is overgrown. You can tell if they have walk-in clients. The street address doesn't give you all that information, so you need to go and use your eyes and see. Someone may be out of business and you don't know that until you've looked. The sign on the door says they've moved. A lot of direct observation is filling in the gaps in what you've discovered.

If your client wants pictures, you have to bring a camera, because you're their eyes. You have to describe the situation to them, and sometimes verbally isn't enough. A lot of times I'll bring a camera and take pictures so they can understand the different angles of the place, what the building looks like.

Are there ethical or legal concerns related to direct observation?

Yes, definitely. First of all, you do have to respect public and private property. It's as illegal for me as it is for anyone else to go onto private property, and I won't do that. If a case is involved in litigation, there are usually other issues. For example, you can't enter someone's office even though it's open to the public.

You don't have the right to do anything you want. As a licensed investigator, I have ethical and general legal constraints, because I can lose my license or undergo professional evaluation or conduct reviews for breaking laws.

Do you have a direct observation success story?

The one I mentioned earlier about checking out this old facility that turned out not to be a warehouse, but basically a storefront. This guy was representing himself as a manufacturer and distributor, collecting money from some major corporations and pocketing a lot of that money. It turned out to be a big fraud case, a major misrepresentation. He didn't have any storage facilities at all. He was getting the product that he was shipping at a retail outlet and marking it up 500 percent. Direct observation was central to discovering that.

Can you gauge what's going on in a manufacturing facility, for instance, by the size of the parking lot, how many cars are there, the number of employees you see?

Exactly. We've checked out factories. Going at different times of day will tell you if the factory is working twenty-four hours, how many shifts there are, when the shifts change, how many employees, what time people get there. You can see delivery trucks coming and going and get an idea, for competitive intelligence projects, of who their vendors are, who they're working with. You just read the names off the trucks.

You can get a sense of the size of a place. You can see if they have things like shipping and loading docks. How are they set up for receiving goods? For example, do they have forklift trucks parked on the lot? Can you see conveyor belts or pipelines for transporting goods within the company? In terms of storage and inventory, you might see things like storage drums outside a chemical facility.

I did one CI project in Germany where all the paperwork said they had a huge facility. But when we checked it out, we realized that they were only utilizing a fraction of their capacity.

You actually flew to Germany and wandered around this facility?

The client knew I'd been successful working here in the States. I told them that I wasn't familiar with public records in Germany, and they said, "It's worth our expense for you to go and take a look." It turns out that, in Germany, there really aren't any public records. Companies are obliged to disclose information, so you go to the companies themselves. In CI work you go with a prepared explanation of why you're there. I met with the company and gave them my explanation, and they gave us a tour of the facility. They turned over their records, as the country's disclosure laws require them to do.

And what explanation did you give them for wanting to visit?

It was a CI project, so my ultimate purpose was to look into their production and where they were getting their materials. But I went there under the bigger picture of representing a group of prospective investors who may have wanted to buy this company.

The client had to send somebody to translate since, in addition to not knowing Germany, I didn't know German. So we set this up. Of course, the people we were interviewing were very skeptical. Competitive intelligence goes on all the time in Germany as well as here, and they're not very willing to turn over information.

I was very up-front. I introduced myself, Alex Kramer with Kramer Research, and made the appointment. By the time I walked into the office, the guy said, "You know, I've been searching the Web and I can't find a Web site for Kramer Research." That was one time I was very happy that I didn't have a Web site. I'm out there in public all the time, dealing with people, going to conferences, giving speeches, writing articles and so on—and I want to be out there, networking, to get the clients. But I don't want to be out there in a way that people can find out everything about who I am in advance.

Did you refer him to other proofs of who you were, or of your validity or competence?

I gave him my card, I gave him my brochure. I was very upfront with him to the extent that I could be. Again, we have ethical concerns and I can't misrepresent, but I can certainly emphasize different parts of the truth that I would like him to know. I am a researcher and I tell people that. Even shopping on behalf of prospective investors, I am a research company.

So they gave you information, you got a tour of the facility, and you discovered that they only use half of the facility. Any other great pieces of information come out of that direct observation?

It was a chemical company, and we found where they were getting their raw products. Even before the interview, we saw this pipeline around the facility, and we saw that they were tapping into an adjacent facility to get their resources. Once we were there, we found information about the pipeline in the company's public annual reports. Because of disclosure laws in Germany, they had to turn that over. So we got all this information, but the actual visual of being there was key. We got a much better idea of the extent of the pipeline, and a better sense of the close contact between the company and the supplier.

How about any direct observation horror stories?

I was working on a domestic case—which, as I mentioned, I generally don't do but feel I should now and then to pretend like I'm on TV. My job was to follow the husband who was picking up the kids for his visitation, because the wife wanted to see where he was living. I get there early and park in the middle of this very suburban area in Maryland. In the city you can blend better, but here I am with D.C. tags, sitting on the street, with no one else around, waiting for the husband to come. All of a sudden this car pulls up right behind me and is also sitting there watching the house. Well, I'm burned. It was the husband, who was so upset about the domestic situation that he had pulled over to compose himself. I couldn't follow him after that. I was parked right in front of him; I was too visible. We had to create other ways to find out what was going on.

We learn from the unsuccessful ones, too. Anything else you want to tell me about direct observation?

It's a useful tool that people just kind of roll their eyes at. Sometimes it doesn't make or change the results that you're finding on paper but, on the other hand, it paints a picture that is more accurate and gives flavor to whatever you're presenting to your client. I find that people are missing out by not doing that. Just doing database work and reviewing the public records, you're not filling in the blanks.

I agree that one of the things primary research does is fill in the blanks. Let's talk about that for a minute. What does primary give you that you can't get online?

It puts things in a different perspective. The way I look at it, there are three steps to every investigation. There's the online, the database searching, which develops the leads. There's the public records, which fills in from the leads and follows up. Then there's the interview process, which confirms, denies, gets the flavor or the meat of everything you've built up so far.

Let's take those three steps, and talk about how you use secondary research to fuel your primary research. It also sounds like you use primary research to double-check your secondary research.

There is some overlap. The secondary research develops your leads. You throw names in AutoTrackXP [12] or CDB [24] or Dow Jones [41] or whatever resource you're using, and you get your leads. You might find a press release on an executive of a company and it says that he came over from this other company, and what he did before. Or, you do a LexisNexis [80] search, which includes public records, and you find that this guy had bankruptcy issues. A lot of times we're not given complete information at the outset. We have the name Risa Sacks and we have to identify which Risa Sacks we're trying to investigate.

There actually turns out to be more than one of me. I came across Risa Sacks Yaffe in Northern Light [97] and thought, "I've got to find out who my alter ego is."

So we have to identify which Risa Sacks we're going after, or which Bill Clinton. Clinton is a very popular name. Are we going after *the* Bill Clinton? If so, we know he has lived in Arkansas. We have various addresses. The secondary research, the database work, helps identify your focus. It gives you a jurisdiction, tells you where to look. Clinton lived in Arkansas, in this jurisdiction; he lived in D.C.; he lived in New York. Now we know. To get a full perspective on him, we need to cover our bases in each of these jurisdictions.

While we're on secondary research, let's talk for a minute about favorite resources. Are there databases or print resources that you tend to go to repeatedly?

"Databases" is easy to answer. I prefer CDB, which is now owned by ChoicePoint. It gives you the nuts and bolts and helps you set the parameters of your investigation.

Any other favorites in the commercial database area?

AutoTrack and CDB seem to be the favorites among my colleagues at this point. CDB has really good coverage of California, and has more current information. AutoTrack seems to be stronger in older information. If you have the luxury of using them all, you would. If you don't, you try to pinpoint which one's going to be most useful for the job at hand. To be honest, I tend to use what I'm comfortable with. The one I've used most, where I've been successful in the past, is the one I go to first.

How about online services like LexisNexis or Dow Jones?

I always search Dow Jones first because of their pricing. Searches are free, you pay for the article you want, and it's a reasonable price. That's a no-brainer. Most of our clients want us to use LexisNexis first. That's the one they're most familiar with and they have unlimited-use contracts, which I don't. I did take the LexisNexis public records research training, and they certainly offer a lot. But because of the pricing, it's not the first service I'd use.

How about favorite CD-ROMs or print resources?

I don't use any CD-ROMs. For print, I use the reference section at the Library of Congress. Some of those sources are online as well, but there's an alcove in the library, off the reference area, with government directories, congressional staff bios, various Who's Who directories. It's all at your fingertips. Since I'm close by, it's my luxury to go and look there. For government sources, the *Yellow Book* [145] is particularly good.

Another huge resource for doing public records is a *Business Control Atlas* [149]. If you're going to search Asheville, you can't just search in Asheville. You have to find out what county it is, the county seat, and the setup of the local government. There are maps for each state, so you know how to set out to do your research.

Any other print sources come to mind?

I use the *Reporter's Handbook* [167] and *Find It Fast* [148] to help set up where I'm going to start looking. I also use *The Guide to Background Investigations* [153], which breaks down cities, counties, and states, and tells you where to find places like courts and state government offices. If you want corporate records or driving records in Minnesota, it will tell you how to get in touch with those information sources.

Do you have any BRB [15] publications?

I do. Primarily, I'll use BRB to find local court and country retrievers. It helps get subcontractors in places I'm not familiar with.

Let's go to the Web. How do you use the Web, and what are your favorite Web-based resources?

Yahoo! [141]. Generally, I'm trying to find either a company Web site or a government agency. Yahoo! will steer me in the right direction. Government agencies are putting a lot of information on the Web. I just did a whole project involving congressional hearings. I went to the committee offices and they sent me home saying, "Go check our Web site." I use other resources, too, but if you ask me which one I use all the time, I would have to say Yahoo!.

What about online discussion forums or newsgroups?

People often set up discussion groups when, for instance, there's a class action suit in the works. I can't talk about specifics because it's hard to give details without disclosing information. But, as a generic example, look at Bridgestone-Firestone. People are talking, trying to get together, so they set up discussion groups. You can see what people are saying, who's taking the lead in the conversation. I might go to Google [59] for the newsgroups you used to be able to get from Deja News. I might also go to the Yahoo! Message Boards [143] for a particular stock to ask a question or pick up on people's opinions about the company.

Tell me how you've used public records or direct primary research to validate or invalidate secondary research.

You get a Who's Who listing that says someone graduated from this college. You call up the university to verify, and it turns out they attended but didn't graduate. You would never have gotten that unless you followed up. That information doesn't exist online.

Or you get a D&B report. D&Bs are based on information the company itself puts out, but people use those reports as if they're God-sent. It's the same thing with an SEC report. An annual report is the company's own reporting. There are regulations; they do have to indicate pending litigation and so on, but they phrase it in a light that's favorable to them. If you go to the court and look at that file, you'll see it's not quite as trivial as the company is making it out to be. By going there and looking at the details and filling in the blanks with primary research, you get additional information that you just don't get from the databases.

I jump up on that soapbox all the time as well. I wonder why it's so hard for people to go beyond database research. Maybe you just get a mind set.

You get your *butt* set. It takes a lot more energy to make an uncomfortable phone call than it does to look in a database. It takes a lot more energy to physically go down to the court and deal with traffic and do all the procedures. I'm not saying it's laziness. I think people just take the easiest route. That's what they're doing when they leave out the public records part.

Also, there's a money factor. Online is a lot more efficient. What might take a couple of hours down at the courts will take you less than an hour searching PACER [102] at your office. But then you're only getting the recent cases and not the historical view. If you do identify the cases, you have to go to the courts anyway. All you can do online is identify public records. You can't review the case files.

You were just talking about making uncomfortable phone calls. Have you had instances where you thought, "I don't want to make this call. This is really uncomfortable?"

Happens all the time! Sometimes I know too much about what I'm trying to get and what's involved. Sometimes, for no real reason, it just doesn't sit right. It just isn't in your comfort zone. You think it's not going to come out smoothly because you're afraid you'll steer the conversation in a direction you don't want it to go.

I might reach out to a colleague and ask them to do a call for me. Other times, I'll talk it over with the client and try to find a better way to go about getting the information. Or I will try to work up a different introduction. But if it doesn't feel right because of something that I question, whether it's a privacy issue or whatever, I won't do it.

Let's say there's a call you're dreading but you've got to make. Is there something you tell yourself, or do you take a deep breath, or walk around the office six times?

I'll procrastinate as much as I can. Finally, depending on the deadline, I'll just do it and pray that I'll get their answering machine. But if you tell the client you're going to do it, you just do it.

If you get their answering machine, do you leave voicemail? And while we're at it, any tips for the telephone?

It depends on the case. Sometimes I find it better to introduce myself, say a little bit about why I'm calling, and let them know I'll call back. Sometimes I want to catch them on the spot so I don't leave a message.

My only tip for the telephone is stand up when you make these calls. I'm standing now. When you sit, you slouch. You slouch, your voice slouches. You're too relaxed, sitting in front of your computer and playing solitaire while you talk on the phone. Stand up!

How do you present yourself when you're doing direct observations?

Depends on the situation. In other areas you might consider this unethical, but lots of times investigators are hired by sex or race or age because you need somebody to fit into a situation. I can't go everywhere in D.C. that I'd like to go to ask questions, because some neighborhoods are heavily Asian or black, and I'd stand out.

You dress the part. Sometimes I do want to look like the lawyer or the corporate person, and sometimes I want to look casual and not intimidating. I don't necessarily show up for an interview with my IBM-looking suit on. You really have to be attuned to your situation, in figuring out your approach.

Say somebody doesn't want to give you the records or answer your questions; how do you handle objections?

Sometimes you have to be willing to say, "That's totally fair," and you move on. Other times you question them: "Wait a minute; I was here yesterday and I got this. Is so-and-so here?" Anyone can do what I do, but not everybody has my experience. Public records are open to the public, but not everybody knows when to question and how to follow up. I know when to say, "That doesn't sound right. That's public information." We'll talk about it, and sometimes I get what I ask for and sometimes I have to go back to my client.

There are times when information or a court case file has been taken in the judge's chambers, and my client doesn't want the judge to know that somebody is looking into it. You have to know when to walk away and when to pursue. Sometimes it's more important to get the information, and if you raise some flags, that's okay.

I would imagine it's important for you to know how much information you're allowed to give out.

Exactly, and you set those parameters to begin with. If I'm going to do a walk-by or a drive-by of a place, I will find out from my client whether they want me to talk to anyone or not. You have legal and ethical concerns and you also have case-related concerns.

There's the issue of confidentiality. My investigative clients know I respect confidentiality and shield their names in all the research I do. I instruct the people who work with me that you're not my employee, you're an independent subcontractor, and there's no reason to affiliate yourself with Kramer Research.

For film or literary clients, I may not have to be as confidential. In fact, sometimes the author or director or producer I'm working with is a name that people would want to help, and they want me to use it. So, I'm at liberty to put it out there.

You have to weigh what you can give out. Sometimes it's to your advantage. My theory is "you gotta give to get." You should always be prepared to give out some information, but you have to know what and how much you can give.

How has the Web changed how you do your job in general?

It's given me more sophisticated clients and more complex investigations. The clients are taking care of the easy stuff. Now they're coming to me when they've gotten more of the details and they need to fill in the blanks or do the intricate work. People are also realizing that there is a whole world of information out there and that it's becoming a necessity, not just a luxury, in doing business. You have to be an informed business person. So the Web is creating more business for us.

If you want to find, for example, any lawsuits relating to a particular company or individual, where do you look for that information?

It depends on what your starting point is. If you don't know anything about it, you would start where the company's doing business or where its headquarters are. Lawsuits are broken down into local, state, or federal level. For instance, most of the cigarette companies are incorporated in Delaware, but they actually do business elsewhere; they manufacture down in Richmond or North Carolina. If I know nothing to begin with, I generally do a dual search. I would search the federal court in Delaware to see what cases have been filed at the headquarters of the companies. Then I would go down to the local level, where the actual manufacturing or whatever is going on, and see what suits are there.

You'll get different types of information at each of these levels because each jurisdiction and each court has its own filing requirements. Cases involving doing business in two states, or involving a government agency, usually go to U.S. District Court, the federal court. But when you go down to the lower levels, the county or state levels, you can find cases like an employee who got into an accident at work and is suing for workers' comp. The nature of the investigation will determine where you go for the information.

For the federal level, for example, do you use PACER, or do you use CDB?

PACER is very reasonably priced, but I don't use it because I've never been well trained on it, and a lot of my clients have it. They've already identified the case and that's why they're calling me to go to the courts. Usually I am in a situation where I need more than just the federal cases. Also, public records in these databases are, for the most part, not archival. They're very current, so your searches are limited. To get a full picture, you probably want to go back at least ten years, and a lot of these courts have put only about three years' worth of their information online. They haven't gone back and filled in the blanks with their older information.

So you have to go to the courthouse. Do they have an index, or do you actually have to go through old records?

You name it, we go through it. Books, microfiche, index cards, anything. I've been to very small courthouses where the case files themselves are the index. We use whatever the courthouse has.

How do you work with court runners in locations where you don't know anyone?

The BRB Local Court and County Retrievers Sourcebook, *The Burwell World Directory of Information Brokers* [17], and the AIIP membership directory all contain listings of people. The problem is that, by the time these directories are published, the information may not still be accurate; someone may have gone out of business or moved. I can't get many people in AIIP to leave the office to do research.

I've got an old library box with index cards cross-referenced by states and then by names, and as I pick up contacts along the way, I file them in there. And I use my colleagues in the investigative world a lot. No matter what case you're working on, you can always call another investigator and ask if they know somebody in Seminole, Florida. There's great willingness to share.

So, it's largely word of mouth. Sometimes you have to pay somebody to drive from two counties over. Sometimes you go there yourself.

How has public record research changed over, say, the last five years?

I have to say that the courts, the recorder of deeds, and a lot of other places are getting more technologically savvy. Up until last year, even in D.C., it was all in books—and D.C. is a pretty big city. But they're automating most of it. The biggest change is that they're using computers in the courthouses now, so it's a lot more efficient to retrieve copies and review indices. Of course some of the courthouses are better than others.

The problem is, some data entry clerk is putting all those things in. There are lots of mistakes in the information that's being automated. Although the error percentage is reasonable, what happens if you're working on a case where there happens to be an error? When you're there in person you can question it, and it's easier to try variations. If there's a misspelling in something, you can see it. It's usually right next to the correct entry, or close enough. You miss a lot by doing it online.

But it is changing, and we are getting more proficient.

Are you finding more restrictions on access to information?

Fair credit and privacy is probably another two-hour interview. Some courthouses won't pull files unless I file a release saying who I am and why I want the file. Very rarely, I've been to places that won't give me information if I'm not a party to the suit, and I question whether they're allowed to do that. But it's me against the clerk, and I sometimes have to take it to their supervisor. It's my understanding that public information is public information but, unfortunately, people are trying to control it and cut it down. There's this craze that says this is all fearful stuff and people can find out anything about you. But all you're doing is protecting people who have committed wrongdoings; you're not confirming people who have clean records.

It's a two-sided issue. You don't want people to get some celebrity's home address so they can go stalk them. On the other hand ...

On the other hand, you can't check your domestic help to make sure they really lived in an area. By restricting public information, you're putting everybody on an equal level. So why not put everybody on an equal level where all the information is public? If the public can't see that someone has a criminal record or has been a party to numerous civil suits, then they're not getting the full picture. Why should somebody with a very clean record have to compete for business, a home loan, or whatever, with a person who has a record that we now can't find out about?

How do you see it changing in the next five years?

Things will probably continue tightening down for another year or two, and then people will recognize that they can't get the information they need. Whether it's domestic help or their kid's boyfriends or whatever, they won't be able to check out anything anymore because of the tightening of the laws. I think people will see the repercussions and we'll have a backlash. I'm just kind of biding my time, waiting for the backlash.

I think it's to our advantage to make this information accessible. The emphasis should be on tightening up how the information is released. If they close off access for legitimate professionals, where do you go to get it? Only criminals, people who don't do it ethically, will have access to it then. PIs used to have some access to financial information on people. Now you can go to court, win a judgment in your favor, and there's no way for you to collect the money. You can't identify the bank account to garnish a person's wages.

How do you see your work changing over the next five years?

It's going to have to change, if we're getting cut off from all these sources of information. For example, a while back, my clients weren't willing to get releases. To run driving records on people in various states, I now need to get a release from the subject we're searching. They used to all want to do it confidentially. Now, if we're doing an employment check on somebody, the prospective employee has to give us a release. More of this is coming. Getting the release seems very fair, but if people want to hide things, they'll get creative. You can't really dig and get the information if you're doing it on their terms.

How do you keep up with the changes in your industry—the laws, the requirements, the resources?

You go to an SLA (Special Libraries Association) [121] conference and see all the vendors out there and you realize, "How do I keep up?" I try not to let it overwhelm me. I try to become focused and specialized and concentrate on what I know. You have to talk to people in the field, and get on mailing lists that will inform you. I'm on a local D.C. detectives' list, and one for

AIIP members. Because I'm out in public so much, I'm constantly talking to the clerks in the courts and the people on the front line, and relaying that information to my clients.

You mentioned SLA. Any other major conferences that you feel are important? For phone researchers and primary researchers, it doesn't seem to be as centralized or well-defined.

Exactly. I think the National Public Records Research Association [91] looks at their world in a vacuum. AIIP and SCIP [114] are important and useful. I want to know what else is out there to help complement what I'm doing now. I go to conferences that pertain to the type of research I'm doing, whether it's competitive intelligence or general business research. There is no one single resource.

What characteristics make a good public records searcher?

Efficiency. Being attuned to details. Knowing how to be complete and how to follow up. You go into a place, and it's a blur of names. You're looking in indices that are sometimes bigger books than I can lift. You have to stay attuned. You have to pick up variations in handwritten indices. If something is misspelled or misfiled or filed inconsistently—like St. John under "ST" one time and under "SA" for "Saint" another time—you could miss important information.

Public places are only open from eight to four, or nine to five. You have to get a lot done in a day. Your day is different when you can stay home and just take a break for lunch and do database work and get back to it later on. You have to be efficient and quick. Your client is paying for you to travel to a place, so you have to complete the job. You have to get everything while you're there. There's a lot of juggling that goes on.

I find that some of the best people in public records research worked in the restaurant business; they can multitask. Writers are not the best because they want all the details. They're not willing to just go in for their assignment. They want to fill in all the blanks while they're there, and read all the papers.

When you're doing public records research or interviewing, you've got to be "up." How do you handle dealing with an absolute creep? What if you're just having a bad day?

If you have a bad day, you can't take it out on other people. It's unfair. They're not going to make the effort for you if you come in there with attitude. I go in to the civil clerk in U.S. District Court for D.C. I know about her gardening, about her mother who passed away, that she's a big Redskins fan. Once you've established the relationships, if you're having a bad day, they know. You have a bad day, you apologize. This is the way I choose to do things, but I also find that it's the way that has helped my business.

If someone's awful, you bite your tongue and thank them. You don't have a choice. You can't take it out on them because you know what happens when someone does. That's the problem with lawyers. They'll go in and demand things, and you watch how the clerks treat them. People think that the clerks are getting paid for this, that it's their job. Well, it's not their job to move fast, and it's not their job to make copies that day if they have a sign on the wall that says it takes three to five days. If you have to, you just go outside, walk around the building and come back with a new approach.

With public records searching it seems so important to have a mentor, to work with someone or to start in an apprentice-type position.

It really is. You go into these places and everybody else appears to know what they are doing. The same runners are there all the time, and the clerks are used to talking to them, all those public records searchers parked all day long at the FAA, the DOT and the courts. You go out with similar assignments, but you don't fit in with these people yet, and you don't fit in with the general public, either. Those searchers can be incredibly helpful and will stop what they're doing, if they have the time, to take you through and show you. But learning along the way is a hard start. Although the searches themselves have been facilitated by modern technology, you don't even know what room to go to, you have to learn the vocabulary. That's why a mentor or a soothing face really helps you out.

How do you find out where to go in a new place when you don't know the ropes?

You know the level of courts—city court, state court, and federal court. So you go to the clerk's office. How do you know to go to the clerk's office? When you tell the marshal or the guard at the door, "This is what I want to do," he will probably direct you there. However, at the Department of Labor, the guard will say, "You don't know where you're going? I can't help you, and you need to sign in with a specific room number."

So you do some legwork before you head to these locations. A lot of them have Internet sites that show you how to do research there. For example, the Library of Congress Web sites provide information including descriptions of the collections, maps, and floor plans. Sometimes you just have to call and see where you get bounced to, and then get some directions from whoever you end up talking to.

I'm so used to doing this now that I can go to any city and find a courthouse without a map or a street address, just by the feel of the layout of the town. You gain it by doing it. I know it's unfair to tell people that, but that's how you do it.

That's the reality of it. Public records is different from online searching in terms of training.

It is. There are books and training courses, but they talk in such generic terms that you don't understand how it's going to apply to you. I grew up in New York, and New York refers to the state court as the Supreme Court, while in D.C., "Supreme Court" means the highest court in the land. The Superior Court in New York is a lower court, and superior court in D.C. is the state court. If you're sitting in a training class and they say, "Go to the mid-level court," all you're getting is general terminology. A mentor is the one who helps you pave the way in your own jurisdiction. I've been a mentor to a lot of people.

My first public records experience was with the two-person firm I mentioned earlier. The second woman had just come back to work. It was very stressful. They had their own personal problems, I was caught in the middle, not very happy, and feeling very challenged by the whole thing. At a few minutes to three on Friday afternoon, the woman who had just come back dropped me off at the D.C. Recorder of Deeds, where all the property records are, and told me to search out this guy. They closed at three. I got in there, and I looked around at this maze. Nobody looked up. Everybody was going through these books and archaic computer terminals. There was absolutely nobody there to help me, and I just went home and cried.

That night, being in my very mature stage, I called and left a voicemail message telling this woman that I quit. So that was my first public records experience. Later, I had somebody who took me under her wing and trained me. I followed everything she said with wide eyes, because she was a guru in public records research. Then it became something manageable, friendly, and great to be involved in.

What recommendations would you make to somebody wants to become a public records researcher?

It's easy enough to do the research. You can go to any title search company and get a job. Doing this on your own, the challenge is getting the business. You have to develop your niche. Learn what public records are. Being in D.C., I'm fortunate to have so many types of public records available. In Paducah, Kentucky, you might only have the local court. But maybe you're close to the capital and your specialty could be state records, corporate records, court records, or the university library, which has some special collections. How do you get started? I got started by doing it, and I think that's how you do it, and then you develop your niche and your proficiency.

Any advice for a novice public records searcher with an assignment?

Put it in perspective. The biggest thing is not to get overwhelmed the way I did, as I cried down there among the property records. Break the assignment down. Public records can be done in steps and phases, and that's generally what we do. Budget constraints, both time and money, help us prioritize: This is phase one, this is phase two, and this is phase three, the follow-up steps.

If you're just starting out, know what you have to offer. Don't just sit there and declare yourself a public records searcher. If you live somewhere in a small county that's not near the state capital, the only thing you have to offer is what's in that county. Know your county. Know that there's a permit office where people get housing permits and occupancy permits. Know that there is a land records office. You might not know how to do the searches, but know what's in these places. Many of them have handouts that they'll give the general public. In small claims court, for example, they deal with hundreds of people who are puzzled and have questions. They don't want to answer all these questions, so they leave a stack of papers on the counter that explains what small claims is. You can go into a courthouse and get their explanation of how the court system works. It's a tool for you, too.

If you're already doing online research and want to branch out to public records, I certainly would take advantage of the training that vendors like LexisNexis offer. It's to their advantage to explain what they have and how to look for it.

Any final thoughts?

People overlook public records and they overlook primary research. It's so easy to stay home and stay online, and of course there are reasons to do that. But you need to be more knowledgeable about what else is out there, because you're not getting the complete picture when you don't tap into public records and public resources. If you don't want to get out there yourself, then find someone to get out there for you. But don't dismiss the value of the information.

Super Searcher Tips

➤ Public records are not an exact science. Something may be written wrong, something may be misfiled. There are so many variables. I tell my clients right off, I work to the "best of my ability." You can only do the best you can.

➤ Clients think that, because I'm so familiar with these courthouses, I can get anything immediately; that if the case is sealed, I can open it; that I can bribe someone to get the information quicker; that there's got to be a way to get around the system because money talks. Money doesn't talk in courthouses, and that's the biggest misconception.

➤ If paint or chemicals are involved, check the local, state, and federal environmental files. In one case, we found a layout of the facility and assembly line included in their environmental report. My client then knew exactly how their assembly line worked.

➤ A Dun and Bradstreet report might say a company's shipping a million dollars worth of construction equipment. You find this facility is an office building. Something's not matching up. There's no delivery dock, no storage area, nothing to indicate this kind of business is going on. You would never get that information from the paperwork.

➤ Checking out factories can provide a variety of information. You can get a sense of the size of a place. How much of the facility they're using may dictate production levels. You can read the names off delivery trucks and get an idea of their vendors, who they are working with.

➤ Every investigation has three steps: The database search, which develops the leads; the public records search, which fills in and follows up; and then the interview process which confirms, denies, gets the flavor or the meat of everything you've been working on.

➤ People will set up online discussion groups when there's a class action suit in the works. You can see what people are saying and who's taking the lead in the conversation.

➤ When you look at public records in person, it's easier to see errors and variations. If there's a misspelling, it's usually right next to the correct entry, or close enough. You miss a lot of that with a database search.

➤ Break down a research project to what you know and start there. Most of us can understand corporate records or articles of incorporation. Latch on to what you can. In public records research, one thing leads to the next. It's a matter of follow-through.

Andrew Pollard

U.K.-Based Competitor Intelligence

Andrew Pollard is director and senior partner of EMP Intelligence Service in Dallington, Northampton, England, and one of the most experienced consultants in competitor intelligence in Europe. He has presented at numerous conferences in Europe, the U.S., and the Middle East. He is author of *Competitor Intelligence—Strategy, Tools, and Techniques for Competitive Advantage* [160, see Appendix].

apollard@emp-is.com
www.emp-is.com

Why don't you begin by telling me something about your background and how you ended up where you are today.

I produced an Open University course in 1985, "Managing in the Competitive Environment." This involved talking to a lot of companies, finding out what they really wanted, and, in the process, reading literally everything there was on competitive intelligence. There wasn't very much, and there was no research done in the U.K. Because the Open University worked with the BBC, we were able to do a lot of interviews with businesses like IBM, British Petroleum, British Caledonian, steel companies, and various other, smaller companies. This involved doing research that had never been done before.

People were very wary in those days talking about competitive intelligence. They thought it was somewhat "not what a gentleman should really do." But they were interviewed, and we put the tapes together with the rest of the course. This went very well and sold something in the region of 10,000 items and made about six million pounds for the Open University. All the work for that led me to collaborate afterwards with a number of others in setting up EMP Intelligence Service in 1988, the year after the course was launched. Since then, we have worked very hard to develop a wide range of courses as well as of consultancy capabilities. We've now had over five thousand people to our seminars, more than anybody else in Europe.

What kinds of seminars do you offer?

We run a two-day competitor intelligence course called "Know Your Competitors," and a one-day course called "Know Your Jungle." Also, we run a two-day exercise on using the Internet, and another workshop on competitive analysis where we focus on the "twiddly bits" as you might say. Analysis is a most overused word in consultancy, but real analysis is much more interesting and much more practical. In the seminars, we focus on practicality rather than the academic theory and all the latest fashions to come from America. EMP also has a consultancy side, a side that sets up CI operations within a company, and a software side.

You mentioned real analysis. That's such a key issue. Would you talk for a minute about what you see as real analysis, the real value-added analysis that you do in competitive intelligence situations?

This is a very big subject. I won't go into the whole area, but the key thing in competition is not absolute strengths and absolute weaknesses. It doesn't matter how good I am if you're better. And it doesn't matter how good you are if I'm better. It's the difference, the relative strengths and weaknesses that really matter. And the analytical techniques to determine that are very limited.

Among the most common types of analysis that people do are Porter [104] and SWOT [126], neither of which is particularly useful. Porter is actually an analysis of the profitability and the factors affecting the profitability of an industry—not a company, and not a market. There's much confusion between the terms "market" and "industry." The Porter model is of some limited use to analyze the competitive environment. Barriers to entry, substitutes, and the rest of the model are only some of the factors that influence the level of competition and determine the degree of competitive threat in a particular industry.

The second analytical tool, SWOT (Strengths, Weaknesses, Opportunities, and Threats) is frequently, in fact, done on just a single piece of paper. It is useful but ignores relative strengths and weaknesses.

What is probably more important is doing sensible things like benchmarking, writing decent profiles on companies, and analyzing the environment in a reasonable manner to be able to predict potential competition. At EMP we developed our own techniques. In England, and in Europe particularly, we're more interested in "does it work?" Does it work, not with a big budget and a big staff and with the CEO sort of cooing in your ear, but does it actually work on a bad day?

Does it work in the trenches?

Yes, with a small budget and with the managing director or the CEO not particularly in favor. For the most part, practical analysis is not taught at the academic level. As a result, most consultants don't teach practical analysis. We don't go for the fancy-looking gobbledy-gook, largely because I haven't got the guts to present it. I much prefer to teach something which can actually be presented in a practical way and where I'm not going to get a lot of people shouting at me, saying it's a load of nonsense.

Say you're going to interview someone. What are the cultural differences between the U.S., the U.K., and Europe when you're doing primary research?

The American culture is much more open and willing to talk. Not in all cases, but you can get much more information from the phone. I would divide Europe into Great Britain and the Continent, and it's much more difficult on the Continent. They will want to know who you are, where you come from, why you want to know, and more. They won't talk as much; in fact, they'll often put the phone down.

Then, of course, there's a cultural difference between northern Europe and southern Europe, with northern Europe much more corporate. There are far more private companies on the Continent than there are in the U.K., and they tend to be more closed anyway. In Germany or France, say, where it's much more hierarchical, they will clam up immediately and refer you upwards. The smaller countries—BENELUX, Sweden—are different. They tend to be much more outward-looking, but they're also very sharp.

In the south, it's mostly the fact that there are far more family businesses, and it's who you know. If you want information on an Italian company, you have to find somebody who has contacts. Contacts are always important, even in America. But in southern Europe, without contacts, you're dead. In Spain, for instance, without a local researcher, you're completely lost. Indeed, it's the rule. If you want to do any research on any European country, you have got to use a local.

How about the U.K.? Are they somewhere between the U.S. and Europe?

They are. And I would say they're drifting towards America. As a little bit of background, the middle class tend to look towards America for the money, and towards Europe for its culture, whereas the working class look to America for both. The middle class will want to live briefly in America, but long-term in Tuscany. Whereas the working class, in my opinion, would go to live in America full time.

How does that affect the way you approach people in the U.K.?

With primary research, they're more likely to talk in the U.K. than they are on the Continent. We have a large sprinkling of American companies and a fair number of Americans over here—somewhere in the region of four or five million Americans live outside of America, and about a quarter of a million of them are in the U.K. So you do expect to get much more information from people on the phone in the U.K., and they will talk.

In America, being talkative is a national disease, I guess.

No, it comes from the fact that you have long distances, and it's still an underpopulated country. You go fifteen miles just to go round the corner, as we would say, when in fact we just wouldn't go those distances. You need the phone, it's part of your life. The truth is, I think, that the younger generation are more likely to talk now than the older generation. There is a trend towards a greater telephone culture in this country now. Therefore if you hit people under thirty, they're more likely to talk.

Do you need to consider the effects of accents and language fluency when interviewing in Europe?

Absolutely so, particularly in France. Indeed, you would never attempt to phone somebody in a French company because, even if you do speak French, you speak with an accent. You're in dead trouble. No company that wants to get information out of a French national should ever use anything other than a French national. A small example: Hoover's [65] asked me if it was really necessary to put their company profiles on the Web in French if they wanted to market in France. I said, "You must be joking. I'm positive. You're dead otherwise. The French will kill you."

One of the things I find unique is the extent to which you like using video clips of people. When I think of the number of times, Andrew, you've sent me off to find some obscure clip of something that happened two years ago ...

Pictures are often worth more than words, and a video, a moving picture, particularly of a key decision maker, can be worth its weight in gold. There is absolutely nobody who doesn't sum up another person on sight. Of course the best approach is to go and see them in the flesh. If you can't, then see them on video. Preferably see them live, if you can get it.

The Internet is wonderful, because you can actually home in on press conferences and so on. We homed in on one in America, and it gave us some wonderful stuff, totally bang-up-to-date. It gave us footage which we were then able to show the client, saying, "This is your competitor's new head man." Senior people in particular like to see the whites of their enemy's eyes. Therefore, I believe that video is important.

I've used sources like Video Monitoring Service, VMS [134], to get video clips in the States. Do you have favorite sources in the U.K.?

We have some sources, but it is more likely that your monitoring a company and their Web site will tell you that there is, for example, a press conference today and that you can hook up to it by clicking here. It's as simple as that. Getting hold of that kind of material is more likely to happen via the Web site of the competitor you're tracking than by any other means. Videos of television or radio interviews, usually quite short, can be obtained. A number of companies in the U.K., including bmcnews [14], provide this service.

How about obtaining corporate records in the U.K.? In the U.S., for example, we have Edgar [46].

You've not got anything as good as Edgar over here. The nearest thing to Edgar is Companies House Direct [30], a division of Companies House based in Cardiff. That's the best place to go to start the ball rolling. It is not available on a twenty-four-hour basis. Remember, this is England and this is the public sector, which is not known for its dedication to long hours and twenty-four-hour service.

What kinds of records can you get from Companies House?

These are the annual filings. We do not have quarterly filings. Larger U.K. companies come out with half-yearly filings as well, called "interims." They do not come out with quarterlies yet. However, because of the increasing importance of international investment capital, and because of the amount of money in America to be invested abroad, and the insistence that companies outside the United States fall into line, increasingly we're seeing companies in Europe starting to go in the direction of quarterly reports. They may not be on quite the same legal basis as the Americans, but they're going that way. It's only a small trend at this stage.

For the most part, someone researching a U.K. company in the States would have to know about the annuals and the interims. In the U.K., you also have to learn new terminology. For "earnings" read "sales" or "turnover," and for "income" read "profits." Also, for profits there are a number of different profit measures or terms.

Do you find any major misconceptions about competitive intelligence and primary research?

Well, let's separate those two. I think the misconceptions with competitive intelligence are much less than they used to be. You may have much more worry in America because I think in some ways you've gone too academic, and you've got too many ex-DIA (Defense Intelligence Agency) and CIA and NSA people who have taken their pensions and gone off to do competitive intelligence, bringing with them the spooky atmosphere instead of the basic commercial research capability. And, of course, this does not give the right image to competitive intelligence. We don't have that kind of worry quite as much now, even though we are a much more secretive country, historically. We're not as open a society as America. I've no doubt that in the U.K. we have ex-MI5, MI6 people in competitive intelligence, but I, myself, have no knowledge of it. If they're there, they're a lot quieter than the CIA people.

On the Continent, I think competitive intelligence is still regarded with rather more suspicion, but that's changing quite quickly. There is much more concern on parts of the Continent about U.S. government economic espionage. There is a lot of talk in Europe, among the French and others, about to what extent the CIA is aiding American companies, because the CIA says quite publicly that forty percent of their work now is economic, and of course they wouldn't be working for the benefit of British companies. I can't believe that that is not taking place over in Europe, but to what extent, I have absolutely no idea.

Now, as to primary research, I don't believe primary research has got a bad name in this country at all. Obviously, people refuse to speak, and that's because they're either too junior, too scared, have been given an order, or are suspicious. This is all reasonable, normal stuff. You're going to get that kind of reaction to a host of different questions for a host of different reasons.

How about client misconceptions in terms of, say, how long primary research takes, or the kinds of results they can get, or the skills necessary to do it?

That's an interesting one. A lot of potential clients are either trying to get more for their money than they really should get, and therefore they expect too much too soon, or they're ignorant about the difficulty of the process. Even when it comes to secondary research, they seem to think that intelligence is just like water: Turn on the tap and it immediately flows. The unreasonable expectations of potential clients know no boundaries at all. This is an international phenomenon; there is no difference between an overdemanding American potential client and an overdemanding European one. One of the biggest factors is sheer ignorance. They don't know how difficult information gathering and sifting and collation and putting together jigsaw pieces really is.

When clients come to you, do they tend to know that they want primary research or secondary research, or do they just say, "I need the answer to this question"?

Most bosses are only concerned with answers. As quickly as possible, as cheaply as possible. Apart from anything else, primary and secondary are very loose terms. I don't believe senior people should worry themselves too much about this unless they are very well clued up. There are situations where they say they want this information collected from certain sources, but I don't believe that happens very often. Most of the time, they couldn't care less as long as they get it.

So when you're looking at a project, are there certain keys or clues that say to you, for this I need to go primary?

We're not giving too many secrets away here. All I'm going to say at this point is that, obviously, you look very carefully at what the appropriate sources are and then go from there. In terms of how you do that, there are a number of really key processes in this whole exercise where, in fact, it's the result of twenty years experience. I'm not giving that away. Sorry.

That's fine. I'll ask the various questions and, if there's any of this you don't want to talk about, we'll move on. Let's switch to something completely different. Do you have favorite print resources for finding experts?

For the most part, we don't. We've been going long enough now that we've probably got as good a directory of contacts, based on our seminar participants and past clients, as you are going to get. We use that to identify contacts. We don't, for the most part, use printed or equivalent online sources.

Do you have favorite ways of getting phone numbers for experts?

There are U.K. directories, but we're not as much a directory country as America is. One of the things that struck me when I was doing a lot of research on information sources twenty-five years ago was that the Americans are reference-mad. I love your reference-mad culture. I think it's fantastic.

It's great for researchers.

You've got lists of everything under the sun. We don't. We have some directories, but we're nowhere near as prolific in publishing this and that and everything. If you can't find information in America, you've got to be a pretty poor researcher.

Are there no good directories for finding people in various government agencies or offices?

Now that's a different ballgame. Government is a key resource. But it's important to realize that government is highly inefficient and full of people who aren't all that well used to dealing with the public. On the other hand, if you get right through to them, they're like flowers that have been kept in the greenhouse for a long time. They quite blossom to a little bit of sweet talk.

The crucial thing, I've found, in getting information out of the government is to use the Internet to get your initial contacts. I recently was doing some background research using government information, and the initial telephone number came from the Internet. It wasn't the right one, but from there I got the right one. The secret is persistence.

The rule is "Don't come off the phone without a referral." I never, ever fail getting stuff out of them. The record was the Home Office, which deals with prisons, immigrations, and the police. They sent me 'round the mulberry bush nine times, but I wouldn't let them get off the phone without giving me a referral. Eventually something clicked, I was put through to the right person, and I got exactly what I wanted.

The phone is very effective in government if you're willing to give the time, if you remember the basic rule about referrals, and if you do your homework. If you're after statistics, go to the libraries, get the statistical publications, and try to see if there are any footnotes, any reference points, so you've at least got somewhere intelligent to phone. Then you can actually throw at them "I was given your name by the *Millennial Abstract of Statistics*." They will probably say they don't collect that data, or they used to do it but don't do it now, or they're not the right person, or they're about to leave, or they're on answer phone, which is what we call your voicemail, or they're about to take early retirement.

And you can get the numbers for U.K. government offices on the Internet?

Not so easily. It's not too difficult to get the general number, in which case you can start right at the front door and talk your way up through the system. That's a pain, but sometimes you have to do that. The biggest problem is getting the right person.

In the States, for example, we have wonderful reference books for government numbers, like

the *Yellow Books* [145]. Is there nothing analogous to that in the U.K.?

No, there isn't. On the other hand, there is a good Web site to start with: open.gov.uk [100]. Get to know that site. It's a very important source, an absolutely vital piece of homework for someone to spend a Saturday morning going through that site. Spend a lot of time on that site and you'll be very well rewarded.

And that will actually give you some good numbers?

No, that will give you a functional, as well as an alphabetical, index to all government operations, local and central, in the U.K. And from there, you may get good numbers. For instance, if you were looking for population forecasting, it's got a search capability which is a bit of a pain, but it will help you find organizations that are relevant to what you're trying to do.

While we're talking about the Net, are there favorite search engines that you use?

To be honest, we tell people to avoid search engines if they possibly can, particularly if you're after corporate-type information. You pick up Web sites, but you can pick up Web sites from Hoover's. If you're after specific academic subjects like SWOT analysis, then search engines are useful. But if, for example, you're after investments in another country made by, say, a Spanish company, you're not going to get that too easily on the Web. Or it's going to be buried within 280,176 hits, which is of no use to anybody. If you're going to use a search engine for very specific things, then Google [58] is good, AltaVista [8] is not bad. Yahoo! [141], although it's a directory, is really a search engine in a way, and it's always worth a try. It's often a good starting point.

You mentioned Hoover's, which brings us to commercial services. Is Hoover's one that you find particularly useful?

For initial quick-and-dirty, as I used to call it, it's not a bad starting point. It's useful for background, as a jumping-off point, and it does have a lot of useful links. But you wouldn't get away with pumping one of their reports in to your client's board of directors.

Are there others you use?

Reuters [112], Dialog [39] and LexisNexis [80]. They're all fine products, in terms of content. It very much depends on the subject matter you're talking about. I find LexisNexis and Reuters very similar, though LexisNexis is far superior when it comes to legal cites. If you want American information, Dialog is your man, as it were.

Absolutely. What type of product do you provide your clients? Do you give them the initial sources, transcribed interviews, summaries, analysis?

We provide all kinds of analysis, profiles, the lot. There's almost nothing we haven't done. There are occasions where people want the background, initial source material, and so on. But that's not common, unlike perhaps in the U.S. We're dealing with a much more analytical, or intelligence, mind in Europe, whereas I think there's much more of an information mind in America. You're information-holics over there. Not only do you produce fantastic amounts of reference books, but you've got, in my perception, many more senior managers who suck this stuff up like babies' milk. Whereas in England and the Continent, as long as they trust you—that's crucial—they don't want anything more than two pages. The twenty-, thirty-, forty-, fifty-page report is still alive and kicking all over the world, and is not wanted by most senior managers. But the Americans, as information-holics, want everything—the transcripts, the docs.

So your final product is really value-added. You're not just giving them the raw data; rather, it's the analysis and the conclusions, the answers to their questions.

If the answer to the question is something that is collected as a piece of raw information, then you just provide it. But the point is, it may be much more subtle than that, or more synthesized in the sense that you have to, for example, assess strengths and weaknesses. Frequently, you've got to analyze the implications of information, for instance, whether having a production site in a certain part of Spain is a strength or a weakness.

I'm not anti-information. There's a huge market for information as well as intelligence in every company. However, I get the feeling that in America the usual thing is to give them all the raw material as well as the analysis. Particularly if you're predominantly a primary research person, because obviously you have to prove that you did something. Whereas over here, there's a greater initial barrier, I think, in terms of credibility, but if you get over that barrier, then they don't expect fifty pages from you, and they're not interested in the raw information. What they want are the conclusions they need to make a decision.

Someone needs to spend time on analyzing the American mind and the European mind. In my opinion, there's a big book here. A lot of good ideas would come out of recognizing the difference between how Americans and Europeans manage. Americans will move forward with three-quarters of the information, whereas in the U.K., they'll wait much longer and get the full information. I don't know what relationship that particular trait has to the different methods of collection, or to the predominance of primary over secondary in America, whereas it's less predominant over here. But I do think it is more important in America because your culture is that way, and because you can get access to more people more easily. Whereas over here, that's not the case. Secrecy is still considerable.

There's a resurgence of primary in the States right now, I think, but there was a period where, when people thought "research," they very much thought secondary.

I know that's the case because fifteen or twenty years ago, primary was probably predominant. Then there was a big online surge. I remember Leila Kight [78] complaining about it at a SCIP [114] conference, saying you can get a lot more by just phoning a few experts up, and she was right.

We had to go full circle to get a balance. How do you evaluate the credibility and reliability of the information you're getting?

This question can be asked about any kind of information from any source. Frequently the standard answer is "corroborated from other sources not likely to form the same loop." In other words, you don't go to newspaper two to check newspaper one because they could both be drawing from the same false source. The same goes, to some extent, for primary research. You've got to be very careful that you don't check source A by talking to source B when they're both misled. They go to the same conferences, read the same papers, and are really, in fact, singing out of the same hymn sheet. The only way to avoid that is try to find either a primary or a secondary source that is likely to be out of that particular loop. In history, they used to call that the external credibility test.

The internal credibility test is to just look at what they're saying, and the phraseology, and then match it up against others. When you start hearing the same phrases, then you start getting suspicious. Especially academics, because they're like sheep. Same goes for government to some extent. Business people may talk to you and tell you everything, but they may be lying to you anyway. I mean, evaluating people, well, blimey, we could be here all night.

Each of these topics could be a book in itself, you're right. We're just giving people a flavor of some of the issues.

It's a flavor of the simplicity, in many cases, of what we're doing. Everybody is always looking for some brilliant technological or analytical solution when, in fact, it's nothing more than just shoe leather, as it were. Phoning, phoning, phoning until you get the right person, and when you get the right person, you forget all the others. In a recent piece of work I did, we used all kinds of sources and it was, of course, sod's law, as always, in the last source. Why didn't we do that first? Everybody makes mistakes. Who cares, as long as you get to the answer?

Have you found effective ways to handle sensitive issues, and does that differ between the U.K. and the States?

Depends on what you mean by sensitive. The most sensitive things are likely to be the ones having to do with intentions, what a company is going to do. That's the kind of thing most people want. The only answer to that one is that you've got to chat them up, in the sense of get them talking. The secret is to get them to talk and win their confidence, and then hopefully they will come out with things that they wouldn't have given you if you'd asked a direct question. Then proceed largely by means of, not open questions, but the standard journalist trick of keeping people talking by just putting a plaster over the last thing they said, referencing what they said, using it as a jumping-off point, and moving forward on that basis. You've used it about four times.

That's very true, Andrew. I want readers to see the techniques we're talking about in action, in the interviews themselves. Another question: How do you know when you're finished with the primary part of a search?

When you've answered all the questions, or got most of the key ones. The truth is, it's when you start running out of contacts. If you get very rapidly diminishing returns, that makes it seem very unlikely that people are going to give you anything. I don't call them experts. I know the Americans do. We just call them contacts because, in many cases, it's not so easy to get the top people. "Experts" is not a term we use over here at all, because the idea of being able to find from reference books the top expert in something is not very great. We don't have the reference book culture that you've got.

Another area that I want to ask you about is direct observation.

I emphasize the importance of going to see places because it's amazing what you can do. Don't forget to take photographs. Photographs are very useful because your memory will not be at all perfect. Get yourself a decent camera, which usually means an up-market SLR that will take decent photographs in zoom conditions in poor light. That means using a fast film as well. ASA400 is probably good enough—a bit grainy, but at least you can take zoom in poor lighting, and take photos from the public highway.

When are the best times to go and look at a facility?

If you were monitoring a transport company and wanted to learn their fleet size and you couldn't find it from any other source, which you probably could, the best day to go and have a look at them is Christmas Day, because all the lorries will be in the car park. As long as you know where their lorry sites are, then you're okay.

But are there set good days and bad days? Because you don't normally know that in advance, you have to go several times. It's essential that you not go just once, because frequently you're not as observant as you think and you will not see everything. If it's a big site and there's a lot to see, then you need to do your homework. Here I'm talking about a factory site rather than an office site or a retail site, because there are different things to look for. But it is vital to go more than once.

On a factory site, you may be interested in issues like who are their key suppliers? Who handles their transportation? How many people work there? You could probably get all that by other means, but it's not a bad idea to have a look and see the ebb and flow of the workforce, to see how big their car parking is, how many spaces they've got. All these can be useful. You need go there two or three times to get a feel. Twice is absolute minimum.

You were talking about doing your homework. How would you prepare for a site visit?

You get all the local planning documents. Also ownership documents are important, as is local press coverage.

Office sites are usually just boring office blocks, or simply a couple of floors of an office block. It's not easy to monitor them, because you might find an office block with five different companies in it. It's certainly not difficult to find out how many floors they occupy and get some feel for the total number of people working there, by simply counting. Retail sites are not too difficult either, because you can see the ebb and flow so easily.

It is important to say that you must not, under any circumstances, break the law and trespass. You must not stray onto private property. That is absolutely crucial because otherwise you're crossing over the line into semi-espionage.

And is that the main legal issue to be concerned about with direct observation?

Stay on public property and you're all right. No one, in fact, can be prosecuted for observation; just make sure you observe from public property. And if in doubt about the legality of something, don't. Most information that's of value can be gathered from ordinary open sources and by open means. You don't need to do anything funny. No one should logically want to go to jail, so let's not go to jail.

How do you see the research world changing over the next five years?

I think the Internet is going to become the most dominant form of information gathering. It is already in some respects. It shouldn't be. The primary telephone sources should be much more important than they frequently are, but people lack the confidence and the ability to carry out interviews on the phone. Telephone interviewing is one of the key skills, and people are not being properly trained. It's one major area of skills shortage in competitive intelligence.

I agree with you. You can go to online searching seminars and workshops, but there are not very many good sources—none that I know of, really—for getting training on telephone research.

That's right. This is not the only major practical skill area in competitive intelligence which is either ignored or badly trained. It's treated as something less sexy than using the Internet, when in fact it is vital. Loads of people just want to go off into the corner and play with a computer all day and produce some fantastic-looking twenty-page nonsense at which everybody would then throw their hands up and say "alleluia."

Over the next five years, do you think there will be more need for primary research, or less?

I don't believe it will go down. If it has already faded and is coming back, it certainly needs to come back a lot more. I believe, in fact, that a lot of research cannot be done except by contact on the phone. You simply can't get certain kinds of information any other way. I think there will always be a demand for primary research. I would hope that, if anything, it becomes more important relative to the Internet. I love the Internet; I'm on it sometimes five times a day. But without direct contact, you don't get the sharpness of information. In published or secondary information, you often don't know the ultimate source.

Do you have a particular success story where this kind of primary contact was really the key?

I have loads of them. Let me give you two examples. One, we were asked to find out when a very important product launch day would be. Of course, it was not available in any secondary source, Internet or otherwise. We got it, not directly in the sense of "April 3rd," but we found enough jigsaw pieces around the missing piece. We got so close that our report said, "We are almost certain" that it was whatever date. And it was.

Who did you talk to, or what kind of information did you get, that allowed you to zero in that closely?

We found that certain prior testing was being done somewhere in the world. This wasn't the only jigsaw piece, but it was one of them. And that meant phoning that country. Now we had little bits of luck; you always need luck. We were able to find information about what happened there, why it was happening, and what the test market was all about. We corroborated that against other sources that weren't in that particular loop, and they started to home in on a particular area. Then we checked it out with another telephone source and—bong!

One of the things our clients did on the strength of our information was book all the advertising space. That stopped the competitor in their tracks.

You mean your client booked all the ad space so that the company that was going to do the launch couldn't advertise it?

Absolutely. That cost money, and they did that on the basis of our advice. As a result the launch was a total failure.

Another case was a competitive bid where a lot of telephoning was done to check out the worth of the target company. Our client wanted to know what to bid for the company. They did their due diligence, but they didn't have all the human intelligence. They wanted to know how well the rest of the industry thought of the company, and how good they were in certain areas, like logistics. This kind of information is not found in secondary sources. It's going to be in people's minds. And the only way to get information out of people's minds is to talk to them. If you can't meet them, you have to telephone them.

Our client had to decide (a) whether to bid, and (b) how much to bid. If our information enabled them to decide that it was worth that extra million because the company had a lot to offer, or that it was not worth bidding any more than a certain sum because of the way they were thought of in the industry, then we have substantially benefited our client in any case. Either we've helped them acquire a worthwhile company, or we've saved them a lot of money. That's what this game is about. At the end of the day, all the telephone research has got to have value added.

It sounds as if what you're saying is that, to help you stay focused on the information you need to get, you need to be very clear about the

purpose of this information, the value-added that you're looking for.

That's right. The hardest thing is to ask the right question. The second hardest thing is to answer it. The third is to stay on the question in the first place. It's easy to wander off, like a cow leaning over the fence because the grass is greener over there.

Are there any other points you'd like to make about doing primary research?

Don't forget the old radio. Radio's important in Europe, more important in England, I'd say, than in America. There are more likely to be interviews of companies that are worth listening to. We've certainly tracked personalities using radio. One of the key target companies on an intelligence project was run by a very unusual senior manager, and we got hold of a two-minute-long interview with the local radio station, which is pretty long. We were able to get quite a lot of information on him, on his style and everything else. We were able to make some guesses that the huge new offices that his company had gone into were as much an ego trip as anything, and would burden the company. And lo and behold, it was a bridge too far for the great man. The debt incurred crippled the company and exposed it to a defensive merger.

You were talking earlier about taking a camera with you. Do you have a success story where going and looking at something, and taking photos, made a key difference?

We were asked to find out about a particular company that was very well-known, had a very big brand name, but when we started to pick the company apart, we discovered that we couldn't find out where it was. It lived in the Yellow Pages. It had offices, and first of all we had to dig up addresses all over the country. At that point we found a dozen addresses which seemed to be their local regional offices. We sent somebody around the whole country, and that took a long time. When we did find the places, they turned out, in most cases, to be tiny.

The company was quite different in reality than we had ever anticipated. It turned out to be not actually a company, but a company plus a number of franchises. It had recently gone through a big retrenchment and cut back from a large part of the country and replaced the big offices in these regions with franchises. That told you a lot about how well they were doing. But it also revealed in fact how big the company was. It was much smaller than we had ever realized. Because they had this big office and had a huge advertising capability, they had an image of being a much bigger and more powerful company.

First we got their accounts. Their accounts seemed not to tell that story. We couldn't understand it. And then it was corroborated by going out into the field, someone driving all around the country with his camera, and when those shots came back, they told a story. And it was those shots that we took to the client. The client realized, for the first time, that they were worrying too much about the competitor. They also saw the weaknesses of this particular company so that they were able to attack it, and to defend against it, much more effectively.

That's a wonderful story, Andrew.

We originally thought it was an English company. Through very good secondary research, we dug up that it wasn't. But the most surprising exercise was when we found that their two offices in Scotland were both tiny little sheds. They were basically one-man franchises up there. The company was more or less dead in Scotland.

That was the greatest revelation, because it was such a well-known company. I thought I knew a lot about it as an ordinary citizen. But in reality, the company turned out to be utterly and completely different. Without having gone around the country with the camera and seeing its facilities for ourselves, we would have never understood that company.

Primary research is absolutely vital and must be given the highest priority even when good Internet sources exist as well. Primary research is absolutely crucial.

Super Searcher Tips

➤ In terms of primary research, the American culture is much more open and willing to talk. On the Continent, they will want to know who you are, where you come from, why you want to know, and more. They won't talk as much; in fact, they'll put the phone down.

➤ There's a cultural difference between northern and southern Europe, with northern Europe much more corporate. In the south, it's far more family businesses and who you know. Without contacts in southern Europe, you're dead. To do any research there, you have to use a local.

➤ Pictures are often worth more than words, and a video—a moving picture—particularly of a key decision maker, is worth its weight in gold.

➤ For public company records, the nearest thing to Edgar in the U.K. is Companies House Direct. Companies have annual filings, and often come out with half-yearly interims.

➤ For government information in the U.K., the best site is open.gov.uk. It has a functional, as well as an alphabetical, index to all government operations, and a search capability to find relevant organizations.

➤ There's a much more analytical or intelligence mind in Europe, and a much more information mind in America, where many more senior managers suck information up like babies' milk. In England and the Continent, as long as they trust you, they don't want anything more than a two-page report.

➤ In assessing credibility, the rule is "corroborated from other sources not likely to form the same loop." Don't check source A by talking to source B when they're both misled. Find either a primary or secondary source that is out of the loop of those you're checking.

➤ Go to see places and take photographs, because your memory will not be perfect. Use a good camera with film that will take decent photographs in zoom conditions in poor light.

➤ Do not, under any circumstances, break the law and trespass. If in doubt, don't. Most information that's of value can be gathered from ordinary open sources and by open means.

John Schwartz

New York Times Reporter

John Schwartz is a technology reporter at *The New York Times*. At the time of this interview, he was a technology and Internet writer at *The Washington Post*. He is co-author, with Michael T. Osterholm, of *Living Terrors: What America Needs to Know to Survive the Coming Bioterrorist Catastrophe*.

jswatz@nytimes.com

Can you tell me a little bit about your background? How did a nice boy from Texas end up at *The Washington Post*?

It's a funny situation. I didn't go to journalism school or take any journalism classes. But about the time that I got into law school at the University of Texas, I realized that I didn't really like law all that much. I started showing up at the *Daily Texan*, a student newspaper, and I really liked that. I got caught up in it, and realized that a day spent among reporters was probably better than a day spent among lawyers. My father and two of my brothers were lawyers, so I said, "We're already giving our quota." I caught the bug and started freelancing. One of the things I did was string for *Newsweek On Campus*, which was a college publication at the time. After about a year and a half of that, I was getting out of law school and I talked to the editor of *Newsweek On Campus*, and asked him if he was interested in having me come work for him. He was encouraging in a bland way, with what I now recognize as the ultimate nice kiss-off line: "You're really high on my list."

I was so stupid I thought he was saying, "I'd like to give you a job." So in April of '85, I called him up and said, "Jerry, my wife and I"—we had just gotten married—"want to come up to New York. That's where we want to live. I'm high on your list, right? So why don't you just hire me?" What I didn't know was that Bill Barol, who had been the first writer hired at *Newsweek On Campus*, had just quit. Jerry said, "Well, okay. I can't hire you permanently, but I've got freelance money, and I'll hire you as a sort of permanent freelancer—without benefits—until we figure out what to do with you." I thought that was the way the world worked. "Okay, sure. Hey, I got that job." So I started to work at *Newsweek On Campus*. A year later, I made my way into the regular *Newsweek* magazine, because once you're there, you sort of call around, say, "You want me to write for you?" they say sure, and after a couple of stories for them, they say, "If we get an opening, I'll keep you in mind." Then the business editor of *Newsweek*, Lewis D'Vorkin called and said, "We just lost a guy, so if you were serious about this, it's gotta be now." So I did the work for him and the work for *Newsweek On Campus* both for about six months, and it all worked, and it was wonderful.

After working for *Newsweek* for a total of about eight years, I heard about a job writing science for the *Post*. I was completely unqualified for it. I was completely unqualified to write about business too, you know. But again, with the *Newsweek* job, I had said, "Lewis, I'm really not sure that I'm your guy, because I don't know anything about business." He said, "Read a book." I said, "Well, okay," and then he hired me. So I had sort of the same feeling, that I could just read a book and would do okay. In fact I got the job at the *Post* in April of '93, and about a year ago I moved over to the business section of the *Post* in order to work full time on technology and Internet stories.

So that's how I got there. I've just accepted a job at *The New York Times*, where I'll be starting on Monday.

What kinds of stories will you be handling at the *Times*?

Since my boss is the technology editor, I'll be writing about technology, but we're still trying to figure out what that means. They do have a staff of technology writers, and we're feeling our way through. The hardest part, I think, is figuring out how to fit in with everybody else who's already there.

Fitting in with people with different expertise reminds me of an article you wrote for the *Post* back in July of '95: "Don't close the book on paper when it comes to research" [163, see Appendix]. It was a wonderful story about your family and the battle of technology. It was so much like Spencer Tracy and Katherine Hepburn in *Desk Set*.

It was fun. It really was a *Desk Set* moment. My wife, Jeanne, is an archivist by training and a historian by interest. She has a master's in history and a certification in archive management, and she believes in paper. I am more of a tech guy. So, over the last ten years or more, as long as there have been computers in the house, there's been a little tension between us. She is the skeptic on all things technological, and I'm the one who says, "No, no, the Internet, that's the way to go, that's how we'll do everything." Of course each of us has modified our views over time. She has begun using the Net in the last year or so; finally she jumped aboard. It was hilarious—one day she called me up at work and she said, "Boy, this Internet thing is great!" That was a wonderful moment, because she had been so tough on me for thinking the Net is the way to do everything.

What I wrote about was a very early skirmish. We were sitting around the house and a movie came on. My daughter was about six years old, and my older son was about three. It was a movie we hadn't seen before. I think it had James Cagney and

Shirley Jones in it. We've got lots of resources around. But I had just gotten a little hand-held Franklin movie guide, so I said, "Okay, I've never seen this before. I'll look it up." She said, "I'll find it faster." And she goes over to the books. And I start punching in information on this device, and she starts going through the *New York Times Directory of Film* [157] and cross-referencing Shirley Jones and James Cagney. Each way takes a little bit of time, and we turn it into a fight. My daughter, who at the time was a Daddy's girl, says, "Go, Daddy, go, yeah!" It was really crazy. I am punching things in and nothing is coming up. This movie is too obscure for the then-pathetic database of these little Franklin handhelds. I'm still looking and looking, and suddenly my wife shouts out, "Never Steal Anything Small!" She won.

My little daughter looks up with those big eyes of hers and says, "Daddy, why did the computer lose?" It's all just horrifying to her. I explained that technology has let us down but Mommy's still wrong. The fact is, though, the paper guides were a better resource. They covered more stuff. Within weeks, Franklin had a new, bigger movie guide out that did include that movie. But the book was still a better way to go.

Nowadays, if I had a fabulous DSL connection or cable modem and could go directly to a bookmarked Internet movie database, things might be different, because I could do it in moments. I could also look at all the ads on the Internet movie database, and all the offers to buy videos. There's still a reason that Jeanne was right: If you want *just* the information, go to the book.

Exactly. Or you might go to another primary source. If Shirley Jones was around, you could've just called her up and said, "Shirley, what is this?" Which brings us to using the best source for the information you need, and how you decide what those sources are.

As I said before, I went to law school, and in law they talk about the best evidence. What's the best evidence? Yes, you could get a facsimile, but where's the original document? Why do you not accept hearsay? Because there's a possibility of corruption of information. So you go for the best evidence. Sometimes the best evidence is locked in a book, sometimes paper is the way to go. Maybe that means that you've got to go to a courthouse somewhere. If you're covering a trial, you do a lot better job of reporting if you go to the courthouse and sit in the room. Beyond that, yes, you can get the final opinion online, but often the briefs are not available online. Then you want to contact the lawyer.

What does primary provide that you can't get in secondary sources?

First, there's no substitute for the real thing. Let's say you're reading depositions in the case, as opposed to just getting a description of it. You're cruising through hundreds and hundreds of pages of questions. You can get a sense of just how testy the different participants are. You can get a sense of the personality of the different players so that when you get into the courtroom, you can say, "Oh yeah, Dan. He's a jerk." You watch Dan, and you know him already. And, my God, lawyers are in the paper production business. They will send you everything they've done.

They'll actually send you copies of the depositions?

If they're not under seal, sure. And there's nothing like seeing for yourself. When I've done stories on adverse events, that is, bad side effects of a particular drug, there is no substitute for going to the FDA (Food and Drug Administration) [50] and filing a FOIA (Freedom of Information Act) [53] request saying, "I want all the adverse event information on this drug. I want to see everything that's come in."

Then you can read the reports for yourself and see how the adverse event has been characterized by a doctor, and whether this makes sense to you. They have to report everything, and some people are very good at reporting and some are not. When you go through these long, long reports, you get a sense of the vocabulary that people use. You find leads that you might follow up. You might see a side effect you hadn't thought about before, and you can follow up on that.

In the Unabomber case, the day that the FBI raided Ted Kaczynski's shack in Montana, we went into full action, and we had a lot of stuff online instantly. We had phone numbers. We had letters that his father had written to the local newspapers. There was a lot online, but remember, Ted Kaczynski had tried very hard to cover his traces. In addition to all the online information, the *Post* had a part-time researcher who worked at the Library of Congress and who was there just at closing time when the story broke. That researcher stayed and was able to deliver Kaczynski's Ph.D. dissertation by seven P.M. Now let's face it, there's no way that even a brilliant reporter was going to be able to read and understand that document. But it included his thesis advisors, it had a tremendous amount of information, and it showed that he was a smart guy. Some things are simply not online, but if you can get them in the real world, you want to be able to hold them in your hand, you want to be able to see them.

I had already done a pretty thorough analysis of the Manifesto, which was available online. I was able to go through the document itself, where he cited works of literature and history. I called up a history professor and said, "Your book is cited in the Unabomber Manifesto."

So there were clues in the document itself, and some of the people I contacted led me to other people who had been briefed, whom the FBI had gone to. There was a web of people that I was able to contact.

Did you find as you worked your way through that web, that one person would hand you on to another?

It wasn't that they were in contact with each other; it was that their scholarship was linked in one way or another, and they would say, "Oh yeah, he cites Ellul …" and "The book to read there is probably …" They helped me get a start, because you don't just jump on Jacques Ellul cold! Then, reading the books that were cited was really useful. I found the antecedents of the Manifesto, found the intellectual underpinnings of it, like those works of Jacques Ellul. I then was able to go to the library and read some of the antecedent works in order to get a sense of whether Kaczynski had gotten it right or not.

This is what you do in the world of paper. You read the sources, you talk to the professors, and you ask, "Did he get it right, and what do you think of his interpretation of your work?" That's where you get the insight. Otherwise you're just doing a once-over-lightly.

Unless you did that, and realized that (a) he was reading incredibly extensively, and (b) his interpretations were crap—that he was so obsessed, that he came in with such a strong set of opinions because he was nuts—then, when you read his stuff, you wouldn't have the basis to show that his interpretations were very shoddy. So the piece that I wrote, based on all this reading and research, said that as a social critic he's actually not that good.

But you had to go to all the primary sources; you were able to go to the professors who'd written the books and get their take on it. When you use both primary and secondary sources, how do you integrate them? Do you start with secondary sources to find primary sources? Do you go back and forth between the two?

I usually start with what's at hand. I keep some books around in my little study at home. I use the newsroom library wherever I am, and I use the Net voraciously. Services like LexisNexis [80], for instance, get you a lot of great secondary sources.

I recently completed a book called *Living Terrors: What America Needs to Know to Survive the Coming Bioterrorist Catastrophe* [159], that I wrote with Michael Osterholm. It's about biological terrorism. A huge amount of the research was done online, first to find clips about interesting things that I could then report out myself, but also to find references to primary works that were available online.

The Office of Technology Assessment's [98] seminal 1993 report on the risk of weapons of mass destruction is online. The chart showing how inline release of anthrax spores could kill three million people in Washington was in PDF form. So the dichotomy of online versus primary doesn't work completely anymore. I had a library on my desktop, and I was able to get Congressional testimony, and a big seminar at which they talked about the risk of biological terrorism, all online.

While we're on the Net, are there favorite search engines or sites that you go to generally, or does it depend on the topic?

It all depends on the topic. Google [58] is where I go when I've got a word, especially if it's an unusual word. Kaczynski was pre-Google, but for a Kaczynski-like search, you go to Google.

If you know specifically what you're looking for, like the New Jersey Department of Motor Vehicles, where I'm going to get my automobile registration information, then you go through Yahoo! [141], which outlines the world for you.

I've never looked up the New Jersey Department of Vehicles. How would you go through Yahoo! for that?

You drill down through government, countries, states, New Jersey, transportation, DMV. Sometimes you need to drill. When someone has done the organizing for you, it's a wonderful world.

But if it's a more free-form search and you've got a distinctive word, then you want to use Metacrawler [86] or Google or something like that.

How do you get started on a brand-new assignment? Do you use any expert sites or online discussion groups to find people to talk to?

Nothing that I monitor all the time. But of course, whenever I interview someone, I need background. When I had to do a news story about the acquisition of a company called Chromatic, I suddenly had to understand dense-wave multiplexing, and I'd never done a story on optical networks before. I was able to find a lot. First thing I would do in a situation like that is go to a couple of technical reference books and read a few paragraphs, so that I'm not completely stupid. And then I would look up an expert. I don't remember how I did this particular one, it may have been through something like *Nelson's Directory of Investment Managers* [93], or seeing someone cited in another article somewhere. Then I contact the guy and he says, "I've done a huge primer on this and it's on my Web site; you ought to look there."

So it's interactive, or synergistic.

Yes. Everything leads to everything else. Then other people say, "Well, you have to read my Web site." And then, of course, once you're linked out there, you can find millions of things. But when you do that, you always have to keep in mind, "Is this the best evidence? Are these trustable, trustworthy sources?"

My daughter was preparing a speech about the subject of leadership. There's a great quote that really works here. The quote is something like: "There go my people. I must find out where they're going so I can lead them." I looked in a book of quotations and I found that it was, I think, Alexandre Auguste Ledru-Rollin. We didn't know much about him, but we put it in the speech. Then we're talking to her speech-writing coach, and he says, "That's a very interesting quote, but you can't just say Alexandre

Auguste Ledru-Rollin, you have to say who he is and document that."

So Elizabeth and I went online and found a few references to him, and one was pretty complete. It said "19th century French politician," and then there was that quote. We looked for a couple of other items on the site, and I said, "Sweetie, look at the context of this quote. Look what the site owner's saying about this." It was a Web site devoted to an anti-Semitic interpretation of history, just completely hate-filled. I said, "Now, what does that say about using this site as a reference?"

In fact the information on who this guy was is correct. But it's in such a rancid context that every fact is suspect. It was kind of a social responsibility issue, too. Do you want to be directing people back to this site? Don't you want the best sources? Don't you want to reference somebody who's right not just on this, but on everything else?

That leads me to the question of how you evaluate your primary sources. You've found some "experts" and talked to them. How do you determine their reliability, their veracity?

If you're talking to them, you listen. You try to figure out whether they're responsible and whether they really have expertise, or whether they're just "dial-a-quotes."

If I see somebody who's quoted in every news story on every topic, I try to keep from overusing them, and save them for what I know they really know. You don't want to just round up the usual suspects every time. Paul Saffo is a brilliant man, but more news stories quote Paul Saffo than Bill Clinton. He's at the Institute for the Future [74], and he is terrific. But I only want to call Paul Saffo when I know it's really, really right, because otherwise I would call him on every story.

That's protecting against overuse, but it's also protecting against calling somebody up just because you know he's good with a quote, and that he'll return your call. A lot of the stock analysts are like that. They sort of feel you out while you're talking to them, to try to figure out what you're looking for them to say. Then they say it, so you'll call them the next time.

I listen for eagerness—those people get subject to a little tougher filter when it comes to deciding what to put in. At the same time, you want people who are helpful, and if the information they're giving you is good, then it's good. You just keep the bullshit detector in place as you talk to these people. Over time, if you develop a beat, you also hear people talking, you read people being quoted, and you sort of evaluate them and decide, "That's a guy I could call."

You develop a sense of expertise over time. For example, there are many fathers of the Internet. If you were going to talk to one of these fathers of the Internet, you know that Vint Cerf is wry and insightful, has terrific depth of knowledge, but is hard to reach sometimes. Dave Farber, who is so important to the development of many of the protocols, is fantastic not just on the technology, but on social implications. Bob Kahn is a great guy on who did what when. His knowledge of technology is unsurpassed. So if you're asking, "How do you know who to call?", I'd say, you learn your sources and your people, you know who's done what and who's out there. In a field that is your regular beat, you develop that over time.

How about a brand-new field, when you are suddenly dropped into an area that you know nothing about?

When I get a story that's due at five and it's thrown at me at two in the afternoon and I've never done anything on it before, I read the clips. I find out who's been quoted. You can read ten clips in twenty minutes, write down who's been quoted, get the Nelson's analysts, do a lot of very quick phone calls, and make sense of it as best you can. You don't get many of those stories. If you have more time and can read a technical paper, and it's written well, so you can actually understand what's being said, that author is like gold, and you call him up.

What are your typical turnaround times? Is there a range, or an average?

Incredible range. I've done plenty of stories that I get at 6:30 and turn in at 7:30. If somebody calls me and says, "Hey, this is happening," I start making calls, and I pound it out and it's done. On the other hand, I had stories at *The Washington Post* that I worked on, and that didn't run, and I continued to work on, and they didn't run. I had one set of stories that was in development for fourteen months.

In what ways does deadline drive your approach to the story?

If it's a fast story, then—it's not that you cut corners, it's just a very straightforward job. After you've worked in newspapers for a while, there's a machine in your head. If you need to bang out an eighteen-inch story on topic A, then you make the calls, you figure out where the quotes go, and you write it. It's quick and wonderful because you don't have time to think about it.

How do you get the phone numbers? Have you got favorite sources for getting phone numbers?

The Net is great for that. I use Switchboard [125]. It used to be a lot harder to get phone numbers, but now, with online access to national phone directories, life is good.

There was a story a couple of years ago where the FDA announced it was pulling a drug called Duract off the market. Duract was just a nonsteroidal anti-inflammatory drug like Aleve. But if you took it for more than ten days, it had the potential to blow out your liver. The FDA had repeatedly warned people about this. But doctors continued to prescribe it for more than ten days. So the FDA gave up and pulled the drug.

That happened at three or four in the afternoon. I got all the information, did my FDA interviews and drug company interviews, but I also went to Deja News [59], and found a discussion on Duract, and I found a couple of people who talked about it. One guy said, "Yeah, I took that stuff. Started feeling awful, went to my doctor and he took me off of it." His name was something like Graylen Jones, a really good name. I went to Switchboard, typed in the name, and there was only one in the United States, in Plaquemine, Louisiana. So I got the guy on the phone, and I said, "I'm sorry to bother you but, you know, you've posted to a newsgroup about taking Duract." He said, "Oh, yeah, yeah, I took that drug, and after I'd been on it about four weeks I swole up like a house." "Swole up like a house?" "Yep, swole up like a house. I went online, and I found out that that swelling was a sign of liver damage. So I went to my doctor and he said, 'Yeah, well, we better take you off of that.'" In a story that was otherwise going to be sort of dry, I had a human being saying, "I swole up like a house."

You did a story recently on universities that conduct student orientation online, where you had some interesting sources. One was an incoming freshman at Worcester Polytech. I could see how you'd locate the directors of admissions and some of the other sources you talked to. But how in the world did you find her?

Some of the schools gave me access to their Web sites, but they hadn't thought it through. Once I got on the Web sites, I was able to contact students. I contacted three people on one Web site, and one of them got upset and complained to the school. The school told me, "You can't do this." I said, "Then why did you let me?" And I told them, "Look, I'm not going to contact this student who was upset again. But I really would like you to contact her and relay my apologies." I still had this other person, though. I said to her, "I hope you don't mind, I'd really love to talk with you about this stuff," and she was terrific.

That brings us to the interviews themselves. Whether it's a freshman college student or a Nobel prize winner or whatever, are there certain techniques that work for you once you get someone on the phone?

In fact, I have no technique. It's a conversation. When I interview someone, they're often surprised because it's so much more like a conversation than a real interview. They're expecting questions in order, with some tight control over the topic, more professionalism. And I don't do that, I talk. Sometimes we go back and forth, but all the questions eventually get asked.

Is there some sixth sense that you've developed that says, "It looks like they're wandering off, but let's follow that one?"

No, because you always get where you're going. And you can always gently guide things back if you just stop and say, "Okay, here's what I really need to talk about." But you can get a lot done just through casual conversation.

I did an arts piece about two and a half years ago about a Canadian band called Moxy Früvous. I was talking with the singer and drummer, a guy named Jian Ghomeshi. He said, "Oh"—you know, he was trying to entertain me—"Schwartz, in fact, I know a Schwartz in Philadelphia who was in his eighties, a guy named Isadore Schwartz, Izzy Schwartz. There's a great story about Izzy. Do you want to hear it?" I said, "I love to hear great stories." He tells me this wonderful story about Izzy Schwartz. They do a private gig, they're playing the Pennsylvania Horsemen's Association, and in the middle of it, somebody comes up to them and says, "You ought to let Izzy play with you." And Izzy is there. Izzy is this little old man who's a violinist. He's with the Philadelphia Orchestra. And we say, "You want to play with us?" He says, "Yeah!" And he gets up and he plays, they give him the chords and the changes, and they play a couple of pieces. When it's over, Jian tells me, people are stomping on the floor, pounding their feet on the floor, saying, "Iz-zy! Iz-zy! Iz-zy!" It was wonderful.

When he finished telling me this story, Jian says, "Don't you want to do the interview?" I say, "Yeah, let's. Where'd you grow up?" and we did the rest of the interview.

The next morning, I call Izzy Schwartz. How many Isadore Schwartzes are there in Philadelphia? And I get him on the phone. "Hello? I'm looking for Isadore Schwartz, the concert violinist." He says, "Well, I'm retired." I said, "I'm writing a story about Moxy Früvous." He says, "Moxy Früvous? I love those guys!" He said, "I tell you, I was at the Pennsylvania Horsemen's Association, and they said I could play with them. I play a couple of songs; at the end people are stomping their feet yelling 'Iz-zy, Iz-zy.' This never happens to a concert violinist!" He says, "It was the last time I ever played in public." So I put Izzy in the story.

A couple of months later I go to a show and there's Jian, and he says, "That story was amazing. I didn't know you were interviewing me. I was just having this long conversation with you, and I thought, well, when are we going to get around to the interview questions? You found Izzy Schwartz!"

And there it was! Do you prepare for a call in some way—write questions out or whatever?

Sometimes I do write things out, if there are specific things that need to be worked through. In business reporting, very often you already know what the questions are because the news event is occurring and you've got stuff that you know you need to bring up: When is this going to happen? How did this happen? When did you catch him with his hand in the till? Those kinds of questions are very straightforward. When it's something like an interview about a band, well, you've got to let that just take its course.

Do you find that interviews have a life of their own?

Yes. And it really depends on who's the person, who are you talking with.

Are there any differences between doing phone interviews versus in-person interviews?

I love in-person interviews, although I rarely have time for them. But again, I say go to the source. There is no substitute for being in the room with somebody. I'll give you an example. In last Sunday's *Post*, there's the final story I did for them, about a guy named Jules Lodish. Lodish is in the late stages of ALS. The story was that he had really set up his life in order to continue living, even though ALS is difficult. He's got round-the-clock nursing care. As a doctor he came up with sterile procedures that have helped extend his life beyond what one could expect for an ALS patient, and he wrote a thirty-five-page training booklet for these nurses. He's really an amazing man. But more than that, he's still there. He's there for his family, and his daughter calls him from college to say "listen to my essay that I just wrote." So he's making the most of a very difficult disease, and he is still himself, no matter what. This is clearly a fascinating guy; he's exactly what you want in a story.

I interviewed him by phone several times, but I felt that for the real interview I had to go out to his house. And it was at his house that I saw him, saw his wheelchair, saw how he's surrounded with equipment, and saw the cartoons on his wall. And I cited the cartoons in the article.

It's that sense of immediacy, of being able to see the whole environment. What if someone doesn't want to talk to you? How do you handle that?

In the Lodish case, he refused to be interviewed at first. He talked to me four and a half years ago, and then he got cold feet. So I withdrew, because it was going to be a profile of him, and I couldn't really do it without his participation. Then I heard about six or seven weeks ago that he might be willing to talk again, and

I called him up. So we just picked up where we'd left off. But some members of his family did not want to talk to me. I talked to two of his kids, but not his oldest, and I talked to his wife, but only after she thought about it for a while.

So you can give them an opportunity to think about speaking with you. How about on a news story as opposed to a personal profile?

Well, if somebody's saying "no comment," all I'm going to get is no comment. You can't cajole the CEO of a corporation into talking with you if the CEO of the corporation doesn't want to do it. You can wheedle and you can say, "Well, you know what I'm going to say in the story; you really need to have your side in here," or "This is the story that's going to be in *The Washington Post* tomorrow. I assume you're going to want to respond to that, because these people are saying awfully nasty things about you."

How do you handle sensitive issues? Do you lead up to them, or talk around them?

Sometimes you save the hardest stuff for last, sure. You certainly don't start with it. You get through the basics first, ask them about themselves and other subjects they can comfortably talk about. Then you say, "Now, here's the part you're not going to like. This is the nasty stuff people are saying about you." I'm pretty straightforward about it when I get to that point.

Do you use silence to elicit information from people?

Silence is an incredibly effective tool, and if I knew how to shut up I would use it. I know that, if I could only hold on the phone without saying anything for another minute, I'd get something. But I'm just not good at holding.

Well, it's good to know your own limitations! I want to segue for a minute, in fact go back completely to a different subject. We talked about using the Net and how that has affected your approach to research and reporting. You also mentioned some commercial services like LexisNexis. Do you use any other commercial database services?

Dow Jones Interactive [41] is fantastic. There are many others, but it really depends on the bottom line, on who's paying for it. At the *Post*, I had access to both LexisNexis and Dow Jones, and I used them constantly.

When you're searching online, do you tend to start narrow or broad, or don't you have a pattern?

I tend to start sort of broad, because one of the things that people like Nicholson Baker [146] talk about with regard to the loss of card catalogs is that there's no serendipity in searching online. But he's wrong. He's a brilliant man; I shouldn't say he's wrong, but he is. In fact, if you do a broad search, serendipity still works. It's just a different type of serendipity. And as you develop your skills, you find these things. I believe there's just as much room for the unexpected.

When you search manually, there's this browsing phenomenon where your fingers are just walking through things. Sometimes I love having the physical books in front of me, and serendipity is one big reason. Yet you can find a kind of serendipity online as well.

That's the beauty of holding an encyclopedia. It's just so luxurious to let the page fall open and the information is there. But serendipity can happen online. You can start out doing a Google search just to check the proper spelling of someone's name, and you get all this additional information, including a complete employment history that shows not only the institution where this person is currently teaching, but all the previous institutions where she worked. Now you have leads to other institutions or universities that specialize in this area.

How has online searching in general changed over the last few years? Have the Web sites and sources that you use become more stable? Can you relocate information easily?

When I did the biological terrorism book, it came time to do the footnotes, and I realized to my horror that I had not done a good enough job of organizing. I was able to go through and find everything again. Now, to anyone who uses a library, that sounds like the dumbest thing in the world—of course you can find everything again. But you remember how it was back in 1992 or so; with some of those online sites, trying to find something twice was like looking for your trail of breadcrumbs. But now I can find it all. Web sites are more persistent, the information is easier to find, the searches are more consistent, everything's better.

How do you see the research picture changing over the next five years?

One big thing is that more and more primary materials, like all those reports from Congressional testimony that I found, are going to be online. There's a Robert Darnton [35] essay on how incredibly useful the Internet is for doing real historical research. He's a hero of my wife's, because she thought he had the most fascinating take on history and made the most innovative use of sources. He's one of the best there is in going to the primary source, to the best source. So for him to come around to this way of doing research was fascinating. For her hero to say, "Boy, there's a lot there on the Net, I found these ancient French Provincial records …"—I must say, it scored a point for me.

Do you think you'll be doing fewer live interviews, using fewer experts, over the next five years?

Not everybody wants to do the job right. People are still better than machines. People can be augmented by machines in interesting ways. Everyone I talk to now says, "Read this on my Web site." "Find this here, I said it better here." It's not true. They said it more fully there, more clearly there, but I still call them up and say, "Look, I know I can get this information on this Web site. I know essentially what you can tell me. I don't want to waste your time, but live people tell better stories." And that issue of serendipity comes in again: Where is this conversation going to lead?

Let me ask you this as someone who both uses sources and might be viewed as a source. I call reporters frequently when I'm doing research, and I adore them. In general, they're wonderful. My experience is that reporters are willing to talk, actually return phone calls and are, on the whole, gracious and knowledgeable. So let's put you in the seat of being a source: Do you mind when someone calls you as a source?

It depends. If it's the day after a story has appeared and I get a call from a law firm and they want a phone number for a publicly traded company—forget it. You guys, use a phone book. I covered tobacco for five years. If it's a college student sending me a note saying, "Please send me all the information you have on cigarettes because I can't believe it but I've got a paper due next week." No. Time to do your own research.

I don't often help TV producers who just want to rip off my story and not even credit the *Post*, or not credit me for having done the work. They call up and say, "Oh, this was such fabulous work." So, sometimes I'm inclined to respond, sometimes I'm not.

What would you tell a researcher about calling reporters for information? If you could say, "This is what we're willing to do" or "This is what you need to have done before you call us?"

The first thing is, you've got to know the schedule. In other words, don't ever call a newspaper reporter after four. They're on deadlines. The *Post* has rolling deadlines because of the online edition. That makes it pretty rough. So the first question you ask a reporter is, "Are you on deadline? Is this a good time?"

The next thing is, know what you really need to ask. Do the obvious first. If it's a company, a person quoted, a college professor, find it yourself first, if possible. There's nothing more irritating than to have somebody ask you for something that they can find in the phone book. I'm sorry, but I could really use my time a lot better than teaching you how to use the phone book.

What kinds of things would make you feel "Okay, it was reasonable for them to call me about this?"

There's plenty. I'm happy to talk with people about other sources, or other ways to look at the material. Sometimes people will ask, "Was there any more? Can you give me more information about this company?" or "What do you think really happened here?"

Sometimes I get those calls and I can tell that the person's a stock speculator. I say, "It's all in the story. I can't help you get rich, I'm sorry." On the other hand, if it's somebody saying, "I'm really fascinated with this company's story and I want to know if you really think … " If someone is sincere, and if their questions are interesting, it goes a long way.

Sometimes I share back information with reporters. If they've quoted someone, and I've just talked to that person and found out that he's changing jobs, I can share that. Or I can give the reporter a great source that I found. Is that kind of thing useful to you?

That kind of payback is a good thing to do. That trading is wonderful.

Are there times when you just find it really difficult to go to the phone? Have there been situations where you thought, "Uh-uh, I don't want to make this call," or where you experienced a lot of rejection or frustration? Or is that something that you just accept as part of the job?

It's not uncommon at all to need to talk to people and find out they're really not interested in talking to you. When a reporter calls you, it's usually not good. For instance, I did an immense piece on silicone breast implants. One of the main researchers on the implants is Louise Brinton at the NIH National Cancer Institute. Brinton had been viciously attacked by the implant companies and the people that defend them. She was accused of bias and she was cited in the *Washington Times* as a biased researcher. I really wanted to get her view, so I called her, and she didn't want to talk to me. She had already had too much exposure, she felt, and there was no profit in her in talking to me. I finally convinced her that, if anybody was going to give her side and explain why she did the research that she did the way she did it, then it would be me. She consented to be interviewed, and we had a very good conversation in her office.

Another time, I found a wonderful tobacco document about studying kids and their smoking habits. The guy had a distinctive name, Claude Teague. I found Mr. Claude Teague and called him up. He said, "Well, first, I don't want to talk to you about this, and there's nothing in that paper that you've got right. You're reading it wrong." He said, "Why would I talk to you? In what way would it ever profit me to talk to you?" I didn't have a good answer, because in fact I can't imagine why anybody would ever talk to a reporter. But in fact he had just had a back operation and was feeling the medicine, and he kept me on the phone for about thirty minutes, and we had a good conversation, and I quoted him in the story.

What are the characteristics of a good researcher? How is it that you're able to get through to people and have them open up to you?

I have no idea. As I said, one of the things that people seem to like about dealing with me is that these are conversations. If I'm doing it right, they are more likely to be at ease. Another thing is that I do my homework. So by the time I talk to them, I tend to know things. Somebody will occasionally say, "That's really good"—they're favorably impressed by the kinds of questions I'm asking. Doing your homework goes a long way. If you've done your homework, it shows, and if it shows, then the person's going to stay on the line.

On top of that, I will shamelessly use the law degree. If I'm talking to a lawyer and they say, "This is a pretty difficult concept for a nonlawyer; I'm not sure you're going to get this," then I'll say, "My law degree is only from a state school, but I think I can keep up."

I talked to Bill Gates once. I've interviewed him several times, but this one time, he said, "Well, I'm not really sure how technical you are," which is about as severe an insult as he can levy. It's his way of saying, "I realize you're an idiot; you probably don't understand what an idiot you are." And then he went into some description of whatever, and it wasn't even all that technical. It was his way of putting me in my place. And in fact I held up my end of the conversation; it was as pleasant as these things can be.

Are there any legal or ethical aspects that you're particularly concerned about in terms of going to primary sources, presenting yourself to people, interviewing them, or using the information you get from them?

No, I don't really see any of those as big issues. You've got to be honest, you've got to tell people what you're doing, do what you tell them you're going to do, and represent what they say accurately. If you do all that, and if they say something libelous, then you have to remember that printing it will be libelous. Well, that ain't brain surgery.

How about privacy issues?

In the Kaczynski case, there were privacy issues that came up. Ted would hitchhike a ride into town on the postal truck and spend hours at the local library, and the FBI and other folks wanted to know what he was reading. I called the librarian and talked with her about "Did he come in?" and "Did he spend time there?" and I said, "Look, I'm really sorry, but I have to ask this question. What did he read?" I talk to ALA (American Library Association) [6] people all the time, and I know their codes of ethics. But if she was willing to tell me, I was going to write it down, because that's my job. She said, "I can't tell you that, that's private." I said, "God bless you." But, you know, I had to ask.

This has been wonderful, John. You've been just a peach. Are there any final things that you'd want to tell somebody about going to the source or using primary research?

I think what we said early on is key—there's nothing like holding it in your hand. And you've got to go to the best evidence. You've got to find out what that is and get it, wherever it is.

You can use online sources to validate primary information—for example, to recheck what someone told you in an interview—and, at the same time, you can use your primary sources to validate the information you've found online.

It really does go both ways. And you can sort of backstop people. If you've talked to somebody, you can see how they've been treated in other articles. You can see what they have told people in the past. But you've got to think about what you're getting, evaluate the source, and know whether you're doing the best that you possibly can.

Super Searcher Tips

➤ People are still better than machines, but people can be augmented by machines in interesting ways. Everyone I talk to now says, "Read this on my Web site. I said it better there." It's not true. They said it more fully there, more clearly there, but live people tell better stories.

➤ I tend to start my online searches broad, because if you do, serendipity works. As you develop your skills, you find that there's room for the unexpected.

➤ You can find out a lot by reading primary documents yourself—the vocabulary that people use, leads to follow up, side effects you hadn't thought about. If you read a technical paper that's written well and you can actually understand what's being said, that person's like gold— call him up.

➤ If you have an unusual term or name, a search engine is a good place to start. For information from an organization or government agency, try drilling down through Yahoo!. For phone numbers, I like Switchboard.

➤ When calling reporters for information, the first question you ask is, "Are you on deadline? Is this a good time?"

➤ I approach interviews as conversations, and if I'm doing it right, people are more likely to be at ease. If you've done your homework it will show, and the person's going to stay on the line.

➤ You've got to go to the best evidence. Find out what it is and get it. It might be online or it might not.

➤ Be honest. Tell people what you're doing, do what you tell them you're going to do, and represent what they say accurately. If you do all that, and if they say something libelous, then you have to remember that printing it will be libelous.

Joe Flower

Researching the Future

Futurist Joe Flower, author of *Prince of the Magic Kingdom: Michael Eisner and the Re-Making of Disney* (John Wiley & Sons, 1993), and co-author of *Age Wave: The Aging of America* (Bantam Books, 1990) and *China's Futures* (Jossey-Bass Inc., 2000), is founder of What If ..., an educational and communications firm in Larkspur, California.

Photo by Joey Tranchina

bbear@well.com
www.ImagineWhatIf.com

You have an incredibly varied background— author, journalist, speaker, futurist. You've written about everything from the Disney kingdom to HMOs and growing new hearts. Can you tell me about how you got where you are today and how all your roles fit together?

I prepared for my background as a health-care futurist and journalist and author of books by taking a degree in poetry. I have a master's degree in creative writing and world literature from San Francisco State, and I must say that very little of what I do now has anything to do with that.

I got into what I do now by marrying into it. I married a woman who took a job with an association of hospitals. Having a degree in creative writing and world literature, you can imagine that I was desperately looking for some way to make a living. She suggested that their journal might need some writers and they might actually pay some money for it, which turned out to be true. I've written for that journal now for almost twenty years.

From being a health-care journalist, I graduated during the 1990s to being a health-care futurist; that is, going out and speaking and writing from a point of view about the future of health care, rather than simply reporting on it.

You have dealt with a number of other areas over the years. Did you just branch out from that one niche of reporting?

It sort of went the other way. When I first began writing, I pretty much wrote about anything that people would pay me to write about. I used to do some sports reporting; I wrote about the L.A. Rams cheerleaders. I did some travel reporting; I went to Tahiti, I reported on the people who make totem poles on the islands off British Columbia. I did business writing. But eventually I began to narrow down the areas that interested me most. I had had enough success that I was able to pursue the areas that fascinated me.

What kinds of projects do you mostly do today?

I work with my wife Patrice Guillaume in our business, which is called "What If . . ." because it's about imagining and stepping into new futures. About eighty to ninety percent of what we do is in health care. We also do some general futures work, mostly in high technology. In the last few years I have edited and co-authored two books for the Global Business Network [56, see Appendix], one on the future of China and one on the future of Japan, both of which had some high-tech elements to them. But they were really broad-focus futures books on those two cultures. And I do some general futures writing, especially about high technology.

I know you do hands-on—or "eyes-on"— research, where you physically go and look at

facilities and exhibits, as well as doing interviews, both on the phone and in person. Do you also look at primary documents, things that you might get with a Freedom of Information Act request or by digging in archives yourself?

Most of the work I do now, because it's futuristically oriented, requires interviewing people, looking at Web sites, and going places where I'm invited. I used to do a number of things that were much more investigative. I first started out in the area of business writing, where you have to be very careful about what you're saying because it affects many people's jobs and the future of their company and such.

Then I did some sports writing, which generally does not have that attitude. Sports writing has a fairly devil-may-care attitude about research, but I didn't know this. On my very first sports article, about a football owner in Canada, I went to all seven regional law courts in the Vancouver metropolitan area and looked up the man's name in discovery proceedings, just as a matter of course, to see if there were any proceedings about him. I discovered, among other things, a palimony lawsuit settlement. It was very detailed and it included a gag agreement where the woman agreed to be silent about it. But I noticed her lawyer had not agreed to be silent about it, so I called him up and interviewed him.

Perfect. That actually brings us to one of my main questions: What do primary sources provide that you can't get online?

One of the important things to realize is that different people absorb information in different ways. Some people absorb information very well by going to a class or reading a book. Other people really have to have their questions answered; they have to have a live person that they can talk to and slow down occasionally and ask, "Well, what's that mean?"

It's important, if you're doing a lot of research, to recognize the easiest path for you to understand something. There's actually an enormous amount of information that you can get publicly, by reading the annual reports of a company or its quarterly securities documents. But for some people, it's very difficult to do this. It's not necessarily about "do you know the terms?" You could get a little book that brings you up to speed on business terminology—for instance, I have one called The Instant MBA, or something like that. But for some people it just goes right in the eyeballs and drains out the ear and does not stick. They would do better if they found somebody who understood the company, say for instance a stock analyst, and said, "I read through the 10-Qs, and I read through the annual report, and I just didn't get it. Tell me what's really going on." They will be able to absorb better that way.

Some people can look at a primary document like a discovery proceeding or some inside memo from a company, and be able to read between the lines and see what's going on there. Other people can look at the same document and it just washes right over them. My advice to people who are doing research is "Don't swim upstream. Recognize what you're really good at."

A lot of it is about the personal style of the researcher, what works best for you. In order to know that, you have to try out a lot of different styles. I have found over time that I can do the primary document thing, but I really absorb information better if I talk to someone. So, in the health-care field, for instance, at conferences, I always go to the trade floor. I wander around the exhibit floor, and anything that I don't totally understand, I go find somebody and ask, "Can you tell me what this is?"

For example, I recently did a fifty-year forecast of the influence of technology on cardiology. I have to admit, at the beginning, I didn't know much about present cardiology technology. So it's very useful for me to wander around the trade floor and see something that looks like a transistor radio but about one-eighth the size, and go over to someone and say, "Excuse me, what is this? Oh, that's a defibrillator. And what does it do?"

The key here is, a very important tool for me is admitting my own ignorance, which is not easy for me. I like to feel like I know everything. Feeling that I know everything is a tremendous barrier to my learning anything. So I have to tell myself over and over again, go ask what it is, even if I think I know what it is, and see if they tell me anything new. And very often they do.

While we're talking about that hands-on, being-there experience, what else do you look for, what do you pick up, in wandering around a trade show or an exhibit?

Going to a trade show gives you an overall gestalt of the industry, which is hard to get anywhere else. For instance, last fall I was invited to Canada to speak about health at a public safety convention. Of course, health and safety are related, but the exhibit floors were totally different. When you plunge into this world of public safety, what they're selling is traffic cones, and the lights on top of police cars, and loudspeakers, and all the apparatus of being a policeman or a fireman. Talking to the salesmen and other people wandering around the exhibit floor, you get a feeling for the industry as a whole, what their concerns are, what's of interest to them, and what's on their radar, which you would not always see from the outside.

Absolutely. You had mentioned that in addition to picking up literature and so on, you also tend to take either a digital camera or a video camera with you.

I do this for two reasons. One is that a picture can say a thousand words. Often it's much easier to remember something you've seen if you have a visual note on it. Frequently, if I have a conversation with someone, I will take their picture. I have a little digital camera that's easy to carry around in my pocket and I take their picture so I can connect their name with a face. You can attach notes to the picture in the computer, saying this is doctor so-and-so who said such-and-such.

The other reason is that, as a speaker, I often want to display something in my talk. Recently I went to a hospital that I had heard had converted their imaging center so that it looked like a collection of beach cabanas. And it was true. It was Sunday, they were closed, but I just walked right in, whipped out my camera and started talking pictures. A janitor came by, asked what I was doing, I told him, he said, "Oh," and walked on.

Had you gotten permission to do that, or did you just think, "I'd like to go see this," and off you went?

I didn't get permission because I hadn't known I was going to be in that town, but I often visit an institution that I've read or heard about. I call up the communications officer and say, "I'm so and so. Could I have a tour? I'd like to see such and so, I've heard such and so." And they often will arrange a tour. I bring along my camera and take some snapshots.

Do they mind that or are they generally fine with it?

Well, keep in mind the kind of work I do. I'm a health-care futurist. Pretty much everything I say is positive. I'm not an investigative reporter. I'm not trying to turn somebody inside out. I'm generally showing that they're doing this wild, interesting new thing in such-and-such a place. I'm almost always helping the people I'm interviewing. I'm helping them explain themselves to the world.

When you go to exhibits or trade shows, do you collect the lists of speakers or exhibitors in case you ever need contacts in that area?

I do, but I find that I don't use them. I work best with personal contacts that I've made myself. If I talk to somebody, I'll take their business card and I'll remember them. I may call them up and ask them further questions, and they'll turn me over to someone else. I don't tend to whip out a list from a conference and start to cold-call everybody on the list.

So you make a personal contact, and they refer you on.

Some people are better than others at cold-calling strangers. I sometimes do this—and let me give you the quintessential case. I once wrote a fictional story about terrorism in which somebody sneaked atom bombs into the U.S. in suitcases. In order to make this credible, I needed to know how small you could really make a suitcase nuclear weapon. This was way before the Web. There was no way to go on the Web and find out how to make an atom bomb. I thought, who would know this? Who has nuclear weapons? Well, the Army. Okay, I looked up U.S. Army in the phone book, and I found the nearest Army base over in the Presidio in San Francisco. It had a general information number and I just dialed it and asked the general information person there, "Could you give me the Office of Nuclear Research?" I just made it up, threw in the word nuclear. And she said, "The Office of Nuclear Research? Oh, could that be the Agency of Nuclear Investigations?" She came back with a very similar title.

I said, "Oh right. Now is that, I'm trying to remember, is that Colonel Johnson still there, or is it that new guy?"

And she said, "Well, the commanding officer is Colonel Robert Wendsmore."

"Oh, very good, very good. So what's that number?" And she gave me the number. I called the number and said, "Is Bob in?"

And the secretary said, "Uh, Colonel Wendsmore?"

"Yes, is Colonel Wendsmore in?"

And she said, just a moment. And then I was on the phone with Colonel Wendsmore. And when I got to Colonel Wendsmore, I confessed completely. I had done all that just to get on the phone with the right person.

I said, "I'm writing a short story. I've got this terrorist carrying around a nuclear weapon in a suitcase and I have to know, is this totally insane or could this be true?" And he said, "Well, that's interesting, let me see here." And I hear him pull some reference work down off a shelf. He found the minimum critical mass of plutonium, and it was only thirty-eight pounds.

And I said, "Well, you'll need more than just the plutonium, right?"

And he said, "Oh, there's the trigger mechanism. I think the minimum weight you could have for a suitcase nuclear weapon would be about seventy-five pounds."

"Well, that's carryable. And how big would this be?"

"It would be like one of those big Samsonites, you know, like people take on airplanes. The big kind."

"And with this you could blow up San Francisco?"

"No, but you could wipe out Candlestick Park."

"Thank you very much, Colonel Wendsmore."

So I tend to get my information best person-to-person, if I can find the right person. I had a question on linguistics a while back and we called up a professor at Berkeley. We looked up U.C. Berkeley and found a professor of linguistics and called him and asked him a question. Sometimes I have to go through primary documents to find out who that person is. In Canada I found that lawyer for the palimony case, and I got most of my information about the case from the lawyer, once I located him.

That brings us to the next point, which is, how do you integrate your primary and your secondary research? Do you begin with people, or with the Web, or with printed documents?

My favorite sources are people, and they quote various figures and facts. Then I get them to send me stuff to make sure I got it right—what the number was that they'd said, and where they got it from. Often they'll have an article that they can send me, especially in the medical area. Very often now people send me PowerPoint presentations, or they refer me to their Web site on which there is an article that I can download.

I go to the people and the people refer me to articles. The thing is, there is so much, especially in today's information environment where it's very easy to get to things like articles and public records through the Web, that I find I am actually turning more to the people, because you need them as a filtering mechanism.

So you tend to start with people.

People are where I start because, even if what I need to know is much more than I can get from any one person, they act as a filter. With cardiology, for example, I was looking for a book to teach me what all the terms were, all the basic ideas of cardiology. I needed to start from scratch. One of the questions I asked people was, "What should I read just starting out? Is there a primary text?" I found out that there were indeed a couple of primary texts. One person I talked to was the publisher of the books that other people had said I should read. He said, "We'll send you a couple gratis," and they actually sent me those basic texts on cardiology.

So when you start with people, they lead you to the print documents or Web sites that you need to look at. Do you find this more efficient?

My experience in going directly to primary sources myself, without anyone steering me, is that I can easily get lost. Especially if it's a field that I'm not familiar with. This goes way back into the '80s; it's one of the things I had to learn slowly. I did an article once on bankruptcy, and I tried to go first to things like the bankruptcy law and court filings. I spent a lot of time because I didn't know what I was looking for. Finally, I cornered one of the bankruptcy attorneys and asked him to have lunch with me and tell me what I should find out.

My first tendency is to go to people as well. I've learned to curb that a bit and to check the Web or other sources for background. But I find, too, that people can be very good guides into whatever new world you want to enter. When you're going to have an interview with someone, are there particular things that you do to prepare?

I try to be as knowledgeable as I can about what I'm asking about and who I'm talking to. I occasionally get tripped up on that. I remember one occasion in which I interviewed somebody who is now in the Hall of Fame as a catcher. Because I had just been turned over to him by somebody else, and sports was really not my field, I had no idea who he was. And I asked some questions that turned out to be embarrassing, which revealed my ignorance.

I try to know as much as I can about who they are, and as much as I can about the field, so that I can ask intelligent questions. Then I usually prepare a few questions. I don't make up a long list, because I find that I don't get to everything on a long list. If I have more than four or five questions for an interview, that's too many. I'll get sort of confused as to what's most important. So I winnow it way down.

The point of having four or five questions is to make sure that you cover all your major points. That you don't hang up the phone and go, "Oh my gosh, I never asked him about such-and-such." Because usually, if you're asking somebody, with true curiosity, about a subject they are passionate about, they can go on forever.

That's what makes it so much fun. That's what makes it a delight each time you talk to someone who is really good at what they do, or really loves what they do.

Right. In my line of work, and I think probably in the line of work of most people doing research, the people you're talking to are not famous, are not accustomed to being interviewed, and don't have pat answers to things. To them it's flattering, finding somebody who actually knows what they do and wants to talk to them. If they have time, they usually like trying to explain what they do, how they do it, and why it's better than something else.

When you say you learn as much as you can about the person and who they are, how do you do that?

The first thing I do nowadays is put their name into a Web search engine. Even if they don't have a Web site or haven't put up anything directly on the Web, if they're at all prominent in their field there will be mentions by other people, and you'll get a general sense of their universe.

Do you have favorite search engines?

I use Copernic [34], which is a search client. It lives on your computer, and it goes out and searches all the other big search engines out there. The advantage of this is that it keeps the search on your computer. If you start researching a particular subject, you set up a search and it brings you back twenty sites, or however many you want. I find that it's very good at bringing back things that are relevant to what I'm looking at. You can edit the search and throw out the ones that aren't relevant. You can save the search, so that you can continue to go back to it and refine it and add other sites about that particular subject until you're done with the subject, and then you can get rid of it.

Do you tend to start narrow or broad when you're researching a subject on the Web?

With a general Web search like that, I try to narrow it as much as possible, because you know how Web searches are. You get back a quarter of a million documents. So I try to think what two or three words I could put in that will effectively triangulate what I'm really asking about.

When you actually start interviewing someone, are there particular approaches that you tend to use, or does it change from person to person?

I'm very straightforward. When I'm doing a more formal interview, I try to arrange it ahead of time, and tell them why I'm calling and what the publication is, and how much of their time I think I'll need. This is very important to people, how long you need to talk to them. If they come back and say, "Well, could you show me some articles?" I'll refer them to my Web site or a Web site where I have published something. Sometimes people want to know what I'm going to ask about, and I'll give them a general idea of that. I don't send them questions ahead of time, because I don't want canned answers.

Do you ever have to deal with sensitive issues, and how do you handle them?

They do come up sometimes. They used to come up more when I did more investigative work. But they even come up sometimes in futures work because people criticize each other's methods. They'll say, "Oh, such-and-so won't work." I always frame it in terms of what other people say. This is a classic journalistic technique. I say, "Well, you know, Dr. so-and-so has been known to say that your technique is not going to work because of such-and-so. What do you say to that?" They always have a response. I make it clear that I'm not questioning whether they know what they're doing.

Oh, heaven forbid—"I think whatever you do is marvelous."

Sure, I think pig hearts are going to work perfectly. That's an example of where there's been controversy recently. I interviewed a doctor who is ready to put pig hearts into humans. The literature shows that this is probably fairly safe. There have been studies done, but there are other people who have actually shut down lines of research into putting pig hearts into humans because they're afraid there might be viruses brought over from pigs. It's a matter of some controversy, so I asked him, "What do you think about these other people who have said that you really shouldn't be allowed to do this?"

And you find that that works? That that's a good tool for getting them to respond?

Right. Because I don't want to soften the attack. I want the attack to be as sharp as possible in order to bring out the sharpest possible response. On the other hand, I don't want it to be an attack from *me*.

Do you have any other hints or keys to your success in getting information?

Be nice. There is an area of journalism that has developed over the last twenty years that seems to equate aggression in tone and manner with being serious about collecting information. That may actually be true for some very minor fraction of investigative journalism. For the most part, though, it's a matter of being straightforward, nice, and persistent. If someone doesn't want to talk to you, that's fine, there are almost always other people to talk to. Be nice to secretaries, to assistants, to publicity people, even though it's sometimes hard. Anybody who stands as a gatekeeper or who may possess knowledge of who else you should talk to may be able to help you in some way. You really have to be gentle and sweetly persistent.

Yes. Getting through gatekeepers is an incredible skill.

The fellow whom I eventually unmasked in the palimony case had become famous at that point because he was a Canadian millionaire buying American sports teams. It turned out, as I found out from his secretary, that I was competing with *Time* magazine, *People*, and *Sports Illustrated*. I was working for a much more minor publication at the time, called *Sport*. But I kept calling. I was ready to go to Vancouver and interview the man, but I wanted an appointment. I didn't have a big enough budget to go up there without an appointment. Eventually I was calling every half-hour. It was just, "Hi, this is Joe, do you think he can talk to me yet?" I'd joke around with the secretary, so my calls were not irritating. My calls were very short, but I was constantly there. Finally I got a call from him. He was in San Francisco and would I come to dinner with him? And I know that he did not, in fact, talk to any of the other reporters. He took me to dinner with friends, and then I went up to Vancouver, and he drove me around town and gave me the whole story, and that's an example of getting through the gatekeepers with sweet persistence.

Sweet persistence is a great term. How about the use of silence when you're interviewing? Do you tend to use silence as a tool at all?

Not as much as I should—I like to talk. It can be very useful. If it's a somewhat adversarial situation, and someone gives you a response that seems evasive or insufficient, simply sitting and looking at them can be very effective.

That's assuming you're sitting across from them. Do you find any difference between phone interviews and in-person interviews?

I don't have a ready answer for that. I try to interview people in person when I can, when I have the budget to go see them or when they're here in the Bay area. But most of my interviews are done over the phone. I've talked to probably between three and five thousand people in the last twenty years.

I noticed that number somewhere and I thought that certainly qualifies you as an expert on interviewing! So you don't find any particular difference in the dynamics, or in your approach, whether you're talking to them on the phone or in person?

When you're there in person you can do a bit more in terms of personal charm. Like when I went to interview Willie Brown, who is now the mayor of San Francisco, about his clothes. He was then the Speaker of the California Assembly. It shows how little I knew Willie Brown at the time, but I thought he might actually be offended by my picking such a trivial thing to interview him about. But I was on assignment for *GQ*. Can you imagine how Willie Brown, a well-known clothes horse, would respond to *GQ*?

I lived in the Bay area for twenty-five years, so I know exactly what you're talking about. You made his year!

Oh, absolutely. I did one important thing. I maneuvered to get his last appointment for the day. I had an appointment at something like four o'clock in the afternoon. The reason was that that's an appointment that's expandable. His secretary would only give me a half an hour to talk to him, and I wanted more. He talked to me for two and a half hours and rescheduled his flight to L.A. so that he could show me more of his clothes.

This was years and years ago, back in the '80s sometime, but there was the article in *GQ* about Willie Brown and his clothes, and the picture that ran with it showed him wearing a full-length black leather coat with a fur collar, standing outside the state capital.

Is there any difference in researching the future as opposed to researching the present or the

past? Do you need to understand someone's thought processes or rationale more deeply?

In researching the future, the main difference is being able to cut through the bullshit to discern what might really be important. I find that especially true in health care. That doesn't come so much from techniques of research as it does from a familiarity with history and with systems dynamics. Things like chaos theory, conflict theory, and adaptive systems theory. History gives you a sense of how things move and change, and how they often don't change, and what influences that. Systems theory lets you see what can disturb a much larger universe than itself, and why that happens or doesn't happen.

I'm constantly deluged by people who have some new medical device or some new business plan that is going to revolutionize health care. At first, I tended to get taken by these. Now I have a much more developed sense of "Gee, I've seen this particular type of thing a number of times before, and it hasn't revolutionized health care before, so what's different about this?"

How do you evaluate the veracity or the reputation of the people that you interview?

One thing I do is I ask other people. Just because somebody else says, "Well, so-and-so is full of hype" doesn't mean that it's true. But it does help place them in the industry. For instance, with the pig hearts, there is more than one guy, but there is one in particular at the Mayo Clinic Xenotransplant Institute, Dr. Jeffrey Platt. He is outside of the mainstream. I know this because I've talked to a number of cardiologists.

In most industries there is some way of evaluating somebody's position by how many articles they have written in the journals, who their co-authors are, who quotes them in the professional literature or the trade magazines, for instance.

What about your own sense of them as you're talking to them?

I look for a certain amount of self-consistency, and I look at what sort of claims they're making. When people make very broad claims for themselves, usually that raises an eyebrow. But the reporter has to be very careful. A case in point—Al Gore was quoted as saying he invented the Internet. I'm just guessing, because I'm completely outside the loop on this, that he was misquoted by a reporter who did not understand the Internet and the process of how it came into being. Al Gore was chairman of the subcommittee that brought out the legislation that enabled the Internet to come into being. So for him to say he had a hand in making it happen is perfectly legitimate, but he was quoted in a way that made him sound like a fool.

So even with "direct quotes" you have to be careful. There's the primary source, what the primary source actually said, what the primary source really meant, what the interviewer heard or inferred, and whatever version you get to see in print. I suppose that's one good reason for going back to the primary source, to the source's mouth, yourself.

One way I differ with the industry practice is that I am perfectly open to reading quotes back to people and allowing them to make corrections under certain circumstances. When I'm doing an adversarial piece in which I have somehow caught somebody dead to rights, and then he comes back and says that he didn't really say that, I will say, "I'm sorry, but you did say that, and it was under this agreement, there was no agreement that I keep it out of print, and I have it on tape." I have done that, though more in the past than now.

But in general, my work is not adversarial. We're just trying to help people explain themselves to the world. I'm perfectly happy to read people's quotes back to them, because sometimes I miss something. I have had very few problems doing this. Almost always, if somebody wants to change something it really is to make it better, to enhance it, or to enlarge on what they've already told me.

For one particular type of article, I do send the entire piece to the person. That is where I've done an interview with them, then edited out my questions and edited down their responses, and it'll be called something like "A Conversation with So-and-So." It just sounds like them talking. The article is almost completely in their words, but because I have edited their words, I send it to them to make sure that it still says what they believe themselves to have said. It's supposed to be a distillation of their thoughts.

I know that you've done many long interviews with top business thinkers.

I've done this for almost twenty years with the *Health Forum Journal* [64], which is the publication I mentioned earlier. The people I interview like the finished product a lot. A number of them, if you were to ask them to send you something that shows what they think, will send you my article. Usually when we interview people, it's to put their thoughts into the larger context of an article about some theme or subject area. But these features I do are really about them, so I represent them as faithfully as I can, using their language and their way of thinking.

After almost twenty years, are there still calls that you find difficult to make, or are you so inured to it by now that anything goes?

On the one hand, I can call almost anybody and ask them almost anything. On the other hand, I do tend to shy away from calling somebody who doesn't know me or might not understand why I'm calling them, especially if I don't have an assignment. It's one thing to call somebody saying, "This is Joe Flower, I'm a reporter for *Esquire* magazine," or "I'm a reporter for the

L.A. Times," or whatever. It's quite something else to call them and say, "This is Joe Flower, I'd like to talk to so-and-so because I'm curious."

How do you handle that? Do you just not make the call, or do you try to find some other way to make contact with that person?

I do generally make the call. You know, it's very funny, I've been doing this for so long, I've interviewed so many people, but I do still kind of hesitate to pick up the phone after all these years. I have to kind of get myself up for it. I feel that way more often nowadays, because more often nowadays it's for a talk or for a column, so I really am calling to check something out. And then I have to explain what a "health futurist" is, because most people have never heard the term. A lot of people have barely heard the term "futurist."

Have you got a particular success story where interviewing a primary source was really key?

There was one recently. I was putting together a talk about how you can profit by using better techniques for satisfying your customer. Hospitals are a primary audience for me, and hospitals are in deep financial trouble. Many of them are facing bankruptcy. So here I am preparing a talk about how to treat your customers better, knowing that much of my audience is likely to think, "Well, that's easy for you to say if you've got a bunch of money in the bank, but we don't have wiggle room."

I called up a guy whom most of my audience would despise. He was a doctor who built a private for-profit hospital to compete against the big hospitals in his area. He has such a beautiful facility that he actually has people writing him to ask, "Could we please come stay at your place, even though we don't need surgery. It's so nice. Can we come there for vacation?" He is doing very well financially. I mentioned to him what most of my audience would think of him, that they would think bad thoughts.

And he came back and gave me a quote saying they would do very well to take a look at what he's doing as a business, because it's people like him that are going to eat them for lunch. That's one of the ways you get good quotes—you represent to them the other people who think they're crazy, and you let them answer that. So now when I give the talk, I take that quote and I put it in bold, full strength, and I read it out to them word for word.

That technique worked beautifully there. The quote certainly has a punch. How about any horror stories or cautionary tales where you were making a call or interviewing someone or using some technique and it didn't work?

One of the reasons why I am so careful about telling people ahead of time how the information they give me is going to be used, what it's for, what the ground rules are—why I try to anticipate any possible problems—is because I have had experiences where lack of clarity made things very sticky and very difficult.

I used to do a series in which every year a trade association picked the up-and-coming young executives in the healthcare area. One person was picked as an extraordinary hospital executive, and she was, because she had done a remarkable turnaround on this particular facility. I spent a day with her, she gave me complete access, and I looked at all the documents. It turned out that it wasn't just a financial turnaround. She had done a great turnaround partly because the facility had been extremely sloppy in terms of things that make a big difference clinically, like whether you read the medical record before you give somebody their medicine. They had really fallen down on the job in terms of clinical quality, and there had been some deaths that were very questionable. There were things that could have gotten the hospital's licenses yanked, and actually did get the licenses of several nurses yanked.

We had no agreement ahead of time about how I was going to report this. The problem was, how could I say she had done a great turnaround if I couldn't say what she had done a turn-around from? It ended up as a three-way screaming match between myself, the editor, and the subject of the interview. It was supposed to be a very laudatory interview. We ended up coming up with some compromise language, but the article was much gutted from what it had originally been.

The lesson I take away from that is not that I should necessarily have been allowed to print all that private information, but that I should have set it up much better ahead of time with the subject. That way we could have had more clarity and come to an agreement about what I could write about and how I could characterize it.

A counter-example of that happened in about the same period, which was back in the early '80s. I did a series of articles about gays in business, trying to counter the then-current stereotype that gays are ineffectual, inconsequential people. In fact, I interviewed people who ran savings and loans, who owned construction companies, who had chains of theaters—very substantial business people. Some of these people were still, at that point, deeply in the closet, including one man who was the managing partner of one of the largest law firms in the country.

I wanted to be able to give a personal portrait, but if you give enough of a personal portrait, you identify the person. So we went through extensive negotiations as to how he would be characterized, what sort of adjectives I would use, what I would say about what his office looked like, his background, and that sort of thing. And it went well. The story was really well done and the people quoted were happy with it. It made its point and it was factually correct, even though it was very carefully edited.

What do you like best about doing primary research, about being able to deal with people directly?

I like the permission it gives me to talk to anybody I want. I'm a very curious person and this gives me cover to walk up to almost anyone and say, "Could you explain this to me? How come this is happening?"

Let me put you in the other seat for a moment, when you act as a source. Do you mind when people call you for quotes or information?

It's happening more these days because I'm being quoted as a health-care futurist. I like people quoting me as a source. However, it depends on the person. For instance, our conversation is very free and open because you came to me through a trusted pathway, and so I trust that when you edit this it will make me look smart and not stupid.

But if I don't know them, or the person who referred them to me, I kind of test them out in the course of conversation. Especially when you're talking health care and the future, the caliber of reporters who call me varies extremely. Some don't test out very high on the experience scale; they might be asking me what a chromosome is. With them, I keep it very short. I don't exactly speak in words of one syllable, but I try to think through what I'm saying so that it will not be misconstrued. Not that they are going to twist it in some evil way, but so that what comes out of it will make sense. I will try to construct a quote with them, and avoid saying anything else that might be used in ways that are not conducive to full understanding.

Are there better times or worse times for calling? Do you have any other suggestions or rules for someone calling any reporter or any expert in a field?

It's especially important if you're calling a journalist to ask them, "Is this a good time? Would there be a better time I could call?" Often people who are on daily or weekly deadlines go through rather wild changes of cycle and you can't know from the outside what that might be. If you call some reporters at three o'clock in the afternoon, it's like murdering them, because they may have a three-thirty deadline.

Is it useful if people who call you share back information?

Yes, it is useful. If you call someone who is an expert in a field, especially if they are somebody who makes their living by writing, it's wonderful to offer them information: "Gee, I was just talking to so-and-so, and I've put together this little interview with him. Would you like to see it ahead of publication?"

For instance, recently I was interviewing someone and they were talking about the financial aspects of a hospital. I had just been to a presentation by the Health Care Advisory Board [62], which has an interesting publication on avoiding financial flash points. I offered to send this person a copy. It was a PDF file on my computer, so it was no problem at all. And they were very grateful.

Part of the image people get is that reporting is about dashing in with a microphone and shouting out questions. In reality, almost all reporting is a matter of forming relationships over years and decades with people whom you can go back to and ask basic questions. People you can call up and ask, "What do you know about this field? Who should I talk to?" Basic sources that will guide you further. Every time you do a story, one of your goals should be to cultivate sources that can help you in later stories.

Now I'm putting you in the futurist role. Do you see any changes in technology that are altering or affecting the way we do primary research?

Teleconferencing and video phones are the first things that come to mind. The ability to find out who somebody is on the Web is a big difference, and it means that savvy people expect you to know who they are. For instance, a few weeks ago in Germany, I found myself suddenly in a car with somebody who had been introduced to me as one of the top—and I remember the word was neuro- something but I hadn't caught neuro- what. And this guy says, "Oh, you must come see my institute." And I can't remember what he is, right? Well, I had to ask him, there was no faking it. It turned out he was one of the top neurosurgeons in the world.

As soon as I could get to a computer I did what I would have done if I'd had a chance in the first place: I entered his name in a search engine, and came up with a whole series of references to papers about a very obscure leading-edge type of brain surgery. This would have told me instantly who this person was. As I said, the expectation that you will know who someone is, and why they are worth talking to, will increase greatly.

The ability to talk to somebody face-to-face, even though you're not physically present, is going to be taken as normal within five years. One of the things we've seen over the past decades is the fact that we can record anybody anytime, so misquoting somebody should become a thing of the past. People have the expectation that you're recording them accurately. Digital cameras are becoming so common that whipping out a camera and taking somebody's picture no longer surprises people.

Do you have any legal or ethical concerns in this area, any issues we should be aware of?

It's always important that your ground rules are clear, for both legal and ethical reasons. Whenever I do something adversarial that somebody might have a legal problem with, I always tape-record it. There are rules around tape recording. In California, at least, you have to tell someone if you're tape-recording them on the phone. And I always do. As you, for instance, at the beginning of this conversation, mentioned you were turning on the tape recorder now.

This has actually come up. I did an article years ago about a man whose career was wrecked and his reputation destroyed in a week of articles by a very prominent newspaper, whose name I will not mention because they are also very litigious. I interviewed the head of the editorial board of the newspaper for about an hour and a half, and had him first take me through the politics of his state, and then through many more general questions. He said he would not comment on the case itself, but by starting with how things worked in that state and who knew who, I was able to lead him to a point where he said that he personally knew the person who had fed them all the information for the attack on the subject of my article. He said that that person had visited the editors of the newspaper and that they felt comfortable with him. In effect, these quotes had the editor putting his arms around the source of the attack. I had a tape recorder sitting out on the desk, in full view, while this was going on. The subject of the attack later sued the newspaper for slander. Lawyers for both sides called me up and said, "Those quotes you have in the article, do you have those on tape?" And I said, "Absolutely, and they are not altered by one word."

Apparently this had a great deal to do with the fact that the man won a settlement. This was because I could see ahead of time that this was a litigious situation. People were already suing each other, so I recorded the conversation. If you are doing something that is potentially controversial or litigious, make sure you record it. In business, this could be almost anything; it depends on what area you're working in. But if you quote a CEO of some business saying that his rival's product really doesn't work, for instance, you should have that on tape, because that could send the stock down, it could cost people their jobs.

You need to be thinking of the consequences of what you write.

You do. You need to be very careful about quoting somebody saying anything that is potentially libelous. If you publish a libel, even if somebody else said it, you are potentially at risk. One way around that is to go to the subject of the libel and say, "So-and-so said such-and-such about you, and I'm going to have to put this in the article. What do you have to say?" That will almost always elicit a response. Even the attempt to elicit a response is something of a safety net on your part. But you need to stay very aware of the effects, consequences, and risks of what you do.

Super Searcher Tips

➤   A very important tool for me is my own ignorance. I have to tell myself over and over again, go ask what it is, even if I think I know what it is, and see if they tell me anything new. Very often they do.

➤   In today's information environment, where it's very easy to get so many things like articles and public records through the Web, I find myself turning more to people as sources, because I need them as a filtering mechanism.

➤   When interviewing, try to know as much as possible to be able to ask intelligent questions. I usually prepare a few questions, no more than four or five. With more than that, you can get confused about what's most important.

➤   Sometimes people want to know what I'm going to ask about. I'll tell them in general, but I don't send them questions ahead of time because I don't want canned answers.

➤ With sensitive issues, I frame it in terms of what other people say. "Dr. so-and-so has been known to say that your technique is not going to work because of such-and-so. What do you say to that?" They always have a response. I make it clear that I'm not questioning them, because I want the attack to be as sharp as possible, to bring out the sharpest possible response.

➤ To evaluate people, I ask other people. Just because somebody else says, "He is full of hype," doesn't mean that it's true, but it does help place him in the industry. In most industries there are ways of evaluating somebody's position by how many articles they have written, who their co-authors are, who quotes them in the trade press.

➤ With the growth of the Web, the expectation by people that you know who they are, and why they are worth talking to, will increase greatly.

➤ Almost all reporting is a matter of forming relationships with people who will guide you further. One of your goals for every story should be to cultivate sources that can help you in later stories.

Photo by Tony Sleep

Wendy Grossman

American Freelancer in London

Wendy M. Grossman is a freelance writer based in London, and author of *net.wars* and *From Anarchy to Power: The Net Comes of Age* (New York University Press, 1998 and 2001, respectively).

wendyg@pelicancrossing.net
www.pelicancrossing.net

Can you start by telling me something about your background and how you ended up where you are today?

Really just pure accident. I knew somebody who knew somebody in a company where they needed people. I was a folk singer, then I did a magazine called *The Skeptic* [119, see Appendix], and then I did journalism.

Have you worked in both the States and the U.K.?

I never worked in the States as a journalist. I do interview people in the U.S. all the time, but I didn't live in the States and work as a journalist. And I never had to make my primary living from U.S. publications.

Do you find cultural differences that affect how you interview experts in the U.S. as opposed to

the U.K.? Do you find that, for example, people in the U.S. are more or less formal?

I never think about it. Actually I think there is this great myth that Britain is more formal than the U.S. If anything, Britain is much ruder and more abrupt than the U.S. If an American has to end a phone call quickly, they will want to make you feel good about it. So they'll say something like, "I would love to keep talking to you, but ..." A British person will just say, "Oh, got a meeting, gotta go." Then they're gone. I think there is this very refined British social sense at all times of the class and background of the person you're talking to. But that's a different thing. Americans make much more effort to be polite and grease the wheels.

In a way, for me, it's a big advantage being a foreigner in Britain because no one can really expect me to know my place. That's one reason that I actually try to prevent my accent from slipping, and I wear American clothes. I might do those things anyway, but I also think that they make me look foreign, and that that is an advantage. Because you are a little bit of an outsider.

In the States, if I feel that somebody's not taking me seriously enough, I just drop the fact that I went to Cornell. I never realized until the last five years or so what going to Cornell meant. But it's really noticeable to me that if I'm interviewing somebody from Silicon Valley, and I mention that I went to Cornell, there's a little switch that clicks in a lot of their brains.

And so they respond to you differently?

I think so. They assume that you're intelligent, that you're more on their level. Also, now that I write for publications like *Scientific American*, it makes it much easier.

Do you find that you have to approach people differently in the U.K., as opposed to the U.S.?

I think I'm really the same with everybody. With everybody I talk too much and interrupt. I tailor things a bit, in the sense that

I'm always looking for a personal connection with the people that I talk to. Because I spent a lot of time as a folk singer, I tend to hate being interviewed; I hated being interviewed as a folk singer, anyway. And I hate answering the same ten questions all the time. It's boring and it's pointless, and you want to say, "I answered those ten questions there, go read that." And I know that's not really what journalists want.

What I try to do is entertain the interviewee a little bit, maybe too much. But I actually want them to enjoy the conversation, and I think of it more in terms of having a conversation with people than doing a precise, structured interview where you work out all the questions in advance. The most I'll have is a list of a few topics that I want to make sure get covered. And as I'm talking to them, because my software is sort of outlining software, if something occurs to me that I want to ask, I'll just space down and type in the question, and go right back to where I was taking notes. Then the question is there so I don't forget it, because one of the reasons I interrupt people is that I think of something I forgot to ask.

So you take your notes on computer while you're talking to people?

Certainly if I'm interviewing them over the phone, which is the case most of the time these days. If I go in person I take a tape recorder—actually, these days, an MP3 player with a built-in voice recorder. But I'll take some kind of recording device, and I will take handwritten notes, in case the tape recorder fails completely. I always worry something will go wrong with the tape recorder. The first interview I ever did with anybody at IBM, something went wrong. I can't remember if I forgot to turn it on or the battery went dead or what, but that was awkward, because you really don't want to call the person back and say, "I boobed the tape."

The handwritten notes give you some kind of guide to what order things are on the tape. Also, taking notes is another way that, if they're talking and I think of something else I'd like to ask them, I can jot it down and go back to it, rather than interrupt them.

Do you find differences between doing in-person interviews and telephone interviews?

The problem with in-person interviews is you have to get to them. By the time you've fought through the transport system, or gotten lost in the car because the directions were incompetent, you arrive with smoke coming out of your ears. So in that sense, the phone interview is a little more relaxed.

You mentioned to me at one point that sometimes you just hate calling.

That's true. But I don't mind getting phone calls. I have trouble getting started making phone calls in the morning. And lots of times I just can't stand to pick up the phone. So what I will do is send out email asking people to call me in the morning. And that works, because most of the time my incoming line is open, because I make phone calls on a different line.

I do the same thing, have the incoming line free. And the outgoing line is my fax line as well.

That's exactly what I do, or what I did. Actually, I had a cable line, which is the modem, and the fax line and the outgoing line were the same. And then that line was converted for ADSL, so now the fax line and the ADSL are on the same one, and I've stopped using it so much for voice calls, because when they converted the line they added a very noticeable amount of hiss. So people have trouble understanding what I'm saying, and I have trouble understanding them. There's a lot of attenuation of the signal. Since I'm not using the cable line for the modem anymore, I've switched to making outgoing calls on it.

I love your strategy of sending out email at the end of the day and hoping someone will call you in the morning.

Actually, I did get into a really silly exchange with, of all people, the PR guy for Team Mobile. I emailed him and said, "I'm working on this piece and they'd like some statistics on how your WAP (Wireless Application Protocol) service is going. Could you call me tomorrow when you have a free moment?" And he sends me back a message that says something like, "Our users are using so-and-so many minutes on average a month, and it's up from such-and-so and it's growing. Call me if you want any more information." So I email him back, and say, "Thanks, but I need something else, call me when you have a minute." We go back and forth like this. Neither one of us ever picked up the phone. And I was sitting there looking at this exchange, thinking, "You work for a phone company! Pick up the phone!"

Well, it's nice to know that, even in the phone company, people can't stand picking up the phone some days.

I actually did try phoning him once, and I didn't get through. So after that I said, "Well, I couldn't get through." It just struck me as really funny. I don't know if it was some kind of power play for him, that he had to be called. You do find people who are just too busy, or who are away and don't see their email, or who are out, or just generally inept at returning email.

But a lot of times that tactic is effective for me, because quite often the people I want to talk to are very busy anyway. My phone line is usually open, and I'm home most of the time. It is more convenient for them, because they can call when they're free, instead of my harassing them when they're in the middle of a meeting.

The most organized person I ever interviewed, by the way, was Sherry Turkle [129]. I had made contact by email, and we had arranged an appointment for a time I could call her, which is another very useful thing to do with email.

I don't know who Sherry Turkle is.

She's a psychologist at MIT, and she does a lot on online identity and role-playing. She's very fashionable, also very good and very interesting. I told her that I was writing a piece about educational issues online, and use of technology in education. So I called her at the time she set, and she said, "Now, I've been thinking about what I wanted to say to you," and then proceeded to talk for twenty minutes. She had worked out what she wanted to say and she said it. She was perfectly happy for me to ask her questions, but she basically had organized the whole thing. Having the appointment, she just prepared for it. It was interesting. It was the first time I'd experienced that; it was very efficient.

Do you ever leave voicemail for someone you're trying to reach?

Depends who it is. If it's somebody whose email address I know, and who I know is good with email, I'm more likely to send them an email message saying, "I just tried to call you." I also have a very low patience threshold. British voicemail seems to have these very lengthy instructions. If the instructions start to get at all lengthy I can't stand it and I hang up. Also, you'll get voicemail that says, "I'm out of the office all this week until September 22."

And it's October 10. I know; did they die or just never listen to their own message again? Sometimes the person left the company six months ago, but their voicemail is still there.

That's the problem with voicemail. I suppose we don't really know if somebody's read our email either, but at least it bounces if it can't get through. Sometimes voicemail is very nice if all you want to do is remind somebody of something. But I'm much more likely to use email. I find it quite restful now that the volume of phone calls has dropped.

Of course it depends on what I'm working on. If I'm working on the kind of article I did recently for *In Business*, where you need to talk to thirty-six people about what their WAP services are doing, then your phone is going to be ringing quite a bit. But, you know, I had two phone calls this morning, both from PR people who called up and said, "I'm calling about the press release we sent." When you get thirty of those calls in a day, it's very difficult to do anything else. I said, "Send me the press releases, just don't make the phone calls."

What are your favorite sources for locating experts?

It depends what kind of expert. I recently did a piece on the future of food for *Smart Business*. The editor wanted primary sources. I went to Cornell, where one of my friends runs the Science News Service, so I emailed him. And Bill fixed me up with a guy at Cornell. And then I remembered that, for years and years, for reasons that are not entirely clear to me, I've been getting the *Science News Digest* from Purdue. I dimly remembered noticing that they did a lot of food science. So I went and looked on their Web page, and sure enough, they have a whole division of food people. So I emailed the PR person on the Web site. I said, "Can you fix me up with somebody?" and she did.

At that point I knew there'd be lots of research going on in Britain, too, but I really didn't know where to start. So I called up a friend who works on *New Scientist*, and she made some suggestions. She suggested that I try the food gallery at the science museum, and I did, and I left a message on their answering machine. They never phoned back. And then at some point I emailed the science correspondent of the *Independent* newspaper, because he calls me up and picks my brain often enough that I felt that he owed me one. And he gave me a couple of good leads. And then I did a certain amount of looking around the Web. Once I knew what kinds of terms I was looking for, I started looking up "functional foods" and things like that. Eventually I found enough people.

The one thing I don't use, which kind of surprises me, is ProfNet [108]. I remember ProfNet when it was an independent little service run by a guy on CompuServe [31], and it was really good. But the last time I tried to submit a query to ProfNet, the woman asked me so many questions about it—"Well, we can't post this without knowing what publication it's for"—I don't think the query ever got posted. When I first sent it out, there would have been time to talk to people. By the time she was finished asking questions, it was either the day of the deadline or the day before, and I found the whole experience very unpleasant. My friend Bill is actually on the ProfNet list, because he's in public relations at Cornell. So I'd be more likely to just ask him. I use quite a few friends as contacts.

If you've got personal sources, you go to them, at least to start you off, and then get referrals from them?

Yes. Also, I do a lot of searching on the Web. But for something like the future of food, it was almost too general a topic. Charles at the *Independent* pointed me to some organizations that do food research, and a couple of them called back with useful stuff. Once I had their names, I could look them up on the Web and see what they did, and see what kind of links they had to other people.

But it's fairly rare that I'm actually researching a topic that I know nothing about, which that one certainly was. If I want to figure out something about WAP, one of the first people I'm likely to call is my friend Simon, who founded the first mobile phone magazine in Britain. If I'm writing about privacy, I would probably call my other friend Simon, who is a privacy advocate. Part of the reason these people are friends is that we met at CFP (Computers, Freedom, and Privacy) [25] conferences and we've been hanging around together for a long time. He started out as a source; now he's a friend, too.

So some sources do become friends, or become long-term sources that you can go back to?

Yes, there's been a discussion about that on The WELL [139] recently, whether sources should be friends. I go to CFP every year, and I always get fuel for an entire year's worth of stories from it, because I see what's going on and what people are thinking about and what the new big issues are. There's somebody like Bruce Koball, whom I see every day on The WELL and I see at conferences, and who has been a source I've used in a number of stories. What is he? Is he a friend, is he a virtual friend, is he a source? Who cares? I think when it comes to reviewing people's books, you need to mention how well you know them. Otherwise, it's not that you trust them because they're your friends; they're your friends because you trust them.

That brings up the issue of how you evaluate how trustworthy someone's information is, how good they are as a source.

That can be difficult. I write largely about specialized subjects. The Internet is increasingly mainstream, but topics like Internet policy and culture and developing technologies like WAP are still specialized subjects. Over time, you build up a base of knowledge and a point of view. That helps in evaluating new sources. If somebody new comes along and says, "We're raising thirty-five million pounds because we have cracked direct email marketing"—when you've been on the Net for ten years, you're going to be very skeptical about that. If somebody comes to me and says, "We've figured out this fabulous new cryptographic algorithm," I can call any number of cryptographers whom I've talked to over the years, and ask, "Does this make sense to you, what this person is saying?"

So I think I'm greatly aided in that I do largely specialize. The world I specialize in is growing much bigger very rapidly, but it's still not huge.

With something like that future of food article, did you evaluate based on the people who recommended them to you, or the positions they held, or your internal bullshit meter?

The future of food was very simple, in a way, because everybody tended to say the same kinds of things. If there had been one person standing out saying we're going to be genetically modifying soybeans to … I don't know …

Wash your dishes for you …

Yeah, or something. Everybody was saying that the future of food is these so-called more functional foods, subtle changes like boosting the levels of fiber-enriched milk, and other things that sound frankly revolting. Everyone was talking about the same kinds of things. They were all talking about subtle changes. The farthest-out project I heard about was a project at Cornell to create bananas that can deliver vaccines in the Third World. And that's a really clever project, because there are so many problems in distributing vaccines. And in that case, they're Cornell, so I believe them.

How about using newsgroups or discussion forums?

In one case, I read a particular organization's newsgroup for months, in order to assess what side people were on and what their points of view were. I was keeping an eye on it long before anybody else would even agree there was a story there. I knew enough to know that where there was this kind of rebellious defiance and heated argument going on, sooner or later there was going to be a story.

So in monitoring the newsgroup, you noticed names of people ...?

You notice names, you notice, for example, the guy with the sig file that says "member since 1974," you notice the guy who used to be a member and is trying to do stuff independently on the Net. You see who they are. And you develop over time a sense of who does what. Absolutely.

Is checking newsgroups something that you do frequently for stories, or just once in a while?

At that time—this was in '94, '95—Usenet [133] was the place where stories happened on the Net. Like the Canter and Siegel [22] green card spamming case. I knew about that because I was reading Usenet, and because this stupid commercial message for a green card lottery kept popping up.

Now, unless I know the newsgroup, I'm probably not going to barge in and ask questions. I researched a piece for a tennis magazine recently, about the disappearance of tennis off free-to-air television—essentially free satellite channels—in Europe. I'm interested in tennis, I've read rec.sport.tennis every day for six years. So I felt perfectly comfortable posting a note there saying, "I'm researching this for a story. Can you get tennis where you live, is it a premium channel, do you have to pay extra for it?" I know there are posters from all over Europe in that newsgroup, and that kind of survey can be very effectively done on Usenet.

I also use CIX [28] quite a lot, which is like London's answer to The WELL. Recently I was trying to get Gnutella [57] to work, and I went to a conference called Noticeboard where you just put up a note and people email you answers. So I put up a note saying, "Has anybody here been able to download a file using Gnutella? If so, I'm using this particular software and I can't get it to work. Any pointers would be welcome." Finally one guy emailed me and said, "I'm using the same software you are," and he called me up and made it work.

I've been asked to write a piece about when IT directors started being called chief information officers or chief technology officers. Again, that's the sort of question that makes sense to put in the Noticeboard topic on CIX because a lot of people who specify large systems for companies will read it, and some of them might have an answer.

Would you then follow up and interview them?

It would depend on what they said. I can't think of any other way to start on this topic. I have no idea how you would find out except ask people who work in that field, and they congregate on CIX, so it's a good place to ask them.

You've talked about using stock analysts, for example, for some of the financial pieces you've written. How do you identify and locate analysts?

I swear there's a box on the wall of the London Stock Exchange that tells them all to scatter. It knows what I'm writing about and it tells them all to go to lunch.

I used to write for an investment Web site that had a subscription to Bloomberg [13], and Bloomberg has extensive lists of analysts that are supposed to cover different stocks. If you're lucky, there's a date that tells you the last time each person wrote a report. The lists are always hideously out of date, and half the time the person's gone. But that gives you a place to start.

Usually, the way you find an analyst is to call any of the leading brokerage houses and ask for the research department. You ask for equity research, and tell them what company you're trying to find coverage on, and either they have somebody or they don't. And you go from there. But it's very tedious.

Analysts were the first people I ever interviewed that only have two minutes to talk to you. Writing about computers and the Internet and living in Britain, you get pampered, because companies tend to be rather anxious for coverage, so they will make time to talk to you. With analysts, it's much more, "You know, I haven't got very long." I'd say, "Well, what do you think about this?" And they'd reel something off and hang up.

I went into it thinking that analysts were full of bullshit, and discovered that that wasn't entirely fair. Often, they actually have done quite a lot of research on the companies they cover, and they have reasons for thinking what they do. Even so, sometimes you get off the phone and you think, "This guy is out of his mind." But that's not your responsibility when you're doing that kind of news. A lot of the time they just want an analyst, any analyst. It doesn't matter whether what he says makes sense. They want some expert opinion in the story. It's what one of my editors described as "cover your ass"—they don't want it to appear that the reporters themselves are giving financial advice.

When anybody talks to me now, I take it as sort of a gift. They don't have to spend their time talking to me.

I think we're a little more arrogant than that. The journalists I meet in Britain are a lot more arrogant than that. The attitude is much more, "We're giving you free publicity." There's some give and take. Yes, the guy does not have to spend an hour explaining the finer points of cryptography to you. But on the other hand, if he wants his company in the newspapers, he does at least have to talk to you.

I think the attitude is a little different in the States, where there are so many more media outlets. If you go on a book tour in the States, you could do a different city every day for three months, and do eight interviews a day with local radio, local newspapers, national newspapers, state newspapers, magazines. In this country, you might spend two or three days. There are four big broadsheet national papers, and probably six tabloids, and ten Sunday papers at most, if you include the tabloids. And that's it, you've got the country.

There's a lot more media in the States. The guy doesn't have to talk to *PC Magazine* because he can always talk to *Smart Business*. If he doesn't feel like talking to *Smart Business* he can talk to *Wired* or *Red Herring*. We just don't have that breadth here.

What do you do if someone doesn't want to talk to you? Do you find that less the case in Britain than in the States?

Different people have different attitudes about that. One of the interesting things on CIX is watching some of these technology hacks get really pompous about how important they are. They'll actually take it as a personal insult that somebody hasn't called them back. Whereas my view is, there might be lots of reasons why they haven't called back. They might be busy. It can be very frustrating. But if they really don't want to talk to you … I mean, I'm not an investigative reporter. I'm not in a situation where, if somebody doesn't talk to me, people are going to die. My view is, if they don't want to talk to me, fine. That's their problem. People have a right not to want to talk to you.

How do you handle sensitive issues someone might not want to talk about, something like a negative report that's come out about their company?

I'm usually talking to people about the technology they do, and obviously they're not going to tell you stuff that's commercially sensitive. If somebody is working on something and they're afraid their competitor's going to get hold of it, there's not a lot you can do. You can't make them tell you.

In the financial news that I've been doing recently, the editor might say, "Find out how much funding they're getting and who it's from." Maybe they're not ready to tell you. I never had journalism training, so I don't know how hard you're supposed to push for these things. My view is that if they've said twice that they're not going to tell you, then you should drop it, because what's the point? They don't want to tell you, and they're not going to tell you, and what's the point of trying to trick them into it? All that's going to happen is the next time you want to talk to them, they won't talk to you at all. I don't see the benefit in that, unless there's a really important overriding public interest.

The thing that may actually make me a very bad news reporter is that I tend to think that if they're not going to announce something for two weeks, well, what's the difference? So you'll know in two weeks. It's really not how you're supposed to think if you're doing news.

There are a number of investment sites where you get the impression that they're jumping on every rumor. And I think that's a disservice to private investors because, in general, most of them will be better served by picking investments that make sense in the long term, in which case today's rumor doesn't really matter that much.

It also sounds like you're willing to respect the boundaries of the person you're talking to.

Well, this is a small country. I have this theory that whenever you're on the outside of something, whether it's Hollywood or the technology industry or London's media, it looks huge and impenetrable. But every single one of those is a small subculture. When I came to London, I figured that London's media is a small subculture, there has to be a way in, and all you have to do is find one end sticking out, and follow that. I think that's pretty much true of almost any subculture. Even something as intimidating as Hollywood is ultimately a small subculture. If you write about the Internet or write about technology in Britain, you are essentially living in a small town.

And this is my second career. I was thirty-six when I started doing journalism. Before that I was a musician. So, having pissed off half the people on the folk scene, it seemed obvious to me that I was going to have to behave differently in a second profession because I probably wasn't going to want to start a third one when I was older than forty.

I'm not saying you should give anybody a soft ride, necessarily. If you think their technology is crap, then you say that. For example, six years ago I reviewed the original version of Autonomy's [11] software. I didn't like it and I said so. This year I interviewed the chairman of the company, Mike Lynch, who is now a software billionaire, and even he agrees that what they do now is much more effective than the way they originally launched the product.

So I think people will accept your not liking what they do or what they say, as long as they feel you're being fair. But in Britain, there's also this kind of culture that is very different from, say, the journalism forum on CompuServe. People are not polite. People are snide, they're malicious, they're cynical, they're rather trenchant in expressing their opinions of other people's postings. They'd be thrown out of the journalism forum if they talked like that in there. And there is a certain element, I think, in British journalism that is much rougher than anything you'll find in American journalism.

I think American journalists go to great pains to establish the facts. For example, British journalists tend to think that Americans are very soft on technology companies, because the American journalists applaud at the end of press conferences and the American journalists are very nice to the people in the companies. But what they don't register is that the American journalist may then go back to his office and spend three weeks digging up whatever dirt there is to be dug, then call the company again and say, "I have the following unpleasant questions for you." Whereas with the British journalists it's more, "Let's see who can ask the nastiest questions at the press conference."

Straight off, go for the jugular.

There's also this sort of culture in British journalism, outside of financial journalism. The business journalists all wear suits. They look like bankers. But in every other area of journalism, the men especially will wear as scruffy clothes as possible, as a way of indicating to the companies that "I'm not your lackey, you can't make me dress up for you." It's very common at technology press conferences here that the male journalists will be wearing torn jeans and tattered t-shirts. PR people have told me that, when they're bringing clients over from the States, they have to sit down with them and say, "I know these are going to look like street people, but they really are journalists. Don't let the clothing fool you." It's this kind of perverse pride: "I'm interviewing the VP of IBM and I don't have to dress."

How have changes in the Net over the last five years, say, affected the way you do primary research?

One of my friends likes to say that the biggest change is that a lot of the information is reliable now. If I'm writing a piece about a discussion over a new government policy, I certainly don't have to take someone's word for what the policy says. I can go read it. A lot of things that would have been prohibitively difficult to do—the amount of time it would take to go to the library and look up the policy, or the amount of money it would take to buy copies—you would have tended not to do. You would have tended to take their word for it.

On the downside, though, the one thing that I do worry about with the growth of the Web is that anything that isn't on the Web is dropping off journalists' radar. It's so much easier to get stuff off the Web, and so much more difficult to go to the library or whatever. So I am somewhat concerned that material that hasn't been digitized and placed on the Web is not going to get included in what people write. It's not going to turn up in searches on Google [58]. It's not going to be linked to. And so, for a lot of journalists, it might as well not exist.

I think it's important to remind people that there's a world beyond online, and you need to be aware of it and utilize it when appropriate.

The difficulty, of course, is simply the volume of work you have to do in order to make a living. And I routinely get assigned stuff that is due in a couple of days. You often don't have the time.

Has the Net changed your research in terms of locating experts outside your area of specialization, or getting background so you can talk to them intelligently?

I wasn't a journalist for very long before the Net came around, and when the Net turned up, it was one of the things I wrote about, so I am a very lazy journalist. But in a way I've turned that into an asset. Nobody is going to shoot me because, for example, in writing about policy about the World Wide Web, I'm not going to the library.

How about for locating experts or finding phone numbers for them?

The first feature I ever wrote was for a magazine called *PC Dealer*. It was about selling computers into the education market in Britain, and I knew absolutely nothing about any of these things. The editor who assigned it had wanted to write that piece for some time but hadn't gotten around to it. So that editor gave me the numbers of the PR people for some companies. I just had to start cold and call these people and say, "I'm writing this feature, can you field somebody for me to talk to?"

The big difference the Web makes is that I rely much less on PR people. Sometimes you go to the Web site and you look up the press release and you call the PR person listed at the bottom of the press release—assuming there is one, because a lot of companies are really stupid about that. And you say, "I want to talk to the person who wrote the report mentioned in this press release." But just as often, you don't have to call the PR people, because you're finding the material you want on the Web site. In one sense, that means you're using a lot more canned material, but you're also looking at what other people are saying about that company or that technology; you're getting input from multiple sources, which tends to minimize the effect of the PR department's spin.

I do think that the barrage of PR material that lands on my doorstep has less and less relevance to anything I do, and in a way that's a good thing. I get more story ideas from items that appear on my mailing lists from people who are actually more like primary sources. I get ideas off The WELL, I use the Net enough that I see things happening. All that has to be good. It means that the stuff that I'm writing is not driven by PR.

You indicated earlier that when you call someone, it's to their benefit to talk to you.

Well, theirs and mine. There was a guy not long ago I thought it would be good to interview. He's a well-known Net loon. He sued Demon Internet [37], the first mass-market consumer British ISP, over a forged posting that appeared to have come from him. The whole thing was ridiculous, and I was really opposed to the way he behaved. Anyway, I suggested to the *Telegraph* that, since he was getting roasted in all the other papers and nobody had actually talked to him, maybe we should do a profile and talk to him about what he did and why. He demanded all sorts of conditions and the *Telegraph* came back and said, "No, look, I'm sorry, we don't do that."

The only reason he considered talking to me was that a couple of our mutual friends were sort of saying to him, "You should talk to some journalist, and if you're going to talk to a journalist, this is the person you should talk to." They apparently told him he was being an idiot. He wanted the right to dictate what we talked about, and he wanted the right to see the article. His attitude was, "Why should I take the time? You'll make money off it, the *Telegraph* will make money off it, I won't get anything out of it, why should I do it?" What we were trying to say to him was, "You've never had a chance to push your side of the story. I disagree with you, you know that up front, but I will be fair." But he didn't go for it.

It was worth a shot, though.

Yes, and as far as I'm concerned, it leaves me free to say what I think of how he behaved. Then if he complains that I haven't given him a chance to defend himself, well, I did, and he didn't take it.

I'm wondering if that would have been a difficult call to make. Do you find some calls or interviews particularly difficult, that you really have to force yourself to do?

People who are really boring. I talked to a journalist once who told me he'd fallen asleep while he was interviewing this guy. I asked him, "Was it a press conference or something?" And he said, "No, one-on-one." And I said, "On the phone?" And he said, "No, in person." And I said, "How did you do that?" And he said, "I was very tired, and he was very boring." I have to confess my instinctive reaction was something like, "Look, it's your job to make the person be interesting."

I mentioned earlier trying to find a personal connection with people. The accents in this country are very identifiable, and I've traveled a lot in Britain, which most people here haven't. So it's quite common that I'll try to place their accent. Most of the time I will have been near where they're from, and I can say something to them about that. If it's an American, it's more likely to be, "What college did you go to?" The point is, it makes people a little more comfortable, you're not quite so alien, once they know that they have some small thing in common with you. You visited their small town.

I talked to a guy on the phone a couple of weeks ago, lovely rich Scottish accent, turned out to be from Paisley. There was a period in the late '70s when I played the Paisley Folk Club every week, and it turned out that he used to hang out at the Folk Club, so we knew some of the same people. So here it's, "Whatever happened to Frasier and Ian Bruce anyway?" That made for a really nice conversation, and he went away happy. It's not my job necessarily to make them go away happy, but it's pleasanter, isn't it?

It's much pleasanter, and I think you get more. People open up much more when they feel a connection with you. I went to the University of Leeds for a while, so whenever I'm talking to someone from England, I have that experience of having lived in one of "Tetley's Houses."

I traveled a lot in the U.S., too. So if somebody mentions a place, chances are I've been there or I've been near there or I have friends there. The other thing is, if all else fails, I drop a mention of either *The Skeptic* or the former folk singer, because people are always curious about that. I find it kind of tedious, because then I have to answer questions about it. But still, people are curious, so then they get curious about me, and they talk to me.

If you can just get the conversation going …

One thing I've realized is that most people are not very good at striking up conversations with strangers. That's why so many conversations at parties are so pathetic. I'm always looking for something that will actually start a conversation as opposed to continue the standard interview. Like the last movie they saw and how annoying it was, or whatever.

When I've asked, "What techniques do you use?" many people, especially journalists,

have said, "Basically I have conversations, I don't do interviews."

That's interesting. I thought I was the only one. It's intriguing, because I always thought what you were supposed to do is have a list of questions, but I think it's really boring when you do that. I also think you miss opportunities. I've had people interview me that way. They come in with a list of questions, and you answer the questions, and that's what they want. But it means that they're essentially rejecting the rest of you that they didn't know to ask about.

When people do interview you, or call you as a source, do you mind?

It depends who it is. Actually, I'm egotistical. I like being quoted, I like being visible. I like showing off in public. I have books to promote. So anytime anybody is looking for quotes on subjects that I can actually say something about, I'll email them and say, "What do you want?"

Sometimes I do get unhelpful. For example, a few years ago I got a phone call from a guy who said he was a researcher for some obscure BBC program that I had never heard of. He had seen my piece about alternative health and finding reliable medical information on the Net. Did I know of any other cases that he could look up, and could I give him some phone numbers? My reaction was, "Why should I do your homework for you? If I were writing this piece, I would have to go survey the Usenet newsgroups, look at Web sites, find these people." It's not as if he was offering to pay me to do research for him. I finally ended up saying essentially that: "I would have to go read the Usenet newsgroups, I would have to go do these other things—so go do them." And he kept saying, "But it's the BBC." I thought, "So what? They can pay me if they want my information." There is a sense of entitlement, among TV people particularly, that can be really annoying.

Here's an example of what not to do. I had one kid from some university email me and ask if I could do an interview with him on the subject of hacking, and I said sure. So he sent me his set of questions, and they were all over the place. Half of them were about hacking as we know it, and the other half were about old-style hacking. They have nothing to do with each other. He obviously had no idea that hacking in the sense of kludging together a computer system was a totally different topic. It was just a bizarre list of questions.

I sent him a note saying, "It would take me hours to explain all this stuff and it's not necessary, because it's already been written. You should read the following background materials: You should read at least some of Bruce Sterling's *The Hacker Crackdown* [123]. You should read the hacking chapter in my book *net.wars* [94]. These things are free on the Net. If you have time, you should look at *Cyberpunk*, by Katie Hafner and John Markoff [154]. Why don't you read this chapter in my book, and read *The Hacker Crackdown*, and then come back to me."

For some reason, he never seemed to get any of my responses. And for months after, I got, "You never answered and you said you would do this interview." Finally I emailed his tutor, whose address was helpfully included at the bottom of the message, and said, "He doesn't seem to be getting my responses. Could you please tell him that he should read this background material and then rewrite his questions." I never got a rewritten set of questions from him, but I got an apology from the tutor.

It's a case of someone literally needing to do their homework before they call you.

I think that's it. To be fair, when I was first doing technology journalism, I knew very little about any of this stuff, and it was not uncommon for me to show up at an interview and have to say, "I have no idea what your company does, could you please tell me?" I spent a lot of time doing things like that, but eventually you learn.

Has the Net changed that? Whereas before, I might have had to call someone and say, "I don't have a clue," now, at a minimum, I should have looked to see if their company has a Web site, and done some basic research before I called.

Yes. It's funny, I had this conversation with my financial news editor the other day, because my ADSL connection was down, and I was being very petulant and having a temper tantrum. She wanted me to write a story about this company, and I said, "I don't know anything about them and my ADSL connection is down and I can't get to their Web site and I want to ..." And she was saying, "I was a journalist for ten years before the Web was around. Just phone them up." And I'm going, "No, no, I can't do that, I have to go to the Web site first, it's a ritual. I have to go to the Web site first." Of course, I still had a dial-up modem set up, so I ended up dialing in and hitting the Web site first.

I hate calling people without knowing anything. It was really funny; I was completely nonfunctional. "No, I have to go to the Web site first. I can't call them. I have to go to the Web site first." Part of that is that I actually panic about calling the wrong person. If the Web site only gives the CEO's name, I hate it. I want to go through the proper channel, starting with the PR flunky. PR people can be very helpful. If you want to talk to a particular person, they can sometimes make it happen where you couldn't, unaided. For that I'm very grateful to them. I just wish they'd stop phoning me at ten A.M. and asking me if I read the press release they sent last night.

Do you find that different personal qualities come into play when you're doing online research as opposed to interviewing?

No. I'm driven by fear. Because if I don't make the deadline, they won't hire me again. It's the only way I get anything done. In fact, if I want to learn about something, I get somebody to commission a piece about it, because otherwise I'll never bother.

Are there any legal or ethical aspects that you're particularly concerned about in terms of interviewing people?

In the interview I did with Mike Lynch of Autonomy, he was talking about altered consciousness. I looked at him and said something along the lines of, "Does this mean you need to do a lot of drugs?" He said, "Well, as a CEO of a public company, I'm not going to answer that." And of course I put that in verbatim. I don't know what I would have done if he had started telling me yes, he'd been experimenting with acid because he thought it was very important. I would have thought that was interesting, but he probably would have asked me not to print it.

And if he had asked you not to print it, would you have not printed it?

Probably. Unless I believed that he was in some way nonfunctional as CEO of this company. I did once interview somebody who was under investigation by the Department of Justice. He granted me an interview at a time when his lawyer didn't want him to grant any interviews. Later he got braver and decided that the publicity he was getting was actually helping him. But at the time, his lawyer was afraid that if he seemed to be courting the press to put pressure on the DOJ, the DOJ would react negatively. He was really afraid that he was going to lose his house and so on.

The thing he was under investigation for was something I agreed with. I thought he probably had broken the law, I thought he had probably done it knowingly, but I also thought he had done a good thing. And I decided I did not want to be the person who had cost him his house. So that's the only time I have ever willingly shown copy to anybody. When he asked me to rewrite the piece to make it appear as though I hadn't spoken to him, I actually did it. I don't think it would have cost him his house if I had done it differently, but I didn't want to be responsible for it.

So you applied your personal moral standards.

Well, if he had done something that I thought was despicable, I'm sure I would have behaved differently. I think people must make those value judgments all the time.

Super Searcher Tips

➤ I think in terms of having a conversation with people rather than doing a precise, structured interview where you work out all the questions in advance. The most I'll have is a list of a few topics that I want to make sure get covered.

➤ I've had people interview me with a list of questions, and you answer the questions, and that's what they want. It's really boring, and they miss opportunities. It means that they're essentially rejecting the rest of you that they didn't know to ask about.

➤ I have trouble getting started making phone calls in the morning, so I will send out email instead. That's very effective, because they call when they're free instead of my harassing them when they're in the middle of a meeting. Or I use email to arrange an appointment for a time for me to call.

➤ Analysts have often done a lot of research on the companies that they cover, and they have reasons for thinking what they do. To find an analyst, call any of the leading brokerage houses, ask for the equity research department, and tell them what company you're trying to find coverage on.

➤ If someone has said twice that they're not going to tell you, then you should drop it. They don't want to tell you, and they're not going to tell you, and what's the point of trying to trick them into it? All that's going to happen is the next time you want to talk to them, they won't talk to you at all.

➤ I do worry that anything that isn't on the Web is dropping off journalists' radar. Material that hasn't been digitized and placed on the Web is not going to get included in what people write. It's not going to turn up in searches. It's not going to be linked to. For a lot of journalists, it might as well not exist.

Photo by Joe Comick

Dan Tynan
Magazine Editor, Freelance Writer

Daniel Tynan is an award-winning journalist and former executive editor for features at *PC World* magazine. Formerly based in the San Francisco Bay Area, he is now a principal of Cynical Communications, an editorial salon in Wilmington, North Carolina.

dan@cynicus.com
www.cynicus.com

Tell me something about your background and how you ended up where you are.

I have to say, first, I'm flattered that you consider me a Super Searcher, because I don't consider myself a Super Searcher. I'm pretty much a working journalist, and I use the Internet and I use direct sources. I interview a lot of people as part of my job, so I've done a fair amount of this. I'm constantly looking for people who are better than I am at it and asking for their tips, so I'll try to give you whatever benefit I have from their experiences as well as my own.

I've been a technology journalist for fourteen or fifteen years, about half that time for *PC World* magazine. When I left *PC World*, I was executive editor for features and was overseeing investigative journalism projects as well as other service stories. In addition, I've freelanced for about five years writing a wide range of stories for a wide range of publications. Some investigative, some very straight business journalism, a fair amount of first-person essays where I go out on the Internet and look for,

357

say, a present for my wife's birthday or advice on how to be a better parent.

What you write appears to be well researched, and the people that you talk to are interesting. But there's something about your writing that's just so much fun to read.

I'm not really a technology writer, I'm a humor writer. So I try to sneak some humor in when I can. I started to develop a specialty where people say, "We need kind of a short funny piece that involves computers," they call me, and I charge them as much as I possibly can.

Laughs are worth it. As far as your straight stories are concerned, I know that you did a number of investigative pieces for *PC World*.

There are two stories from when I worked for *PC World* that I want to talk about in particular. One is the "Bobby" story, and the other is a story I did about three and a half years ago that won a bunch of awards. That one involved a group of companies in Southern California that I believe were moving stolen computer goods. I actually want to talk a little bit about my wife, Christina Wood. She's the one who figured out what these guys were doing and put together this whole ring of companies.

What's her background?

She was one of the two primary consumer editors at *PC World*, which is where all the magazine's investigative reporting is done. Most of it comes out of letters from readers. She put together a bunch of letters from readers about these different companies, all in Southern California, that were all selling memory and all had the same story to tell. She started doing background research, calling these companies. As she talked to them, she got the same spiel from each one, as if it were scripted, and she decided these guys were all in business together.

This is great primary research. She got letters from readers and then she used those to track down the companies?

She had an advocacy column. Her job was to go through reader letters—she got two hundred to three hundred a month—and pick the ones that seemed like they'd make good stories. Usually people didn't get the product they paid for, or it didn't work after they got it, or they needed support for it but the company had disappeared. She forwarded all the letters to the appropriate companies, then pursued the complaints for a handful of people every month and tracked down the companies to get them to respond.

What techniques would she use to track down the companies?

Generally speaking, my philosophy about research is, get someone else to do the legwork for you whenever you can. It saves you a lot of time. People who have been wronged by a company or by another individual are very motivated, and some of them are very good at ferreting out information. We would not get just a letter, we'd get a packet of materials including every piece of correspondence, receipts, and phone records. Often it's a simple matter of making a phone call, unless the company's hiding or it's gone belly-up. That's when you have to start digging. I use a lot of the same sources Christina did to do that.

Should we talk about sources now, or do you want to save that for later and go on with the story? What's your preference?

I'd like to talk about the memory story because it's a good example of starting with some primary research, going on the

Web and doing some online research, then coming back to primary sources. It gives that full picture.

I inherited the memory story because no one at the magazine really had time to do it. Christina had started the story but wasn't able to continue with it. I worked alongside a woman named Angela Navarette, who was a fact-checker for *PC World* at that time. This was her break, her opportunity to do a story. We researched it as a team, which I find very helpful. If you're going to do investigative journalism it is kind of a cliché, the whole Woodward/Bernstein thing—but it helps, because you're twice as efficient, can call twice as many people, and you can also compare notes and bounce things off each other. It's much harder to do this sort of investigative stuff on your own.

So I walked into that story with a lot already done. I helped push it through, and I got a lucky break here and there. But the final result was the work of a lot of different people. Angela had managed to get hold of a Secret Service agent who confirmed some information for her about these guys, and that's rare.

How in the world did she even know to look for a Secret Service agent?

It was a reader who told her about the Secret Service's involvement; he even gave her the name and location of the agent investigating the case. The Secret Service is a branch of the Treasury Department, and apparently they handle interstate commercial fraud. Some of these companies were based in Nevada, some were based in California, and so the Secret Service was brought in by the credit card companies.

What happens with Internet scams is that a lot of these companies take credit card payments, then people get ripped off and start canceling their charges. If the credit card company gets too many cancellations against a company's account, they either close down the account or they pull money out of it. They'll say, "We're taking one hundred thousand dollars from you, to hold in escrow." So, once the credit card companies get involved, if they get ripped off, they will contact the federal authorities.

Are you actually able to call a credit card company and ask them what's going on with such-and-such a company?

You can imagine the wall you run into there. Here's the classic line from somebody running a scam: "I'm a legitimate business man, I was just trying to serve my customers, I got a little behind, I got too many orders, I couldn't fill them, and then the credit card company shut me down." That is the classic "mea culpa but I'm not really guilty" response. "Suddenly all my money was gone because the credit card company sucked it all up." They sucked it all up because he wasn't delivering product.

Then you call the next company and they give you the exact same spiel, and the next company says the same thing, and you think, "I see a pattern here." That's how Christina put together this story. The key was connecting the dots among all the companies. Taken individually, you couldn't say whether each of them was a legitimate business that had just hit a bad patch, or if they were badly run, or if they were a scam. Just looking at their behavior, they could easily be just some company that got in over its head. But when you connect them to another company that did the exact same thing, and then connect that company to a third and a fourth and a fifth, then it seems pretty clear that something funky is going on.

And you connected all these companies because of the readers writing in?

It was a combination of things. One was reader letters, although most of the time these readers were just dealing with one company and didn't know anything about the other companies. But it helped, because sometimes they'd give us names. "I talked to Jack at this company." Then we'd use the Dun and Bradstreet database [42, see Appendix]. Dun and Bradstreet collects information on businesses. You can see a payment history, how quickly it pays its creditors, what kind of financials it has. But Dun and Bradstreet is not a quotable source. Part of their agreement with our magazine was, "You can use Dun and Bradstreet as background, but you cannot use it as primary source; you cannot quote us." So we used it to research the histories of the principals involved in the companies, or the companies they used to be involved in, because usually the report would provide some background on these individuals. We looked to see if some of these guys had worked at the same company in the past, and they had.

That was brilliant.

I don't know if it was brilliant or not, but it worked. The information Dun and Bradstreet provides is given voluntarily by individuals, so if somebody's lying, there's no way to know. But these guys were so stupid, they didn't lie; at least some of them didn't. So that was two of the dots we connected: These two or three guys all worked for the same predecessor company. You look up the predecessor company and find it went bankrupt, with a whole bunch of creditors, people with liens against the company. So you call the people who have liens on the company, and ask, "What about these guys? Were they legit?" Sometimes they'll talk to you, sometimes they won't. But oftentimes they'll say, "I talked to so-and-so at this company; he was our contact and this is what happened."

Now you have a lead on a name, and you work with that. We also went to the fictitious business name filings, or DBAs, and believe it or not, we looked at the signatures on the forms. We hired a handwriting analyst, because a couple of these companies were registered by different principals who turned out to have the same handwriting. The handwriting analysis told us, "Yep, these two are the same guy."

You went to the Secretary of State's office to look at the handwriting, or they sent you photocopies?

We got copies from the Secretary of State's office. We got hold of credit applications they had made. For the credit applications you have to give three or four references for companies you've done business with. Well, guess what? They gave each other as references.

All of this said, "These guys are all in business together." That background research indicated, one, that consumers were being ripped off. Two, that all these businesses had the same modus operandi. Three, they're all connected by personnel. That is generally enough for the postal service to suspect mail fraud. That's three out of maybe five criteria they have. It doesn't mean the companies are actually involved in mail fraud, but it's reason enough to investigate.

Then, for the story, we decided to purchase products from some of these companies. We hired people to do it—"operatives," I like to call them—because we didn't want our names exposed since we knew at some point we were going to talk to these guys. We said, "We want you to buy a product from these companies and then ship it to us." This is where the lucky break comes in. We bought a few memory cards from these companies, thinking we'd pay them money and they won't arrive. Well, they arrived. They were perfectly legit, they worked, and we're going, "Oh well, what do we do now?"

And I'm sitting here, looking at this memory board, and I flip it over, and there's the name of the company that built the board on it. So I called them. I looked them up, I don't remember if I used the Internet or what, but I found where they were located and called their offices with just a general question. "I know you're board manufacturers, not memory manufacturers, but I'm wondering whether there's any way to trace stolen memory? Would I be able to find a serial number and track it back to a stolen shipment?" They said, "Just a minute." I was on hold for five minutes. Next thing you know I'm talking to the company president and he knows all of these guys. He's known about them for ages. He's done business with them for years, they have a reputation and it is not good. He has all the dirt, the inside story.

There's that incredible sense of hitting paydirt.

Yes, absolutely. He's saying, "You're the first guy who's actually talked to me about this," but inside their tight-knit little circle of high-tech companies, it's pretty well known what these other guys are doing. So that was confirmation. It was something I couldn't use in the story, but it told me I was right. In the story I had to be very careful about what words I used. We had a lawyer read the story twice before it appeared in print. He said things like, "You can't use the phrase 'ring of companies' because that implies they're part of organized crime." But the president's information gave me more confidence, and that—along with the Secret Service and the fact that these companies were also being investigated by local police departments—confirmed what we'd figured out. The key was making that extra phone call and just getting lucky.

You make your own luck as well. You tracked down the leads and actually had the physical board in your hand, as opposed to just hearing about it or getting a picture of it. So you could turn it over, and there was the company name.

I always intended to follow up on that story because there was a lot more to it that I was never able to tell. When the story appeared in print, I got a whole bunch of phone calls from people, including employees of these companies. That's another really good inside source, if you can get employees willing to talk to you. They often have a gripe and you have to weigh that against what they say, but it gives you the kind of information you'll never get from just looking at documents.

And I got tips from one guy that seemed totally out of the ballpark. He said that one of these men, the main principal of this group of companies, who started the original company twenty-five years ago, once did federal time for selling bad computer chips to the U.S. government for use in defense equipment. I could never even come close to verifying that, though I really wanted to. Two years later, two of the guys involved in my story were arrested for selling bad computer chips to the U.S. government for use in missiles. I really wish I had broken that story.

Is there any way to find out someone's federal prison record?

That's what I tried to do. I didn't even know if that was public record or not, though I assumed it was. I know the name of the prison where he's supposed to have been, but I couldn't get through to them. Also, one of the big problems here, and an issue to talk about when you're tracking people, was that trying to track down someone with a very common American surname proved next to impossible.

Online listings of court cases might show someone's name but, particularly with a common name, you can't tell if that's your "John Smith."

Yes. Now this person had a unique middle name, which helped a little bit, but most records aren't indexed by middle names. You can provide a middle name but they won't search by it. I discovered that, much to my chagrin, after spending several hundred dollars doing online searches that ignored the information I was entering and gave me every single "Smith" found. You want some piece of unique identifying information about that person. Phone numbers with area codes are really good. That leads to my "Bobby" story.

Is there anything else you want to say about this one, just before we go on to "Bobby?"

Investigative journalism is expensive and time-consuming, and it sometimes doesn't pan out. So it's very hard to get a publication to commit to it because they don't want to spend money and scarce staff resources on a story that might not happen. And the only way to know if a story is going to happen is to actually do the research. So give some credit to the editors of *PC World* magazine for being willing to fund it.

One final note was that we did ultimately contact or attempt to contact all of the individuals I talked about in the story. And the way we did it—we considered it due diligence—we waited until the last possible minute, two days before the story was set to be laid out. We FedExed letters to each of the individuals saying, "Hi, we're planning to write a story on this topic. We'd like to speak to you about this company. Please contact us by this date," thinking that everyone would ignore us. Ten out of the eleven called me. Naturally, they all blamed the others. "Those guys are dirty but I'm clean." And of course the one who didn't return the call was the ringleader who ended up getting arrested two weeks later.

Let's go on to the Bobby story. I got to play Brenda Starr, girl reporter, for a couple of days on this. Can you run through the genesis of it?

It began with a letter from a reader, forwarded to me from *PC World*'s Webmaster. The letter started out by saying, "I tried to sign up for this Internet service provider on the Net and they ripped me off. How could you name these guys as one of your best buys?" Best buy? I had no idea who this company was. When I was at the magazine we did a review of ISPs, and we definitely did not name them as a best buy. But I had to make sure we hadn't screwed up badly here. *PC World* is published in twelve countries, and I thought maybe one of the foreign editions had named this company as one of its best buys.

I started searching, and went to the ISP's Web site, and sure enough there was the *PC World* "Best Buy" logo, along with a link to www.pcworld.com. I clicked the link and it didn't work. I got a 404 error. There were three or four links to other magazines that had allegedly recommended this ISP. They also didn't work. And then I clicked another link to an independent ISP rating service called Inverse Technologies [75]. That link did work: It went to a page that discussed at length how well the ISP did, with all these reports.

I thought, that's weird. I knew about this rating service because we had used them ourselves for part of our ISP review. They do nothing but dial up ISPs all day long, from locations across the country, and measure how long it takes to get through, and the speed of email, and so forth. I called them and asked, "What's the deal with this company?" And they said, "Let me tell you. These guys ripped off Web pages from another ISP." That ISP was ibm.net, which had gotten the legitimate Best Buy from *PC World* and received an excellent rating from Inverse. The bogus ISP downloaded those pages from the Web, replaced "ibm.net" with its own name, and posted the pages on its Web site.

I never heard of anyone doing anything like this before—essentially hijacking someone else's Web site and passing it off as their own—so I started to do research. The next day I went to the bogus ISP's Web site. It was gone, and I thought, "This story's over." Then, a couple days later, I went to the Web site and it was back again, but with an entirely different look. This was, as it turns out, another Web site that they had ripped off. That's what started me on the story.

I called the person who'd written the letter and talked with him about it. He'd paid for his account by check. I asked him to send me a copy of the cancelled check, so I could see who'd endorsed it and where their bank was located.

I also went to the WHOIS [140] database, typed in the Web address of the ISP, and got the name and contact info of the guy who allegedly owned it. We'll call him Pat Bickels. WHOIS is one of the primary sources, these days, for information on companies.

You can put the domain name in WHOIS and it will give you identifying information about whoever owns the domain?

You can do a lot with WHOIS, but that's their primary thing. If you want to find out who has registered HotBot.com, for example, type in HotBot and you get a name, address, phone number, and email address and then links to other information. But you can also search by a person's name. So if it's John Doe who registered HotBot, you can search by John Doe and find out all the sites he's registered. A lot of people don't know how much WHOIS lets you search for.

So I went through the links on the WHOIS page for this ISP, and each one featured a different address and phone number in various states—Maine, Florida, Colorado, Georgia, North Carolina. The same name—"Pat Bickels"—kept appearing. There was one, though, that sounded like a very corporate address in Atlanta, and I thought maybe these guys are legit, maybe this is just some weird snafu.

Let's say the name of the ISP was BogusNet with an address at One Bogusnet Way. I searched for "Bogusnet" on the Internet and turned up hundreds of hits for different sites, including all through Latin America, and a large telecommunications company in Southern California. So I called the telecommunications company in Southern California and said, "Are these guys a division of yours?"

Who did you talk to there?

Just a PR person. I did the usual, made four phone calls only to end up with the PR person. The PR person said, "We know something about these guys but I'm not sure we can talk to you; let me check." Half an hour later an attorney calls me. He wants to know how to find these guys because he's trying to serve them a subpoena, and he is a fount of information. Although he's very circumspect and careful not to give me too much, he tells me a lot about how long they've been looking for these guys, and the problems they've heard from different customers. People got ripped off by this little guy in North Carolina and looked around, like I did, and found the big guys in Southern California. Then they called and complained. I said, "Can you give me the names of one or two people who have complained, so I can call them?" And he did.

One woman I called turned out to be a former reporter. She was one of those users who got these guys in her teeth and wasn't going to let go. She'd done an enormous amount of digging. She'd talked to all sorts of people, including the State Attorney General and the Georgia Bureau of Investigation, because one of these addresses was based in Georgia. She gave me the names and numbers of everybody—the local sheriff's department of the North Carolina town where they were based, the name of a teenager who seemed to be involved—we'll call him "Bobby"—the private cell phone number of Bobby's mother that she'd sweet-talked out of the phone company's customer service department. This is another example of having someone else do your legwork for you.

I called everybody, and each one gave me a little bit more of the story, confirming that this was not a legitimate business operation, this was a scam. I also went to the site where you could sign up for this ISP. The only way to pay for the ISP was through an Internet checking transaction—you click a link and fill out information, a third party check company draws money from your bank account and sends the check to the ISP. It's for people who don't have credit cards, or don't want to use credit cards on the Net. I talked to the Internet checking company and they shared all this information with me on how many complaints they'd gotten, how many checks they'd written, and what their own internal investigation had turned up.

Meanwhile I've been staying in contact with the guy who originally wrote the letter, trading information. He's a techie with a very well-known high-tech company and knows the Internet extremely well. At this point we didn't know who Pat Bickels was or what his relationship to Bobby might be, so the techie and his buddies have a contest in the office, trying to track these guys down. They're constantly searching and every so often they'd email me, saying, "He's got a new ISP now, it's called this."

Did they use some particular software to track this guy down?

No, they just know how to search the Internet. They'd search for different types of files, or they'd search for logos. The guy would take someone else's logo, modify it, and post it as his own. So, somehow, they managed to find him through the use of logos. He closed down shop and opened up again four times in the space of my investigation, each time with a new name, and each time ripping off somebody else's Web site.

Then the lawyer from the Southern California company told me that his tech person found a site called PatBickels.com, which they thought was possibly one of Bobby's aliases. There were pictures we thought were "Pat Bickels." At the time, we just didn't know his real name. And there were pictures of a house and a town.

That's the point where I came into it, because we thought the house might be in the mountains of North Carolina, near where I live. I took the pictures from the Web site and went to locals, to see if they knew where it was around here. One of them said, "That's not North Carolina, that's Kalispell, Montana."

And I had the name of a local North Carolina reporter who had written about the original ISP. I sent him the Web site URL for PatBickels.com, because he had met Bobby, and he identified Bobby as the person we'd been calling Pat Bickels. Then I asked you to go talk with that reporter.

The reporter referred me to a member of the local police department. Although the family had left town, we were able to get Bobby's whole history, including his real name and his

mother's name, since he was still a minor. Bobby was almost a local legend. He'd had a whole series of problems starting when he was barely a teenager, from running up debts to riding his bike through town with a police band radio blaring from his handlebars.

> You were able to get public records because you checked the mother's court records and found proof that she was his mother, her connection to the companies, and her car registration and when it had gone "not current."

Also, the police person had heard that a friend had visited Bobby in Montana, and had a possible phone number for him. We looked at the Web site together and she identified Bobby. We did a reverse lookup on the phone number and found another small town in Montana. We looked that up on a map online and could see its relation to Kalispell.

> Then the police called around to law enforcement people in Montana and found an official based near Kalispell who knew of Pat Bickels and his mother "Trudy." We traced the house Bobby and his mother had rented. I talked to the rental office and they knew them, although they knew them as Pat and Trudy. I got a lot of information from them, too. But Trudy and Bobby had left town two days before—owing rent.

From the local police and court records, we also had the names of the officers who had worked on Bobby's earlier cases. We ended up not contacting them, but we could have. It was a small town, where everybody knows almost

everything, and he was certainly a well-known character.

There were a couple of things about this story, in terms of searching, that I'd like to mention. Twenty-five different ISPs turned up that this guy had started, all basically the same operation using different names and different URLs. I found them using a very handy tool called Copernic [34]. It's software that you download from the Internet. There's a free version and two pay versions. It's especially useful for finding older archived pages. It's particularly good because you can save your search results and run the searches again later. With traditional search engines, once you run a search, everything else is gone forever.

I searched on phone numbers given in the WHOIS database. It turns out Bobby, not being that bright, used the same 800 number for most of the businesses. And the phone numbers he used were either phony or they all routed to the same voicemail-box, which I think was a cell phone, so he could be mobile. Talk about unique identifiers; the ten-digit phone number is a very useful, unique identifier. As in the earlier example we discussed, one company going out of business could be anything. Twenty-five companies doing the same thing, there's probably something fishy.

Here's my favorite part of the entire investigation. I had gotten the cell phone number of his mother from that reporter who had been a customer. I called it and said, "Hi, am I speaking to Trudy?" The woman answered the phone, "Nope, sorry, can't help you. Don't know anyone by that name. I've only had this number for about ten days, blah, blah, blah." Very pleasant. And I said, "Sorry," and hung up.

Then I called the cell phone company and I pretended to be her son. I said, "I just tried my mom's number and I got this strange woman answering and I'm not sure if her account's still active or what, and I was wondering if you could check for me?" And they asked for the name on the account, I gave it to them, and the customer service rep said, "Yes, that account is still active, it's been active for at least six months."

So there's my one little bit of lying for the story. I just verified that, first, the number is legit, and second, I know she's lying. So she probably had something to hide.

Using Copernic that way and checking the phone numbers are great investigative techniques. Anything else you want to say about the Bobby story?

Again, I had a lot of help. I had three or four sources I went back to several times, all of whom had done the legwork or had gotten big pieces of the story. In a way, that's what you do as a researcher or a journalist—find people who have big chunks of a story, then get the whole story by putting together all those pieces.

This wasn't really part of my regular job at *PC World*. I just took it on as a special project, and I worked on it late at night because it was so much fun.

It really was fun. It was frustrating to miss them by two days, though.

It was frustrating to miss them. It was really frustrating not to be able to say everything I wanted to say about them. Again, the story got published, and I was contacted by more people who said, "I have more of the story to tell you." I have talked to some of them. Every so often I think about diving in and really digging out the rest of the story. But something like paying work usually interrupts.

Who do you do work for now?

Mostly magazines. I've also done a few pieces for Web magazines or Web versions of print magazines.

Do you find any difference in how you approach things as a freelancer as opposed to when you were with *PC World*? Any difference in the resources available to you?

One of the advantages of working for *PC World*, a big magazine with 1.2 million circulation and high revenue, is that they
can spend money on a story. They don't gag at ten thousand dollars and, although they don't do it all the time, they can. That
attitude is kind of unusual and it helps a lot. They also have
resources like Dun and Bradstreet. I don't use Dun and
Bradstreet as a freelancer because I'd have to pay for it out of my
own pocket. I use different sources for information on the
Internet, like Hoovers.com [65], which has a lot of the information you can get from D&B, but is mostly free. It helps to be able
to hire someone like you and say, "I can't get my feet on the
ground there, I'm not going to drive or fly across country for this,
but I called so-and-so, and he recommended you."

Only because I happened to live in an obscure town in the hills of North Carolina, next to the obscure town that this guy lived in.

Right, exactly. But having the resources to say, "I really want to
do that," and then be able to do it, is a major advantage of working for a big publication.

Otherwise, what I find as a freelancer is that I am only as influ-
ential or as important to the sources as the publication I'm writing for. If I'm writing for a big national publication, I probably get
better, faster treatment than if I'm writing for a tiny regional
publication. It confuses people, especially if I call them again
and I'm writing for somebody else, because everyone assumes
you're on the staff. They assume you know everything about the
magazine you're writing for and that you are one of the editors
there. I have to let people know that I'm a freelance writer and I
work for a lot of people.

When a magazine comes to you with a story assignment, do they tend to know exactly what they want, or do they leave it to you? Do you have to dig out from them what's really going on and what they actually need?

It varies. *PC World* has a tortuous, exhaustive process where they basically write most of the story for you before you can get the assignment. It's story-by-committee. I used to be part of that committee, so I was part of the problem then, and now I get to complain about it. They do this because they have a very specific idea of what their reader wants, and they really do want to touch all the bases.

With most of the magazines I have freelanced for, the editor calls and says, "I need a story about this and that," and gives you maybe a two-sentence description. They say, "What do you think? Can you do it?" Or they send me email two or three sentences long. Then I have to go and talk to them a little more and ask, "What do you really want? How about this? What about that?" And then I say, "Okay. What's your deadline, what's the word count, and what are you paying?" Those things are key. Also: Am I interested in the story? Do I know anything about the subject? If not, is it something I want to learn about? Do I want to write for this publication? Sometimes I take a story just so I can say I wrote for a particular publication and have a clip from them. I sit there and take notes on the conversation on my word processor. When I'm writing the story, I go back to the file I created to make sure the story I'm writing is the one they've asked for.

So you try to find out what they really want, and you also have to take into account deadlines, budgets, word count?

Yes. But for me, aside from those other questions, the key question in taking almost any story is, "How research-intensive will this story be?" Research is the single biggest time drain in what I do. I go back to my mantra, "Have other people do the leg-work for you." If I don't have to start from scratch, if I can get a running start, I might cut a week out of the process. If I cut a week out of every story, I can do more stories, make more money, and take more time off to spend with my kids. So it all ties in.

Another thing we haven't talked about, which is really primary for me, is that when I get a story assignment on a topic I don't know a lot about, I see what other people have written about it.

I'm sitting here with a bunch of cards, and the next one is exactly "How does your approach differ if it's a topic that you know nothing about?" Here we go, take it away.

Basically, a lot of what I do is to start from complete ignorance on a topic and arrive at a point of incomplete ignorance. I get to know a little bit about it, enough to synthesize and summarize for people who know nothing about it. One of the first places I go is *The Wall Street Journal* Publications Library [135] online, which costs money. You have to subscribe to *The Wall Street Journal* online; that's around sixty bucks a year, less if you have a sub-scription to the *Journal* in print. You pay three bucks for each arti-cle you download, or a monthly fee of ten bucks for fifteen articles a month. I go and search the Publications Library, which has just about every major newspaper in the country, all the major maga-zines, and all the major trade publications. I search on a topic and it gives me a list of hits, which is free, but as soon as I click on one to view the complete article, then I have to pay for it.

That is a great way to get up to speed. You get the story, you get a summary of the topic written for general audiences, par-ticularly if it's from a newspaper and not a trade publication. You usually get the names of people who have been quoted, so you have sources. You print out six or ten of these stories, then go through them and see that this guy gets quoted in every story. He must know something about it. So you write his name down, and then you go to the next person, and you develop a list of sources that way.

Do you tend to start your search broad or narrow?

Generally, I think the best way to do a search is to start as narrow or specific as possible, then broaden backwards. If you get lucky right away and find exactly the article you're looking for, you can save yourself a lot of time. Most of the time you don't. So, if you began with six keywords, in the next search you use five keywords, then four, and so forth. You get less and less restrictive in your terminology. You might search the entire database first or you might narrow down to the three or four publications that you think really will have the information.

Do you use other commercial databases, or do you mostly stay with the Web?

I don't usually venture off the Web. I've never used LexisNexis [80] or Dialog [39]. I've used D&B. There are sites where you can actually purchase D&B one-off. I have never used any of the private-eye sources on the Web. I've never had to dig that deep; I've never needed anyone's Social Security number. I also have personal issues about using that stuff. I don't think it's really ethical. I did try KnowX.com [79] because they gave me a hundred dollars worth of free searching so I could try it out. I used it pretty exhaustively, mostly on the Bobby story, and I didn't find it so useful. It let me know the information was out there, but it didn't give me enough of it to be helpful.

Do you have other favorite Web resources?

One source I use is ProfNet [108]. It's for PR people and for journalists, a place where you can go to find experts. There's a database, and if you search on a particular topic you'll be provided with a list of experts, including academics. I wrote a story about MP3 and the Web, so I looked for experts on copyright on the Internet and got some lawyers in Nashville who do nothing but that.

The other way to do it is to post a query saying I am so-and-so writing for this publication and looking for a person who knows something about this. And then people email you directly with information. I did a story on how dot-coms get their names for a magazine called *The Industry Standard* [70]. It was a fun story to write, got a lot of good feedback. I put a query on ProfNet and got a hundred and fifty emails. Too many.

That can be a problem.

Yes, but that was just because of this particular topic. Everyone who had started a dot-com wanted to tell the story of how they got their name. So I got a lot of stories. I got almost all my anecdotes through ProfNet. I was able to filter and say, "Okay that's boring, and that's boring; oh, that's a good one."

Do you have anything else to say about finding people?

I use 555-1212.com [1] as a reverse directory. There's a bunch of them out there. That sometimes works. But all too often I find myself frustrated by the Web, especially when it comes to phone numbers, because the Web directories are incomplete. I tried, a couple of weeks ago, to find my high school French teacher on the Internet. I thought, I'm reasonably intelligent and know something about the Internet, I should be able to find her. Unfortunately she shares a last name with a famous dead rock guitarist, so I found a lot of references to that guitarist and very few to her. I found the email addresses of fourteen people with her first initial and last name, but none of them turned out to be her. I thought I was being clever. I looked at all these associations for language teachers in California and nationally, and did all the things I thought a PI would try to do. Nothing. Didn't turn up anything. I finally looked up the site for the high school, which is a very scary Web site, because it has lots of misspellings. And she's one of only two teachers left from when I went to school there.

That's a perfect example of when using the direct approach works best.

The Web gives you a lot more flexibility in terms of how comprehensively you can search, but it's still easier sometimes to go direct.

Let's talk about ethical concerns, like privacy.

I've found, when I've gone digging on an individual, that it's hard to know where to draw the line. How much investigating is too much? Are you investigating a story or are you investigating a person? With Whitewater, they started out investigating a potential crime, or at least a shady real estate deal. They ended up investigating a person, Bill Clinton. I think they went way too far, and that's why it spiraled out of control.

As a researcher or a reporter, you have to be very careful about what your motives are, what your goal is, and how you achieve that goal. One of the areas I write about is privacy on the Internet, so I think about this. I wonder, am I violating people's privacy in doing my job? Am I serving a greater public good or am I just satisfying my weird little curiosity? I don't think there is a clear-cut rule on what to do and not do.

I would worry if we didn't all have these concerns.

It's true. You end up doing real property searches, which is great in a way, because it's public information and it can get you a really solid grasp on somebody and their location and what they have. At the same time, do you really need to know that for the story you're doing?

And once you know it, how much of it do you make public? How much information

do journalists have that doesn't make it into a story?

Probably the most frustrating part of doing investigative journalism is what you can't say. There are three different levels of every story: what you can say in print, what you're pretty sure you know but you can't say, and what you really suspect but can't prove. What appears in print is always the smallest. It's "Here's what the lawyer said I could say," which translates into "Here's what I have documentation on from three different sources, including a bus full of nuns." You have to be careful about it. There's the bigger picture that you really want to present, but you have to approach stories like the ones I have done with the idea that you're going to get sued.

Do people ever call you as a source?

People have called me as a source a number of times. I've done a fair amount of TV, mostly seven-second sound bites, because *PC World* was very aggressive in promoting itself to the media, and local news stations would call us whenever there was a story. A computer virus would break out or a big company would get hacked and they would call us for comments; often I would be the designated talking head.

Reporters quote reporters a lot, especially in broadcast media because they're piggybacking on the magazine's reputation. They're saying, "We trust you, you did the research." I think about this and it makes me even more cynical than usual, because I know how much I know about a topic. They either think I know a lot more than I do, or they don't care. To the viewing public, I look like I know what I'm talking about, and that's all that matters to them.

Then you might get someone like an attorney saying, "We're trying to track these people down. What do you know about this?" In the Bobby story, I leaned on one attorney pretty heavily for information, and he leaned on me. It was kind of a quid pro quo—I'll tell you this, if you tell me that. You barter information with people. That's the only reason some people will talk to you, especially when they don't want to be quoted.

When a researcher, or someone who's looking into a company or a topic, calls you because of something that you've written, are you open to that or does it bother you?

Given my mantra of "Have other people do your legwork for you," it would be hypocritical to say, "Nope, sorry." I'm usually pretty generous when people call, because I've been in that position and understand what it's like, especially if you're new to a topic. What you really want for your first interview, your first source, is someone who has a good general knowledge of a topic, can give you the basics, and will point you in three or four different directions.

And who speaks plain English.

Speaks English, sort of knows your pain, and will help you through it. If you call the world's leading expert on a topic and you know nothing, you'll probably burn that source, because you're not going to ask them the right questions. They might not ever answer your call again. If they're the patient type, they might explain things, but more likely they won't, because they're too busy. So that's literally the last person you want to call. You want to wait and call that person when you feel pretty confident about your knowledge of the topic. So, in a way, I'm happy to be the first source for someone on a topic because, like I said, I've been there.

Because you're so dear.

Because I'm so dear. Because I know they'll owe me for the rest of their lives. Someday I will ask for that favor to be returned. I am part of the Information Mafia.

For people who might call a journalist, do you have any suggestions about how they should be prepared or what kinds of questions they should ask?

A journalist should be a kind of stepping stone. They shouldn't actually be a source per se. I don't think journalists should quote journalists. I think they should say, "I'm doing this story, can you help me out here?" And as a journalist I respond, "Yeah, talk to so-and-so, he knows a lot about this; talk to her, she knows a lot about that. Here, check out this Web site." That should be the extent of it—sources, other leads, referrals, and general information. But I really don't think they should be leaned on. That's like Tom Brokaw saying, "Peter Jennings at ABC News says ..."

You mentioned sharing information with that attorney. When someone calls you, does it help if they have something they can share back?

Yes, try to make it a mutually beneficial exchange if you can. In any case, I like to hear the sound of my own voice, and to be avuncular, and I love the idea of mentoring someone. So if it's a student, it's "Oh sure, I'll do it." I get to puff myself up and feel like an expert for fifteen minutes.

How do you prepare for a call or an interview? Do you write out questions in advance?

Sometimes, not often. If I'm feeling less confident about it, if it's an early interview in the process. If it's a highly complex or technical topic and I don't know a lot about it, I'll go to the print sources first, or to online versions of the articles, and pick out terms and concepts, get somewhat familiar with them, and then I'll probably type up some questions. But I almost never just go lock-step through asking my questions.

After a certain point I usually chuck the questions, because I've gotten conversant enough. If you want a good interview, if you want good quotes, you have to have a conversation with somebody. You don't want it to be question-answer, question-answer, question-answer. People get defensive, and you'll get either terse answers or very canned answers that they've given to this same question a million times before. But if you get them engaged in conversation, you can get them laughing, you talk about various things, you even admit you're totally ignorant about something, you just sort of be human with them. Then, all of a sudden, they'll tell you something that sounds real, that they haven't told anyone else.

How do you evaluate the validity or the truthfulness or the usefulness of the source?

A bullshit detector is important. I once asked a guy who was some years my senior and a really excellent reporter, "How do I know if they're telling me the truth?" He said, "You just have to right-brain it," by which he meant follow your gut. You also need to look at every source from their perspective. What are they selling? What's their vested interest in talking to you? Are they trying to get famous? Do they just want to see their names in print? Do they have a product or a company they're trying to push? What's their point of view and what's their likely motive?

You have to weigh all that against what they tell you, and then you also have to weigh it against what other people tell you. You're going to talk to multiple people on a topic. If everyone tells you the same thing, one, you know it's probably true, and two, it's probably too boring a story to write. You want to find a real story, where people disagree, where there's conflict.

Do you use different skill sets or characteristics in online searching, as compared to primary research?

They both involve curiosity, certainly. You have to really want to know. You have to be creative in your approach, and ingenious. If you run into a brick wall, in both areas you have to figure out how to get around the brick wall.

A lot of people who live in front of a computer screen either don't have, or lose, their interpersonal skills. They think they can communicate with a person the same way they can communicate with a computer, which is why geeks have the reputation they have. You know you can't. Interpersonal skills are really important. Your ability to charm somebody, your ability to make them feel at ease, to make them feel that you like them and that you're interested in what they have to say, is really important. You don't have to convince your computer that you like it.

You can snarl at your computer, although sometimes I've found that charming my computer helps as well. But it doesn't help to snarl at the person you're trying to get information from.

Unless snarling works. Sometimes it does. It's possible that, if you get pissed off and brusque with someone, they will actually respond to you. But I don't recommend it.

Are there times when it's still difficult for you to make telephone calls?

I used to be terrified of making phone calls. When I first started, I wasn't really writing or editing. I was copyediting, and looking at the prospect of having to phone people as part of writing a story, and thinking, "I could never call a complete stranger. How could I do this? I'd freeze up."

But I did it. It was hard the first dozen times, and then it got fairly easy. It even got to be fun, because sometimes you run into really interesting people, and if the person's a dud, you end the call as quickly as possible, say, "Thanks for your time," and move on. You end up making connections with people, and then they lead you to other people, and it's a lot more interesting than just sitting in a room alone tapping a keyboard.

How did you get yourself to make those first calls?

Usually you have an editor with a whip. You have all this pressure and expectation: "Oh my God, I've got to do this story. They're expecting this of me." One of the first stories I did when I was trying to be a writer was a story on computers and celebrities. People always try to do these stories, and they never work. Celebrities don't use computers, they hire people to use computers for them. But I suggested Hunter Thompson. And they said, okay, call him. So first I had to find him.

He was writing a column for the San Francisco *Examiner* at the time. I called his editor at the *Examiner* who said, "Oh boy, you don't want to talk to him. I don't have his home number but I'll give you the number of the bar where you're likely to find him." So I call the bar and the bartender answers the phone, and I say, "Hi, I'm blah blah blah and so on and so forth, I'm looking for Hunter Thompson." I could hear him saying something to someone, and in the background I hear someone's voice and to my ear it was Thompson, because I've heard him talk. He has a very distinctive voice, kind of a barking mumble. Then there was a click, and I thought maybe he didn't mean to cut me off. So I called again, and click.

That's as close as I got to Hunter Thompson, and that was crushing to me because he was a hero. I thought, "Oh I'm a failure as a journalist." But I recovered. I got over it. I lived to call again.

Now, after years of making phone calls, if there's still a phone call that's hard to make, how do you get yourself to do it?

The first phone calls on any story are hard. You haven't quite gotten into it. There is a form of procrastination going on, which is useful. I think procrastination is a very good tool in researching or writing, although too much of it is not a good thing.

So I try to make the first phone call a friendly one. I try to call someone I already know, whom I've spoken to before. Or I'll make the first phone calls to PR people if I need to get to somebody. These people are the gatekeepers, and they're paid to be friendly even if they don't like you. More often than not you'll get someone who says, "Sure, let me help you." And that helps.

Okay, I've made that first call and I feel like a valid human being now. I'm working for an actual magazine, or something like it, I have some sort of imprimatur and also some pull here. This person is going to spend part of their day helping me out. Of course they may not.

But it doesn't matter. It's gotten you over that hurdle and then the next calls are easier.

I've given my spiel. I've probably stumbled three or four times, but I'll do it again, and after a while I get the spiel down to where I can say it in about twelve words on their voicemail. Ninety percent of my first calls end up in voicemail.

Do you have any voicemail strategies?

I leave voicemails, I leave emails. I have my own little etiquette as to what I do. I've never really harangued anyone, but the catchword I like to use is "polite but persistent." You never go into an interview demanding someone's time. You never assume that they want to talk to you. You're always very polite. "I'd be really appreciative if you could spend a few minutes with me," and give as much detail as you can without overloading them.

I like to do voicemail first, then email, then voicemail again. I'll leave a voicemail and then, if I have their email address, I'll immediately write an email because I can give more details in an email message, along with all my contact information. Then they'll have it and they don't have to re-listen to it, because they can read it. Then I'll wait twenty-four hours, and try again. I usually don't try more than three times unless I absolutely have to have this person or source in the story, in which case I'll be polite and very persistent.

Then there's also this trick of when you catch them.

Yes, perfect. Next issue—timing of calls. Go for it.

I've worked out of my home for five years and you hear your business line ring at 4:00A.M., or you hear it ring really late at night, and you know exactly what's happening. Someone's returning your call at a moment when they're absolutely certain you're not there because they want to, one, say they returned your phone call, and two, not talk to you. It's classic behavior, and sometimes I surprise them because I pick up the phone.

I find that a lot of people don't leave for lunch. They actually can get some work done between twelve and two, because people assume they're at lunch. So I often call people right around noon or right around two, when they've gotten back from getting their sandwich, and they can talk to me because no one has scheduled them for that time.

Beginning and end of day is better, if you can figure out when they start their day. Some people like to get into the office early to get some work done. Little do they know that I'm going to be calling them. You can reach a lot of people between 5:00 and 6:00P.M., or right around 6:00. Especially executives who consider 6:00P.M. still relatively early in the day, but after all the meetings have been scheduled.

Also, I give them a lot of options. If I'm going through a PR person, I'll try to give as many options as possible: Here are the windows I am available. And usually I'll get them on their cell phone in a car or an airport. I have fifteen minutes with them, here's when they can do it. Flexibility is really key.

What about days of the week?

Monday and Friday are both pretty bad. Forget Friday afternoons. Forget Monday mornings. You've really narrowed the week down. I never try to call people at home unless they've given me their home number and I don't know it's a home number. I try to not be too intrusive. You're not going to get a good interview or good information from someone who's pissed off at you.

It comes down to being polite. I am asking people to give me their time. They're getting far less out of this exchange than I am, probably, so I want to be as courteous and as considerate as possible. And they're helping me get some knowledge. So I am appreciative.

I think that comes through. Let's go to a different subject completely—trade shows. I know you've covered a gazillion trade shows in your life. What kinds of information do you get from them, and what tips can you give?

Stay in your hotel, watch movies, order room service—or better yet, just stay home. I'd say there are a couple of reasons to go to trade shows. One is to go and schmooze and hang out with your pals, all your fellow researchers or reporters. Another reason is to put a face to a voice. If you've talked to these people on the phone all year long, it's nice to go and meet them. You can meet them all in the same place; it saves you both a lot of time and frequent flier miles.

Also, if you have a very specific agenda in mind, if you want to get a really good view of a particular marketplace, kind of a snapshot in time, a trade show is a good place to do that. The trade show I've gone to most often is Comdex, which is also known as hell on earth, in Las Vegas every November. About two hundred thousand people come to it, and God knows how many vendors and square miles of product. If you try to cover the entire show, you're going to die. But if you are looking very specifically at, say, cell phones that access the Internet, you can do that. Visit the fifteen or twenty vendors, get the materials, get a good view of where things are today.

Since technology is one of your areas, what technology changes have you seen in the last five years that have affected how we do research? And what do you see coming down the pike?

The obvious answer is the Internet. It went from a novelty—"Hey, we have a Web site"—to an expectation. Now it's not just "We have a Web site," but "Here's what we expect from your Web site." You're considered backward if you don't have a Web site; that's the biggest single change. By the way, I am constantly appalled at how many Web sites don't give you any way to actually reach the company. That information should be on the front page. I want email addresses, I want phone numbers, I want their real property holdings, I want everything.

The Internet has made my job much easier and made it possible for me to move three thousand miles and take my job with me. The number of resources on the Net is continuing to expand, and I think we'll see more of that. We'll see more people who have email addresses, who have some information on the Web about them. But public records are extremely spotty on the Internet. It's worse, in some ways, to have some of this information available on the Net than to have none, because you don't know whether what you're looking for exists at all, or if it's just not online.

In terms of technology, we're starting to see a variety of ways and devices to use the Internet, including being able to do it wirelessly. I'm still not sure anyone doing real research will want to do it from anything other than a PC on a desk, or at least a PC they can carry with them, because how much work can you really get done on a cell phone or a Palm handheld? You want to be able to store that information, too, not have to go back and find it again. You want to be able to print it out, which also implies having some sort of computer.

How about things like caller ID, when you're doing phone research?

When I worked at *PC World*, they had caller-ID blocking. They didn't want people to know they were calling from *PC World* because oftentimes we'd be testing out vendor services or customer support. We didn't want them to treat *PC World* better than they would treat someone else. So when you're pretending to be just a civilian, you don't want them to know who you are. Or if you're doing an investigation, you might not want them to know that they're being investigated yet. So there are good reasons to block caller ID.

How about the general need for primary research, five years down the line? Do you think there will be more need for it, more use of it, or less?

What's happening now is that people are relying a lot more on getting information from Web sites, and that's a slippery slope because we all know that the Web is full of lies. There are lots of nutso people out there who are putting up Web sites. We talked earlier about how you know when your sources are leading you on and not telling you the truth. It's even harder with a Web site, especially if the Web site is not from a recognized source. I see reporters relying more on what they read on screen, as opposed to talking to a person. I don't think that's necessarily a good thing.

Do you think that people will maintain an awareness of the need for primary research?

People in general think, "Oh, the Web is a substitute for ..." and they're mistaken. I don't think daily newspaper reporters will make that mistake. You always want to talk to the person, talk to the victim, get that gut-wrenching quote.

But a lot of other people will just rely on the Web, and the hoax potential is so high. That's why Hillary Clinton and Rick Lazio got nailed. Somebody posed a question to them in an online debate about how they felt about the proposal to tax every piece of email. Anyone who knows anything about the Internet knows about the so-called email tax. It's a well-known urban legend. They both responded, "That's a terrible idea." They both came down firmly opposed to this fictional tax, and they looked like idiots.

We're going to see much more of that on a smaller scale, more people who will say, "Look at this. It must be true." We'll see more of the Pierre Salinger syndrome, where he "uncovered" the cause of the TWA Flight 800 explosion by reading an old, fictitious posting on the Internet.

People who have a point of view that doesn't encompass the whole breadth of an issue can so easily put up something on a Web site that expresses their point of view. Then someone else picks it up and accepts it as gospel.

People think, because it's on the Internet, it has some validity that it really does not have.

Yes. It's published so it must be true. God knows that isn't so. And as more people get on the Web who are new to it, the more of that we'll see.

Back to other kinds of primary research you've done, I just have one more question: Can you think of a case where a visual inspection was key? Have there been any instances where, for example, somebody went to check out a company and found it was a storefront or somebody's house?

In fact we did that at *PC World* fairly often. We had reporters do a drive-by and find out it was a mail drop. That's the typical M.O. of a scam company. It doesn't mean that just because you have a mail drop you're a scam company, but if you're acting like there's a storefront there and there isn't, you might be trying to hide something. The reverse can happen, too. You think, "These guys are shady" and you drive by. Then, seeing the big store with lots of machinery in it, looking like they have paid the rent, might change your point of view. Actually touching something, seeing something for real—you can't substitute for that on the Internet.

Super Searcher Tips

➤ I like WHOIS for domain registration information; Copernic for finding archived pages and saving searches; Dun and Bradstreet for business background; and other people, as much as possible, to do the research legwork for me.

➤ If a business went bankrupt, call the creditors who have liens on the company. They may give you the name of their contact there. Now you have a lead on a name. Employees are another good inside source, if they're willing to talk.

➤ I start from complete ignorance on a topic and I arrive at a point of incomplete ignorance. One of the places I start is *The Wall Street Journal* Publications Library online, to look at what others have written and what sources they provide.

➤ Digging on an individual, it's hard to know where to draw the line. Are you investigating a story or are you investigating a person? Be very careful about your motives, your goal, and how you achieve that goal. "Am I violating people's privacy? Am I serving a bigger public good or am I just satisfying my weird little curiosity?"

➤ In evaluating sources, look at their perspective. What's their interest in talking to you? Are they trying to be famous? Do they have a product or a company they're trying to push? What's their point of view and their likely motive? Weigh all that against what they tell you, and against what other people tell you.

➤ I'll leave voicemail, then immediately write an email giving more details, including all my contact information. That way they'll have it and not have to re-listen, because they can read it.

➤ I'll try to give as many options as possible for when I'm available. I'll get them on their cell phone, in a car, or an airport. I have fifteen minutes with them. Flexibility is key.

➤ For your first interview, you want someone who has a good general knowledge of a topic, can give you the basics, and will point you in three or four different directions. If you call the world's leading expert on a topic when you know nothing, you'll burn that source, because you're not going to ask the right questions. Call that person later, when you feel confident about your knowledge of the topic.

➤   After a certain point, I chuck the prepared questions. If you want a good interview, you want a conversation. Otherwise you'll get either terse answers or very canned answers that they've given a million times. In conversation, they'll tell you something that sounds real, that they haven't told anyone else.

Appendix
Referenced Sites and Sources

ONLINE RESOURCES

16 Million Businesses Phone Book
see infoUSA

1. **555-1212.com**
    www.555-1212.com

2. **ABI/INFORM (Dialog File 15)**
    library.dialog.com/bluesheets/html/bl0015.html

3. **ACM**
    www.acm.org

4. **AIIP (Association of Independent Information Professionals)**
    www.aiip.org

5. **AIM (Administrators in Medicine) DocFinder**
    www.docboard.org

6. **ALA (American Library Association)**
    www.ala.org

7. **Albert**
    www.albert-inc.com

8. **AltaVista**
    www.altavista.com

9. **American Board of Medical Specialties (certified doctors)**
    www.abms.org

10. **AnyWho**
    www.anywho.com

11. **Autonomy**
    www.autonomy.com

12. **AutoTrackXP (DBT)**
    www.autotrackxp.com

13. **Bloomberg**
    www.bloomberg.com

14. **bmcnews**
    www.bmcnews.com

15. **BRB Publications**
    www.brbpub.com

16. **Bureau of Labor Statistics (U.S. Department of Labor)**
    stats.bls.gov/blshome.htm

17. *Burwell World Directory of Information Brokers, The*
    www.burwellinc.com

18. **Business and Industry (Dialog File 9)**
    library.dialog.com/bluesheets/html/bl0009.html

19. **Buslib-L (Business Librarians mailing list)**
    To subscribe, email: listserv@listserv.boisestate.edu
    In message body type: subscribe buslib-l firstname lastname

20. **California Docfinder**
    www.docboard.org/ca/df/casearch.htm

21. **California Secretary of State**
    www.ss.ca.gov

22. **Canter and Siegel green card spam**
    www.nyupress.nyu.edu/netwars/pages/chapter02/ch02_.html

23. *Carroll's Directories*
    www.carrollpub.com

24. **CDB Infotek (owned by ChoicePoint)**
    www.cdb.com

25. **CFP (Computers, Freedom, and Privacy)**
    www.cfp.org

26. *Chain Store Guides*
    www.csgis.com

27. **ChoicePoint**
    www.choicepointinc.com

28. **CIX**
www.cix.org or www.cix.net

29. **CNET**
www.cnet.com

30. **Companies House Direct**
www.companieshouse.gov.uk

31. **CompuServe**
www.compuserve.com

32. **Computer Select**
www.computer-select.com

33. *Connections* **(AIIP newsletter)**
Contact AIIP Headquarters (email: aiipinfo@aiip.org)
to request reprints of articles

34. **Copernic**
www.copernic.com

35. **Darnton, Robert**
"No Computer Can Hold the Past," *The New York Times*, June 12, 1999.
www.uwm.edu/~gjay/darnton.htm

36. **DBT**
www.dbtonline.com

DBT AutoTrackXP
see AutoTrackXP

Defaulted docs
see Health Education Assistance Loan Program List of Defaulted Borrowers

Deja News
see Google newsgroups

37. **Demon Internet**
www.demon.net

38. **DialIndex (Dialog File 411)**
library.dialog.com/bluesheets/html/bl0411.html

39. **Dialog**
www.dialog.com

40. **Dogpile**
www.dogpile.com

41. **Dow Jones Interactive**
djinteractive.com

42. **Dun and Bradstreet (D&B)**
    www.dnb.com

43. **Duns Business Locator**
    ceased

44. **ECMSA (European Chemical Marketing and Strategy Association; formerly ECMRA)**
    www.ecmra.com

45. **Economist Intelligence Unit**
    www.eiu.com

46. **Edgar**
    edgar.sec.gov

47. *Encyclopedia of Associations* **(Dialog File 114)**
    www.gale.com or library.dialog.com/bluesheets/html/bl0114.html

48. **EPA**
    www.epa.gov

49. **Fashion Institute of Technology (FIT)**
    www.fitnyc.suny.edu

50. **FDA (Food and Drug Administration)**
    www.fda.gov

51. **Federal Fair Credit Reporting Act (FCRA)**
    www.ftc.gov/os/statutes/fcrajump.htm

52. **Federal Information Center**
    www.web-pub.com/library/brochure/fedinfo.html

53. **FOIA (Freedom of Information Act)**
    www.usdoj.gov/04foia/index.html

54. **Free Pint Bar**
    www.freepint.co.uk/bar/

55. *Gale Directory of Publications and Broadcast Media* **(Dialog File 469)**
    www.gale.com or library.dialog.com/bluesheets/html/bl0469.html

56. **Global Business Network**
    www.gbn.org

57. **Gnutella**
    www.gnutella.wego.com

58. **Google**
    www.google.com

59. **Google newsgroups (was Deja News)**
www.groups.google.com

60. **Guidestar**
www.guidestar.org

61. **Headquarters USA**
www.omnigraphics.com

62. **Health Care Advisory Board**
www.advisory.com

63. **Health Education Assistance Loan Program
List of Defaulted Borrowers ("Defaulted docs")**
www.defaulteddocs.dhhs.gov

64. *Health Forum Journal*
www.healthforumjournal.com

65. **Hoover's**
www.hoovers.com

66. **HotBot**
www.hotbot.com

67. **I-95ers (DC-area information professionals)**
For information or to be notified of meetings, email: mbates@BatesInfo.com
or send a self-addressed stamped envelope to: Bates Information Services,
1829 Mintwood Place, N.W., Washington, DC 20009-1907.

68. **ILI**
www.ili-info.com/us
www.ili.co.uk/en

69. **Individual Reference Services Group (IRSG)**
www.irsg.org

70. *The Industry Standard*
www.thestandard.com

71. **Information America (ChoicePoint)**
www.infoam.com

72. **infoUSA**
www.infousa.com

73. **InSite 2**
www.insite2.gale.com

74. **Institute for the Future**
www.iftf.org

75. **Inverse Technologies (merged with Visual Networks)**
www.visualnetworks.com

76. **IRSC**
www.irsc.com

77. **Kassel, Amelia**
www.marketingbase.com
Author of *Super Searchers on Wall Street*, Medford, NJ,
CyberAge Books, 2000
www.infotoday.com/catalog/books.htm

78. **Kight, Leila**
www.scip.org/about/awards2000.html

79. **Knowx.com**
www.knowx.com

80. **LexisNexis**
www.lexisnexis.com

81. **The Librarian's Yellow Pages**
www.librariansyellowpages.com

82. **Library of Congress**
lcweb.loc.gov

83. **Likert scale**
www.cultsock.ndirect.co.uk/MUHome/cshtml/psy/likert.html

84. **LLRX (Law Library Resource Xchange)**
www.llrx.com

85. **Merlin**
www.merlindata.com

86. **Metacrawler**
www.metacrawler.com

87. **Myers-Briggs Type Indicator (MBTI)**
www.tradertype.com

88. **National Archives**
www.nara.gov

89. **National Gallery**
www.nga.gov

90. **National Institutes of Health**
www.nih.gov

91. **National Public Records Research Association (NPRRA)**
www.nprra.org

92. **National Trade and Professional Associations (NTPA)**
www.columbiabooks.com/ntpa.html

93. *Nelson's Directory of Investment Managers*
www.nelnet.com/catalog/dim.htm

94. *net.wars*
www.nyupress.nyu.edu/netwars.html

95. **New Jersey Division of Revenue**
www.state.nj.us/njbgs/

96. **Newsletter Database (Dialog File 636)**
library.dialog.com/bluesheets/html/bl0636.html

97. **Northern Light**
www.northernlight.com or www.nlsearch.com

98. **Office of Technology Assessment**
www.access.gpo.gov/ota/index.html

99. **OneSource**
www.onesource.com

100. **open.gov.uk**
www.open.gov.uk

101. **OSHA**
www.osha.gov

102. **PACER (Public Access to Court Electronic Records)**
pacer.psc.uscourts.gov

103. **Peterson, Lynn**
"Navigating the Maze of Criminal Records Retrieval"
www.llrx.com/features/crime.htm
"Online Personal Information: Access vs. Excess"
www.llrx.com/features/personal.htm

104. **Porter, Michael**
Author of numerous books, including:
Competitive Strategy: Techniques for Analyzing Industries and Competitors,
Simon & Schuster, 1998.
ils.unc.edu/daniel/237/Competition.html

105. **Price, Gary**
Direct Search: gwis2.circ.gwu.edu/~gprice/direct.htm
Price's List of Lists: gwis2.circ.gwu.edu/~gprice/listof.htm

106. *Price Watcher*
No longer published. Contact BiblioData for reprint information:
www.bibliodata.com/pw/pwdata.html

107. **Privacy Rights Clearinghouse**
www.privacyrights.org

108. **ProfNet**
www.profnet.com

109. **PROMT (Dialog File 16)**
library.dialog.com/bluesheets/html/bl0016.html

110. **PRRN (Public Records Retrievers Network)**
www.brbpub.com/prrn/

111. **The Real White Pages**
www.realwhitepages.com

112. **Reuters**
www.reuters.com

113. **Rugge, Sue**
info.sims.berkeley.edu/sfsla/bulletin/novdec99/rugge.html or
www.infotoday.com/it/jul99/tribute.htm

114. **SCIP (Society of Competitive Intelligence Professionals)**
www.scip.org

115. **SCIP Code of Ethics**
For a copy, email: ysuh@scip.org

116. **SCIP Peer-to-Peer Network**
www.scip.org/marketplace/peer_search.html

117. **Search Systems (Pacific Information Resources)**
www.pac-info.com

118. **search.com**
www.search.com

119. *The Skeptic*
www.skeptic.org.uk

120. **Sources and Experts**
www.ibiblio.org/slanews/internet/experts.html

121. **Special Libraries Association (SLA)**
www.sla.org

122. *Standard Periodical Directory*
www.oxbridge.com

123. **Sterling, Bruce**
The Hacker Crackdown
www.eff.org/pub/Misc/Publications/Bruce_Sterling/Hacker_Crackdown

124. **Superior Online**
www.superiorinfo.com

125. **Switchboard**
www.switchboard.com

126. **SWOT**
www.marketing-intelligence.co.uk/aware/services/swot.htm

127. *Thomas Register*
www.thomaspublishing.com/pagetr.html

128. **Trade & Industry Database (Dialog file 148)**
library.dialog.com/bluesheets/html/bl0148.html

129. **Turkle, Sherry**
http://web.mit.edu/sturkle/www

130. *Ulrich's International Periodicals Directory*
www.ulrichsweb.com

131. **Ultimate People Finder, The**
www.knowx.com/free/peoplefinder.htm

U.S. Department of Labor
see Bureau of Labor Statistics

132. **U.S. Party/Case Index**
pacer.uspci.uscourts.gov

133. **Usenet (see also Google Newsgroups)**
directory.google.com/Top/Computers/Usenet/Web_Based

134. **Video Monitoring Service (VMS)**
www.vidmon.com

135. *Wall Street Journal, The* **Publications Library**
Full access requires subscription. See also Dow Jones Interactive.
public.wsj.com or www.wsj.com

136. *Washington Information Directory* **(Congressional Quarterly)**
store.yahoo.com/cq-press/wasindir19.html

137. **Web-Ferret**
www.ferretsoft.com

138. **Web4Lib**
sunsite.berkeley.edu/Web4Lib/

139. **The WELL**
www.well.com

140. **WHOIS**
www.networksolutions.com/cgi-bin/whois/whois

141. **Yahoo!**
www.yahoo.com

142. **Yahoo! for the U.K.**
uk.yahoo.com

143. **Yahoo! Message Boards**
messages.yahoo.com

144. **Yahoo! People Search**
http://people.yahoo.com

145. *Yellow Books*
www.leadershipdirectories.com

BOOKS AND ARTICLES

146. **Baker, Nicholson**
"Discards." *The New Yorker*, October 14, 1996. Reprinted in The Size of Thoughts, Vintage, 1997.

147. **Barone, Jeanne Tessier and Jo Young Switzer**
Interviewing: Art and Skill, Allyn & Bacon, 1995.

148. **Berkman, Robert**
Find It Fast: How to Uncover Expert Information on Any Subject, HarperCollins, 2000.

149. *Business Control Atlas*
American Map Company, 2000.

150. **Culligan, Joseph, J.**
You, Too, Can Find Anybody, Research Investigative Services, Miami, 1998.

151. **De Mey, Dennis L. and James R Flowers**
Don't Hire a Crook: How to Avoid Common Hiring (and Firing) Mistakes, Facts on Demand Press, 1999.

152. **Dyctwald, Kenneth and Joe Flower**
Age Wave. Bantam Doubleday Dell, 1990.

153. *Guide to Background Investigations, The*
TISI (Total Information Services, Incorporated) Staff, TISI—National Employment Screening Service, biannual publication.
For information or to order: www.usetheguide.com

154. **Hafner, Katie and John Markoff**
Cyberpunk, Touchstone Books, 1995.

155. **Levine, Stephen and Barbara Newcombe**
Paper Trails: A Guide to Public Records in California, California Newspaper Publishers Association, 1995.
For information, or to order: www.cnpa.com

156. **Levis, John**
"The Economic Espionage Act of 1996 and the Information Professional."
AIIP *Connections*, Fall 1998.

157. *New York Times Directory of Film*
Random House, 1971.

158. **Nolan, John A. III**
CONFIDENTIAL: Uncover Your Competitors' Top Business Secrets Legally and Quickly—and Protect Your Own, HarperCollins, 1999.

159. **Osterholm, Michael T. and John Schwartz**
Living Terrors: What America Needs to Know to Survive the Coming Bioterrorist Catastrophe, Delacorte Press, 2000.

160. **Pollard, Andrew**
Competitor Intelligence—Strategy, Tools, and Techniques for Competitive Advantage, Financial Times/Prentice Hall, 1999.

161. **Ray, Don**
Checking Out Lawyers: What You Should Know before Choosing an Attorney, Military Information Enterprises, 1997.

162. **Rugge, Sue and Alfred Glossbrenner**
The Information Broker's Handbook, 3rd ed., McGraw-Hill, 1997.

163. **Schwartz, John**
"Don't close the book on paper when it comes to research." *The Washington Post,* July 31, 1995.

164. **Stewart, Charles J. and William B. Cash**
Interviewing: Principles and Practices, 9th ed, McGraw Hill College Division, 1999.

165. **Tannen, Deborah**
Talking from 9 to 5, Morrow/Avon, 1995.
That's Not What I Meant, Ballantine Books, 1991.
You Just Don't Understand, Ballantine Books, 1991.

166. **Walther, George R.**
Phone Power: How to Make the Telephone Your Most Profitable Business Tool, Berkeley Books, 1987.

167. **Weinberg, Steve, ed.**
Reporter's Handbook: An Investigator's Guide to Documents and Techniques, 3rd edition, St. Martins Press, 1995.

About the Author

Photo by Patrick O'Connor

Risa Sacks, owner of Risa Sacks Information Services, specializes in custom tailored phone inquiries, manual and online research. She has provided research and writing services to business, government agencies, and individuals for over twenty years, and frequently acts as subcontractor, covering primary aspects of research projects. Risa has a BS and MS in communications from Northwestern University. She has made many presentations on primary research at national conferences and written numerous articles on using the telephone to gather information.

In addition to her research work, Risa has done technical writing and developed and presented training programs for companies from Apple to Xerox on subjects as diverse as loading helicopters, fixing diesel engines, running mainframe computers, and making loans. She currently offers half-day, full-day, and two-day programs on telephone research.

After many years in the San Francisco area, she now lives with her husband in the Blue Ridge Mountains of North Carolina. She can be reached at risa@rsacksinfo.com.

About the Editor

Photo by David Torres

Reva Basch, executive editor of the Super Searchers series, is a writer, researcher, and consultant to the online industry. She is the author of the original Super Searcher books, *Secrets of the Super Searchers* and *Secrets of the Super Net Searchers*, as well as *Researching Online For Dummies* and *Electronic Information Delivery: Ensuring Quality and Value*. She has contributed numerous articles and columns to professional journals and the popular press, and has keynoted at conferences in Europe, Scandinavia, Australia, Canada, and the U.S.

A past president of the Association of Independent Information Professionals, she has a Master's in Library Science from the University of California at Berkeley and more than twenty years of experience in database and Internet research. Basch was Vice President and Director of Research at Information on Demand and has been president of her own company, Aubergine Information Services, since 1986.

Reva lives with her husband and cats on the northern California coast.

Index

C

D

More CyberAge Books from Information Today, Inc.

The Invisible Web
Uncovering Information Sources
Search Engines Can't See

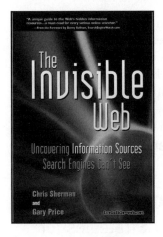

By Chris Sherman and Gary Price

Most of the authoritative information accessible over the Internet is invisible to search engines. This "Invisible Web" is largely comprised of content-rich databases from universities, libraries, associations, businesses, and government agencies. Authors Chris Sherman and Gary Price introduce you to top sites and sources and offer tips, techniques, and analysis that will let you pull needles out of haystacks every time. Supported by a dedicated Web site.

2001/450 pp/softbound/ISBN 0-910965-51-X
$29.95

Super Searchers Cover the World
The Online Secrets of
International Business Researchers

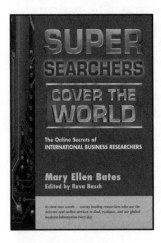

By Mary Ellen Bates
Edited by Reva Basch

The Internet has made it possible for more businesses to think internationally and to take advantage of the expanding global economy. Through 15 interviews with leading online searchers, Mary Ellen Bates explores the challenges of reaching outside a researcher's geographic area to do effective international business research. Experts from around the world—librarians and researchers from government organizations, multinational companies, universities, and small businesses— discuss such issues as nonnative language sources, cultural biases, and the reliability of information. Supported by the Super Searchers Web Page.

2001/320 pp/softbound/ISBN 0-910965-54-4 $24.95

The Extreme Searcher's Guide to Web Search Engines

A Handbook for the Serious Searcher, 2nd Edition

By Randolph Hock
Foreword by Reva Basch

In this completely revised and expanded version of his award-winning book, the "extreme searcher," Randolph (Ran) Hock, digs even deeper, covering all the most popular Web search tools, plus a half-dozen of the newest and most exciting search engines to come down the pike. This is a practical, user-friendly guide supported by a regularly updated Web site.

2001/250 pp/softbound/ISBN 0-910965-47-1
$24.95

International Business Information on the Web

Searcher Magazine's Guide to Sites and Strategies for Global Business Research

By Sheri R. Lanza
Edited by Barbara Quint

Here is the first ready-reference for effective worldwide business research, written by experienced international business researcher Sheri R. Lanza and edited by *Searcher* magazine's Barbara Quint. This book helps readers identify overseas buyers, find foreign suppliers, investigate potential partners and competitors, uncover international market research and industry analysis, and much more. Supported by a Web site.

2001/380 pp/softbound/ISBN 0-910965-46-3
$29.95